12/95

THE LAND OUT THERE

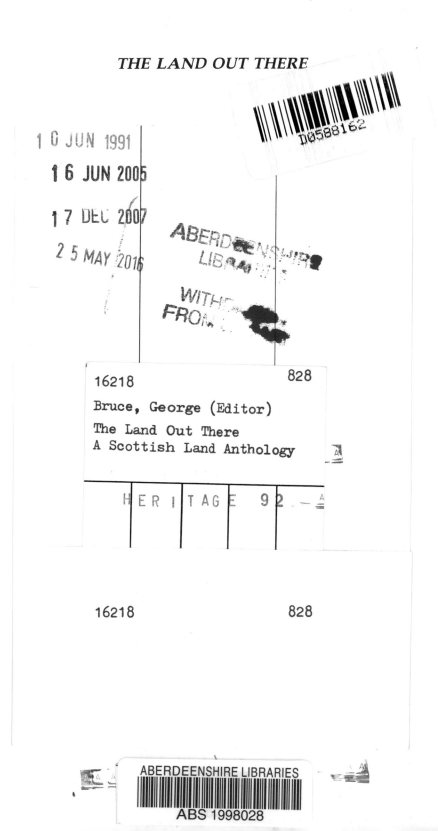

Other Titles by AUP

GLIMMER OF COLD BRINE
A Scottish Sea Anthology
edited by Alistair Lawrie, Hellen Matthews, Douglas Ritchie

THE SCOTTISH DOG
edited by Joyce and Maurice Lindsay

GRAMPIAN HAIRST
An Anthology of North-East Prose
edited by William Donaldson and Douglas Young

THE SCOTTISH CAT
edited by Hamish Whyte

HIGHLANDS AND ISLANDS
A generation of Progress
edited by A Hetherington

THE LAND OUT THERE

A Scottish Land Anthology

edited by

George Bruce

with the assistance of Frank Rennie

ABERDEEN UNIVERSITY PRESS

Member of Maxwell Macmillan Pergamon Publishing Corporation

First published 1991
Aberdeen University Press

© George Bruce and Frank Rennie 1991

British Library Cataloguing in Publication Data

The Land out there : a Scottish land anthology.
  1. English literature. Scottish writers – Anthologies
  1. Bruce, George   II. Rennie, Frank
  820.809411

ISBN 0 08 040907 5

Printed in Great Britain
by Bell & Bain Ltd, Glasgow

CONTENTS

FOLK

THE YIELD OF THE LAND

CHANGE

EMIGRATION AND THE CLEARANCES

CUSTOMS AND TRADITIONS

BIRDS, BEASTS, FLOWERS, INSECTS

RECREATION

WHOSE LAND

LAND AND 'THE SEEING EYE'

LIST OF BLACK AND WHITE ILLUSTRATIONS

LIST OF COLOUR ILLUSTRATIONS

PREFACE

The Land Out There is a companion volume to *Glimmer of Cold Brine, A Scottish Sea Anthology*, yet it can run parallel to it in only a few respects for there are radical differences in the effects of land and sea on the people who live by them. There is the time-scale of the effects: the fisherman knows in a day or night the richness or poverty of his catch: the farmer must wait from the planting of the seed to the harvesting of the crop. So this anthology acknowledges the significance of the time factor by beginning from the making of the land itself.

The first section takes account of the geological process, 'In the Beginning'. It seemed natural to the Editors to move immediately to 'Beginnings'—the perception of the land by those growing up on it, and of their environment, at which point diversity must be acknowledged. A variety of ways of living stem from the varieties of conditions—from lush pastures to bare hill-sides—and then, beyond productivity, the impact on the mind and spirit of living in these circumstances. So not only must reference be made to the producers from the soil, but to all who have come under the influence of the land, be they hill-walkers, sportsmen or visitors come to discover and enjoy Scotland. All these interests are represented in some measure but at the heart of the book is 'The Yield of the Land', its changes and how these have affected the lives of the people.

Ultimately, as there is in *Glimmer of Cold Brine* and in *The Land Out There* the expression of admiration and wonder at what is presented by natural forces, so there is common concern that bounty is impoverished by wanton uses. This was not the motive for the book, it rises through the humours and contrary opinions of the contributors, even in the last words in the anthology, penned by an ill man in bed, William Soutar, the poet from Perth: 'Joy is met and shared—it cannot be buried or hoarded.'

George Bruce

ACKNOWLEDGEMENTS

An anthology of this kind requires not only the permission of authors but also the help of friends and friendly institutions. Our thanks are due to Kathleen Austin of the Saltire Society, Alison Bowers of the Encyclopaedia of Language and Linguistics, University of Edinburgh, Alexander Fenton, Duncan Glen, Dairmid Gunn, Chilton and Marjorie Inglis, Maurice Lindsay, Nuala Lonie, Farquhar Macintosh, P H Scott and Mrs Cath Wilson, also to the Edinburgh and Scottish Departments of the Central Public Library, Edinburgh, the National Library of Scotland, and the Scottish Film Council.

We are grateful to the former Director of Aberdeen University Press, Colin MacLean, to his successor Colin Kirkwood for suggestions and work on the production of the book and to Marjorie Leith for unstinting effort and patience with the Editors.

The publisher acknowledges subsidy from the Highlands and Islands Development Board through its Education Liaison Programme.

In April 1991 the work of the Highlands and Islands Development Board was merged with that of the Training Agency and the land renewal functions of the Scottish Development Agency in the northern half of Scotland to form Highlands and Islands Enterprise.

Prologue

THAT IS THE LAND OUT THERE

That is The Land out there, under the sleet, churned and pelted there in the dark, the long rigs upturning their clayey faces to the spear-onset of the sleet. *That* is The Land, a dim vision this night of laggard fences and long stretching rigs. And the voice of it—the true and unforgettable voice—you can hear even in such a night as this as the dark comes down, the immemorial plaint of the peewit, flying lost. *That* is The Land—though not quite all. Those folk in the byre whose lantern light is a glimmer through the sleet as they muck and bed and tend the kye, and milk the milk into tin pails, in curling froth—they are The Land in as great a measure. Those two, a dual power, are the protagonists in this little sketch. They are the essentials for the title. And besides, quite unfairly, they are all so intimately mine that I would give them that position though they had not a shadow of a claim to it.

I like to remember I am of peasant rearing and peasant stock. Good manners prevail on me not to insist on the fact over-much, not to boast in the company of those who come from manses and slums and castles and villas, the folk of the proletariat, the bigger and lesser bourgeoisies. But I am again and again, as I hear them talk of their origins and beginnings and begetters, conscious of an overweening pride that mine was thus and so, that the land was so closely and intimately mine (my mother used to hap me in a plaid in harvest-time and leave me in the lee of a stook while she harvested) that I feel of a strange and antique age in the company and converse of my adult peers—like an adult himself listening to the bright sayings and laughter of callow boys, parvenus on the human scene, while I, a good Venriconian Pict, harken from the shade of my sun circle and look away bored, in pride of possession at my terraced crops, at the on-ding of rain and snow across my leavened fields. . . .

LEWIS GRASSIC GIBBON

In the Beginning

WORTH A BAG OF GOLD

. . . a bag of gravel is a history to me, and . . . will tell wondrous
tales. . . . I need say no more of this; only, mind, a bag of gravel is
worth a bag of gold.

JAMES HUTTON

1 James Hutton 1726–1797 by Sir Henry Raeburn. Courtesy of the
Trustees of the National Galleries of Scotland.

THE OLD RED SANDSTONE

The first scene in the 'Tempest' opens amid the confusion and turmoil of the hurricane,—amid thunders and lightnings, the roar of the wind, the shouts of the seamen, the rattling of cordage, and the wild dash of the billows. The history of the period represented by the Old Red Sandstone seems, in what now forms the northern half of Scotland, to have opened in a similar manner. The finely-laminated lower Tilestones of England were deposited evidently in a calm sea. During the contemporary period in our own country, the vast space which now includes Orkney and Lochness, Dingwall and Gamrie, and many a thousand square mile besides, was the scene of a shallow ocean, perplexed by powerful currents, and agitated by waves. A vast stratum of water-rolled pebbles, varying in depth from a hundred feet to a hundred yards, remains in a thousand different localities, to testify of the disturbing agencies of this time of commotion. The hardest masses which the stratum incloses,—porphyries of vitreous fracture that cuts glass as readily as flint, and masses of quartz that strike fire quite as profusely from steel—are yet polished and ground down into bullet-like forms, not an angular fragment appearing, in some parts of the mass, for yards together. The debris of our harder rocks, rolled for centuries in the beds of our more impetuous rivers, or tossed for ages along our more exposed and precipitous sea-shores, could not present less equivocally the marks of violent and prolonged attrition than the pebbles of this bed. And yet it is surely difficult to conceive how the bottom of any sea should have been so violently and so equally agitated for so greatly extended a space as that which intervenes between Mealforvony in Inverness-shire and Pomona in Orkney in one direction, and between Applecross and Trouphead in another, and for a period so prolonged, that the entire area should have come to be covered with a stratum of rolled pebbles of almost every variety of ancient rock, fifteen storeys' height in thickness. The very variety of its contents shows that the period must have been prolonged. A sudden flood sweeps away with it the accumulated debris of a range of mountains; but to blend together in equal mixture the debris of many such ranges, as well as to grind down their roughness and angularities, and fill up the interstices with the sand and gravel produced in the process, must be a work of time. I have examined with much interest, in various localities, the fragments of ancient rock inclosed in this formation. Many of them are no longer to be found *in situ*, and the group is essentially different from that presented by the more modern gravels. On the shores of the Frith of Cromarty, for instance, by far the most abundant pebbles are of a blue schistose gneiss: fragments of gray granite and white quartz are also common; and the sea-shore at half-ebb presents at a short distance the appearance of a long belt of bluish-gray, from the colour of the prevailing stones which compose it. The prevailing colour of the conglomerate of the district, on the contrary, is a deep red. It contains pebbles of small-grained red granite, red quartz rock, red felspar, red porphyry, an impure red jasper, red hornstone, and a red granitic gneiss, identical with the well-marked gneiss of the neighbouring Sutors. This last is the only rock now found in the district of which fragments occur in the conglomerate. It must have been exposed at the time to the action of the waves, though afterwards buried deep under some succeeding formations, until again thrust to the surface by some great internal convulsion, of a date comparatively recent.

HUGH MILLER

LEWISIAN GNEISS OUTCROPS

A landscape of lumps of stone.
Yes, I know there's grass
and a few scrubby trees,
but the rock is everywhere,
poking its bones out at all angles,
and man squats uncomfortably between.

It's called 'close to Nature'
or 'the bare necessities'
this continually being nudged to awareness
of where we come in the end.

Yet out of this place have grown
the tongue's impassioned flowering,
grace-notes of elation.

JOHN KILLICK

THE PRESENCE OF THE PAST

Among the many contrasts which geology reveals between the present and the past there is surely none that appeals more vividly to the imagination than that which the records of the Ice Age bring before us. These records are so abundant, so clear and so indisputable, that there can be no hesitation in accepting the picture which they present to us of the condition of this country at a comparatively recent geological period. Everywhere the trail of the ice meets our eye and sets us thinking of the difference between what is now and what was so lately, that there has not yet been time for nature to efface its vestiges. The contrast perhaps appeals most to our sense of wonder when it meets us among scenes rich in human associations and full of the life and bustle of modern civilisation. To sit, for instance, on one of the Highland hills that overlook the Firth of Clyde, and watch the ships as they come and go from all corners of the earth; to trace village after village, and town after town, dotting the coast-line far as the eye can reach; to see the white steam of the distant railway rising like a summer cloud from among orchards and cornfields and fairy-like woodlands; to mark, far away, the darker smoke of the coal-pit and the iron-work hanging over the haunts of a busy human population; in short, to note all over the landscape, on land and sea, the traces of that human power which is everywhere changing the face of nature;— and then to picture an earlier time, when these waters had never felt the stroke of oar or paddle, when these hillsides had never echoed the sound of human voice, but when over hill and valley, over river and sea, there had fallen a silence as of the grave, when one wide pall of snow and ice stretched across the landscape; to restore, in imagination, the vast ice-sheet filling up the whole wide firth, and creeping slowly and silently southwards, and the valley-glaciers into which this ice-sheet shrank, threading yonder deep Highland glens, which today are purple with heather and blithe with the whirring of grouse and woodcock; to seal up the firth once more in ice as the winter frosts used to set over it, and to cover it with bergs and ice-rafts that marked the short-lived Arctic summer; to bring back again the Arctic plants and animals of that early time, the reindeer, the mammoths, and their contemporaries; and thus, from the green and sunny valley of the Clyde, with all its human associations, to pass at once and by a natural transition to the sterility and solitude of another Greenland, is an employment as delightful as man can well enjoy.

ARCHIBALD GEIKIE

LOCH CORUISK

Picking your steps carefully over huge boulder and slippery stone, you come upon the most savage scene of desolation in Britain. Conceive a large lake filled with dark green water, girt with torn and shattered precipices; the bases of which are strewn with ruin since an earthquake passed that way, and whose summits jag the sky with grisly splinter and peak. There is no motion here save the white vapour steaming from the abyss. The utter silence weighs like a burden upon you: you feel an intruder in the place. The hills seem to possess some secret; to brood over some unutterable idea which you can never know. You cannot feel comfortable at Loch Coruisk, and the discomfort arises in a great degree from the feeling that you are outside of everything—that the thunder-smitten peaks have a life with which you cannot intermeddle. The dumb monsters sadden and perplex. Standing there, you are impressed with the idea that the mountains are silent because they are listening so intently. And the mountains *are* listening, else why do they echo our voices in such a wonderful way? Shout here like an Achilles in the trenches. Listen! The hill opposite takes up your words, and repeats them one after another, and curiously tries them over with the gravity of a raven. Immediately after, you hear a multitude of skyey voices.

'Methinks that there are spirits among the peaks.'

ALEXANDER SMITH

facing page
2   Loch Coruisk, William Daniell [Watercolour]. Courtesy of the Glasgow
Art Gallery & Museums.

AULD WARLD SHELLS

To Hugh Miller, Thurso

. . . 'But what got ye?' I hear you say. 'What got ye?' Well, I will tell you every word about it; and, believe me, unless I had the opportunity of telling it to you, I would never have gone a footstep in search of auld warld shells.

Well! on arriving at the eastern side of Dunnet cliffs, I made direct for a precipitous cliff at least 150 feet high; where, some years ago, I sat on a big boulder of sandstone, making my breakfast on cold rolls and cheese. In the present instance, I wound along the foot of those breakneck rocks, which, unless the tide had been out, I would not have been able to do,—for the tide comes close in under the cliff.

Then I went on to the cottage built beside the small, neat landing-place on the sea shore at Brough Haven . . . A very little to the west of this cottage there is a small burn. The burn has cut its way through the boulder clay. I went into the ravine and stood looking around me. No sight could give me so much pleasure and surprise. I found on walking along the little rill that there was a tiny cascade about eight or nine feet deep, down which the mossy water leapt dashing over a perpendicular wall of real, blue, stony, boulder clay! . . .

There are moments when a real heartfelt pleasure amply repays us poor mortals for years of sorrow. And such a moment was mine now. There I stood with evidences of Old World convulsions and changes environed round about me on every side. And yet there was a living cascade, merrily piping away the sunny hours at my feet, the crystal drops bedecking my clay-soiled boots. Columbus had never cast anchor here. No philosopher had ever entered this paradise. It was all a new world. To me for the moment it was The World. And I triumphed in the felt conviction that a humble individual like myself had, under Providence, 'done the State some service;' for the evidence that it brings to bear on geological science is not to be gainsaid.

ROBERT DICK

CAITHNESS AND SUTHERLAND

As the Eastern sage has it, 'Haste is an attribute of devils'. Let us see one thing well; let us, then, as we turn east from Tongue, keep our eyes on Sutherland's own mountain—Ben Laoghal. Ben Hope comes before for contrast. And moors and sea-inlets and skylines keep us company. Around is all the grandeur of all the fabled West—with Ben Laoghal added. Watch Ben Laoghal play with its four granite peaks on the legendary stuff of history, or is it of the mind? Sometimes they are the battlemented towers of a distant Mediaeval Age; in the smoke-blue drift of the half-light they are the ramparts to the high hills of faery; a turn in the road or in the mood, and they have become perfectly normal again, unobtrusive and strong as the native character. Let me add that once going down towards bleak Kildonan, I unthinkingly glanced over my shoulder and saw them crowned with snow. I have never forgotten the unearthly fright I got then.

From that background, or as it were from that door, you walk out upon Caithness, and at once experience an austerity in the flat clean wind-swept lands that affects the mind almost with a sense of shock. There is something more in it than contrast. It is a movement of the spirit that finds in the austerity, because strength is there also, a final serenity. I know of no other landscape in Scotland that achieves this harmony, that, in the very moment of purging the mind of its dramatic grandeur, leaves it free and ennobled. The Pentland Firth, outreaching on the left, is of a blueness that I, at least, failed to find in the Mediterranean; a living blueness, cold-glittering in the sun and smashed to gleaming snowdrift on the bows of the great rock-battleships of the Orkneys, bare and austere also. The wind of time has searched out even the flaws here and cleansed them.

NEIL GUNN

THE ROCKS OF SUTHERLAND AND ROSS

I have already dwelt upon the peculiarity of the landscapes of the Archaean gneiss, which forms part of the Outer Hebrides and stretches as a broken belt along the western coast of Sutherland and Ross. I would only repeat here that nothing can well be more impressive for its monotonous barrenness than an expanse of this grey, cold, bare rock, protruding from the heather in endless rounded crags and knolls, and dotted over with tarns and lochans, which, by their stillness, heighten the loneliness and solitude of the scene. Only at one locality on the mainland does it rise into an eminence that can rank with the more prominent hills of the younger rocks. In Ben Stack in Sutherlandshire, it reaches a height of 2,364 feet and, in its rugged declivities of crag and scar, shows its conspicuous veins of dark hornblendic rock and pink pegmatite.

ARCHIBALD GEIKIE

SUTHERLAND: JANUARY 1973

From eternity these stones have been,
Gaunt, hard, heavy on the iron hills.
Loch Eriboll lies lashed by wind,
Waters of light hard hostile green
Where foaming tongues lap jagged teeth;
Down the long slopes the waters pour
From slab to slab in silvered sheets;
The stones run water, water leaps.
Foams, roars, flies out in spray,
Settles in slow black deeps.
The wind blows from a cold lemon sky.
But something else is here,
A desolate dwarfing fear.
Where, in what place, far or near
Lie now the bones that cowered
In dull mute suffering, watching
Stone upon stone flung down?

ANNA G

from *ON A RAISED BEACH*

We must be humble. We are so easily baffled by appearances
And do not realise that these stones are one with the stars.
It makes no difference to them whether they are high or low,
Mountain peak or ocean floor, palace or pigsty.
There are plenty of ruined buildings in the world but no ruined stones,
No visitor comes from the stars
But is the same as they are.
                . . .   .
This is no heap of broken images.
Let men find the faith that builds mountains
Before they seek the faith that moves them. Men cannot hope
To survive the fall of the mountains
Which they will no more see than they saw their rise
Unless they are more concentrated and determined,
Truer to themselves and with more to be true to,
Than these stones, and as inerrable as they are.
Their sole concern is that what can be shaken
Shall be shaken and disappear
And only the unshakable be left.
What hardihood in any man has part or parcel in this latter?
It is necessary to make a stand and maintain it forever.
These stones go through Man, straight to God, if there is one.
What have they not gone through already?
Empires, civilisations, aeons. Only in them
If in anything, can His creation confront Him.
They came so far out of the water and halted forever.
That larking dallier, the sun, has only been able to play
With superficial by-products since;
The moon moves the waters backwards and forwards.
But the stones cannot be lured an inch further
Either on this side of eternity or the other.
Who thinks God is easier to know than they are?
Trying to reach men any more, any otherwise, than they are?
These stones will reach us long before we reach them.
                . . .   .
What happens to us
Is irrelevant to the world's geology

But what happens to the world's geology
Is not irrelevant to us.
We must reconcile ourselves to the stones,
Not the stones to us.
　　　　　　· · ·　· · ·　· · · ·　· · ·

—I lift a stone; it is the meaning of life I clasp
Which is death, for that is the meaning of death;
How else does any man yet participate
　　　　In the life of a stone,
How else can any man yet become
Sufficiently at one with creation, sufficiently alone,
Till as the stone that covers him he lies dumb
And the stone at the mouth of his grave is not overthrown?
—Each of these stones on this raised beach,
　　　　Every stone in the world,
Covers infinite death, beyond the reach
Of the dead it hides; and cannot be hurled
Aside yet to let any of them come forth, as love
　　　　Once made a stone move
　　　　(Though I do not depend on that
　　　　My case to prove).
So let us beware of death; the stones will have
Their revenge; we have lost all approach to them,
But soon we shall become as those we have betrayed,
And they will seal us as fast in our graves
As our indifference and ignorance seals them;
　　　　But let us not be afraid to die.
No heavier and colder and quieter then,
No more motionless, do stones lie
　　　　In death than in life to all men.
It is no more difficult in death than here
—Though slow as the stones the powers develop
To rise from the grave—to get a life worth having;
And in death—unlike life—we lose nothing that is truly ours.
　　　　　　· · ·　· · ·　· · · ·　· · ·
　　　　　　　　　　　　HUGH MACDIARMID

ROCKS AND MEN

The Flight in the Heather: the Rocks

Sometimes we walked, sometimes ran; and as it drew on to morning, walked ever the less and ran the more. Though, upon its face, that country appeared to be a desert, yet there were huts and houses of the people, of which we must have passed more than twenty, hidden in quiet places of the hills. When we came to one of these, Alan would leave me in the way, and go himself and rap upon the side of the house and speak a while at the window with some sleeper awakened. This was to pass the news; which, in that country, was so much of a duty that Alan must pause to attend to it even while fleeing for his life; and so well attended to by others, that in more than half of the houses where we called they had heard already of the murder. In the others, as well as I could make out (standing back at a distance and hearing a strange tongue), the news was received with more of consternation than surprise.

For all our hurry, day began to come in while we were still far from any shelter. It found us in a prodigious valley, strewn with rocks and where ran a foaming river. Wild mountains stood around it; there grew there neither grass nor trees; and I have sometimes thought since then, that it may have been the valley called Glencoe, where the massacre was in the time of King William. But for the details of our itinerary, I am all to seek; our way lying now by short cuts, now by great detours; our pace being so hurried, our time of journeying usually by night; and the names of such places as I asked and heard being in the Gaelic tongue and the more easily forgotten.

The first peep of morning, then, showed us this horrible place, and I could see Alan knit his brow.

'This is no fit place for you and me,' he said. 'This is a place they're bound to watch.'

And with that he ran harder than ever down to the water side, in a part where the river was split in two among three rocks. It went through with a horrid thundering that made my belly quake; and there hung over the lynn a little mist of spray. Alan looked neither to the right nor to the left, but jumped clean upon the middle rock and fell there on his hands and knees to check himself, for that rock was small and he might have pitched over on the far side. I had scarce time to measure the distance or to understand the peril before I had followed him, and he had caught and stopped me.

So there we stood, side by side upon a small rock slippery with spray, a far broader leap in front of us, and the river dinning upon all sides. When I saw where I was, there came on me a deadly sickness of fear, and I put my hand over my eyes. Alan took me and shook me; I saw he was speaking, but the roaring of the falls and the trouble of my mind prevented me from hearing; only I saw his face was red with anger, and that he stamped upon the rock. The same look showed me the water raging by, and the mist hanging in the air: and with that I covered my eyes again and shuddered.

The next minute Alan had set the brandy bottle to my lips, and forced me to drink about a gill, which sent the blood into my head again. Then, putting his hands to his mouth, and his mouth to my ear, he shouted, 'Hang or drown!' and turning his back upon me, leaped over the farther branch of the stream, and landed safe.

I was now alone upon the rock, which gave me the more room; the brandy was singing in my ears; I had this good example fresh before me, and just wit enough to see that if I did not leap at once, I should never leap at all. I bent low on my knees and flung myself forth, with that kind of agony of despair that has sometimes stood me in stead of courage. Sure enough, it was but my hands that reached the full length; these slipped, caught again, slipped again; and I was sliddering back into the lynn, when Alan seized me, first by the hair, then by the collar, and with a great strain dragged me into safety.

3   Corrie Ghaoll from the Bridge of the Three Waters, Glencoe. Reproduced with permission from the George Washington Wilson Collection in Aberdeen University Library.

1   Cromarty and the Cromarty Firth from the South Sutor. Photograph courtesy of Dr Charles D Waterston.

2   Primroses in Ancient Birch Wood. Loch Call an Uidhean in background. Inverpolly National Nature Reserve, Wester Ross. Photograph by Peter Davenport.

3   Skara Brae, Orkney. Photograph by Peter Davenport.

4   Stones of Stenness, Orkney. Photograph by Peter Davenport.

Never a word he said, but set off running again for his life, and I must stagger to my feet and run after him. I had been weary before, but now I was sick and bruised, and partly drunken with the brandy; I kept stumbling as I ran, I had a stitch that came near to overmaster me; and when at last Alan paused under a great rock that stood there among a number of others, it was none too soon for David Balfour.

A great rock I have said; but by rights it was two rocks leaning together at the top, both some twenty feet high, and at the first sight inaccessible. Even Alan (though you may say he had as good as four hands) failed twice in an attempt to climb them; and it was only at the third trial, and then by standing on my shoulders and leaping up with such force as I thought must have broken my collar-bone, that he secured a lodgement. Once there, he let down his leathern girdle; and with the aid of that and a pair of shallow footholds in the rock, I scrambled up beside him.

Then I saw why we had come there; for the two rocks, being both somewhat hollow on the top and sloping one to the other, made a kind of dish or saucer, where as many as three or four men might have lain hidden.

All this while Alan had not said a word, and had run and climbed with such a savage, silent frenzy of hurry, that I knew he was in mortal fear of some miscarriage. Even now we were on the rock he said nothing, nor so much as relaxed the frowning look upon his face; but clapped flat down, and keeping only one eye above the edge of our place of shelter scouted all round the compass. The dawn had come quite clear; we could see the stony sides of the valley, and its bottom, which was bestrewed with rocks, and the river, which went from one side to another, and made white falls; but nowhere the smoke of a house, nor any living creature but some eagles screaming round a cliff.

R L STEVENSON

THE OLD CALEDONIAN FOREST

Often towards nightfall
there's a feeling in the air . . .
of the oldness of the land.

Two simple lines make the valley:
it is twilit, the edge becoming lighter
where the dark part ends.

The ground, an earthy, clayey red,
the sky, a mineral ruby red;
they are a general field of cadmium.

History vitrifies in its fires.
By hindsight, we are looking back
through this glassy evening

back through the acre and a quarter
of original forest,
to the people of its designs.

users of the wood.

                    Further still, our
native tree shoots up young and small
to tip with spires of fir again.

Old age it is, that makes him
tall but mature, flat-topped,
impersonating us.

Contorted creature, pine tree,
grow in your power
of mimicry.

Whatever we see,
whatever we may signify, or be.
every fir since has grown from these;

their flaky bark, bluish needles cover the hill,
their ground slopes off to our level
in the time it takes the pointed cone to fall.

VALERIE GILLIES

RONDEAU: THE FOSSIL TREE

Compacted into one stone, the round-stemmed bole
Of the tree is petrified in form recognisable for good.
A hand could chafe it till it yields a hard and scented wood,
Tells of the essential change it felt once in the stopped sap
When, resin hardening from volatile oils, and leaf blown ago,
Its bark was sheathed in tufa, and the ribbing lapped
in blue clubmosses as the live grain mottled like pink roe
Compacted into one stone, age around age wound on in whorls.

Rock-former, age, ossify this hand of mine in ringed bone:
Reveal hard annulations, in the hoop of a gold cincture shown
Around a fossil finger. Begin, end, make up my circle incorruptibly,
Conform me to such nature as in the body of that tree
Compacted into one stone, substances are married whole.

(For the five fossil tree-stumps in the Cathedral of Trees, near Oban,
Argyllshire)

VALERIE GILLIES

THE GEOLOGIST PAUSES

One who is familiar by report with the ruggedness and sterility of Highland scenery can hardly fail to be vividly impressed by the first sight he obtains of the singular landscapes of these basaltic districts. Instead of ruggedness, he sees with increasing wonder the long level lines of terrace that rise one above another, with strange regularity, sometimes twenty or thirty in number on a single slope, and wind along the hillsides till they are lost in the distance. Instead of sterility, he beholds grassy slopes, to which, for the exquisite brightness of their verdure, contrasting with the lines of brown crag and the dark blue sea, he would with difficulty find elsewhere a counterpart. I can recall the first impression of astonishment and delight which in boyhood these scenes printed indelibly on my memory. The penning of these lines brings also to my recollection many a subsequent hour of reverie spent among them. Often after a long day of geological activity among the Inner Hebrides have I paused on the homeward journey, to mark how the sinking sunlight, striking along those terraced and crag-crowned slopes, revealed with a vividness that was lost in the glare of noon, their union of dark projecting bars of rock and strips of lovely sward, to see how each little brook, that came tumbling down in white cascades from the uplands beyond, had cut for itself a notch in these bands of cliff, and to conjure up in the imagination a succession of pictures of the same scene from the time when the basalt rolled out in successive streams of molten lava down to the legends of Fingal and Columba. In such musings, hours sped quickly past, until hill-top after hill-top would lose its flush of sunset, as if the dying day were slowly climbing the steps cut along the flanks of these terraced hills, and the chill shadows, struggling upward from dark and lonely glens, would creep up the same gigantic staircase until the whole landscape melted into grey gloom and the night began to fall.

ARCHIBALD GEIKIE

'MEN ARE RACY OF THE SOIL IN WHICH THEY GROW'

The Quirang is one of the wonderful sights of Skye, and if you once visit it you will believe ever afterwards the misty and spectral Ossian to be authentic. The Quirang is a nightmare of nature; it resembles one of Nat Lee's mad tragedies; it might be the scene of a Walpurgis night; on it might be held a Norway witch's Sabbath. Architecture is frozen music, it is said; the Quirang is frozen terror and superstition. 'Tis a huge spire or cathedral of rock some thousand feet in height, with rocky spires or needles sticking out of it. Macbeth's weird sisters stand on the blasted heath, and Quirang stands in a region as wild as itself. The country around is strange and abnormal, rising into rocky ridges here, like the spine of some huge animal, sinking into hollows there, with pools in the hollows—glimmering almost always through drifts of misty rain. On a clear day, with a bright sun above, the ascent of Quirang may be pleasant enough; but a clear day you seldom find, for on spectral precipices and sharp-pointed rocky needles, the weeping clouds of the Atlantic have made their chosen home. When you ascend, with every ledge and block slippery, every runnel a torrent, the wind taking liberties with your cap and making your plaid stream like a meteor to the troubled air, white tormented mists boiling up from black chasms and caldrons, rain making disastrous twilight of noon-day,—horror shoots through your pulses, your brain swims on the giddy pathway, and the thought of your room in the vapoury under world rushes across the soul like the fallen Adam's remembrance of his paradise. Then you learn, if you never learned before, that nature is not always gracious; that not always does she outstretch herself in low-lying bounteous lands, over which sober sunsets redden and heavy-uddered cattle low; but that she has fierce hysterical moods in which she congeals into granite precipice and peak, and draws around herself and her companions the winds that moan and bluster, veils of livid rains. If you are an Englishman you will habitually know her in her gracious, if a Skye man in her fiercer, moods.

No one is independent of scenery and climate. Men are racy of the soil in which they grow, even as grapes are. A Saxon nurtured in fat Kent or Sussex, amid flats of heavy wheat and acorn-dropping oaks, must of necessity be a different creature from the Celt who gathers his sustenance from the bleak sea-board, and who is daily drenched by the rain-cloud from Cuchullin. The one, at his best, becomes a broad-shouldered, clear-eyed, ruddy-faced man, slightly obese, who meets danger gleefully, because he has had little experience of it, and because his conditions being hitherto easy, he naturally assumes that everything will go well with him;—at worst, a porker contented with his mast. The other, take him at his best, of sharper spirit, because it has been more keenly whetted on difficulty; if not more intrepid, at least more consciously so; of sadder mood habitually, but *when* happy, happier, as the gloomier the cloud the more dazzling the rainbow;—at his worst, either beaten down, subdued, and nerveless, or gaunt, suspicious, and crafty, like the belly-pinched wolf. On the whole, the Saxon is likely to be the more sensual; the Celt the more superstitious: the Saxon will probably be prosaic, dwelling in the circle of the seen and the tangible; the Celt a poet: while the anger of the Saxon is slow and abiding, like the burning of coal; the anger of the Celt is swift and transient, like the flame that consumes the dried heather: both are superior to death when occasion comes—the Saxon from a grand obtuseness which ignores the fact; the Celt, because he has been in constant communion with it, and because he has seen, measured, and overcome it. The Celt is the most melancholy of men; he has turned everything to superstitious uses, and every object of nature, even the unreasoning dreams of sleep, are mirrors which flash back death upon him. He, the least of all men, requires to be reminded that he is mortal. The howling of his dog will do him that service.

In the stories which are told round the island peat-fires it is abundantly apparent that the Celt has not yet subdued nature. In these stories you can detect a curious subtle hostility between man and his environments; a fear of them, a want of absolute trust in them. In these stories and songs man is not at home in the world. Nature is too strong for him; she rebukes and crushes him. The Elements, however calm and beautiful they may appear for the moment, are malign and deceitful at heart, and merely bide their time. They are like the paw of the cat—soft and velvety, but with concealed talons that scratch when least expected. And this curious relation between man and nature grows out of the climatic conditions and the forms of Hebridean life. In his usual avocations the Islesman rubs clothes with death as he would with an acquaintance. Gathering wild fowl, he hangs, like a spider on its thread, over a precipice on which the sea is beating a hundred feet beneath. In his crazy boat he adventures into whirlpool and foam. He is among the hills when the snow comes down making everything unfamiliar, and stifling the strayed wanderer. Thus death is ever near him, and that consciousness turns everything to omen. The mist creeping along the hill-side by moonlight is an apparition. In the roar of the waterfall, or the murmur of the swollen ford, he hears the water spirit calling out for the man for whom it has waited so long. He sees death-candles burning on the sea, marking the place at which a boat will be upset by some sudden squall. He hears spectral hammers clinking in an outhouse, and he knows that ghostly artificers are preparing a coffin there.

ALEXANDER SMITH

WATER

So I am on the plateau again, having gone round it like a dog in circles to see if it is a good place. I think it is, and I am to stay up here for a while. I have left at dawn, and up here it is still morning. The midsummer sun has drawn up the moisture from the earth, so that for part of the way I walked in cloud, but now the last tendril has dissolved into the air and there is nothing in all the sky but light. I can see to the ends of the earth and far up into the sky.

As I stand there in the silence, I become aware that the silence is not complete. Water is speaking. I go towards it, and almost at once the view is lost: for the plateau has its own hollows, and this one slopes widely down to one of the great inward fissures, the Garbh Coire. It lies like a broad leaf veined with water courses, that converge on the lip of the precipice to drop down in a cataract for 500 feet. This is the River Dee. Astonishingly, up here at 4,000 feet, it is already a considerable stream. The immense leaf that it drains is bare, surfaced with stones, gravel, sometimes sand, and in places moss and grass grow on it. Here and there in the moss a few white stones have been piled together. I go to them, and water is welling up, strong and copious, pure cold water that flows away in rivulets and drops over the rock. These are the Wells of Dee. This is the river. Water, that strong white stuff, one of the four elemental mysteries, can here be seen at its origins. Like all profound mysteries, it is so simple that it frightens me. It wells from the rock, and flows away. For unnumbered years it has welled from the rock, and flowed away. It does nothing, absolutely nothing, but be itself.

The Dee, however, into which through its tributary streams all this south-eastern side of the Cairngorms is to drain, takes its headwaters not from one only but from both halves of the central plateau. The gash that divides the two halves (the Cairntoul and Braeriach from the Cairn Gorm–Ben MacDhui side), the Lairig Ghru, is so sheer and narrow that when mists roll among the precipices, lifting and settling again, it is sometimes hard to tell whether a glimpse of rock wall belongs to the mountain on which one is standing or to another across the cleft. High on the Ben MacDhui side, though 300 feet lower than the wells on Braeriach, two waters begin a mere step from one another. One runs east, falls over the precipice into Loch Avon and turns north to the Spey; the other, starting westwards, slips over the edge as the March Burn and falls into the Lairig Ghru. Eventually, turning south and east, and having joined the water that flows out of the Garbh Choire, it becomes the Dee. But where it falls into the narrow defile of the Lairig, its life seems already over. It disappears. A little further down a tiny pool is seen, and still further down two others, sizable pools, crystal clear and deep. They have no visible means of support, no stream is seen to enter them, none to leave; but their suppressed sparkle tells that they are living water. These are the Pools of Dee. The March Burn feeds them, the young Dee, a short way beyond the lowest of the pools, is plainly their exit. I can conceive of no good reason for trudging through the oppressive Lairig Ghru, except to see them.

Through most of its length the Lairig Ghru hides its water-courses. On the other side of the watershed, towards the Spey, this havoc of boulders seems quite dry. One is surprised when suddenly a piece of running stream appears in the bottom, but it is soon swallowed again. Finally, where the precipitous sides of the gash widen out, and the storms of centuries no longer have rained successions of broken boulders on to the stream beds, the burn at last gushes into the open, a full strong stream of crystal water.

It is not only in this narrow defile that the fallen and scattered boulders cover the watercourses. I have sat among boulders on an outer face of the hill, with two low sounds in my ears, and failed to locate either. One was the churr of ptarmigan, the other the running of water. After a long time, I saw the ptarmigan when he rose with a movement of white wings from among the grey stones he so closely resembles, but the water I never saw. In other places, a bottle-neck gurgle catches my ear and where I thought there were only stones, I can see below them the glint of water.

The Cairngorm water is all clear. Flowing from granite, with no peat to darken it, it has never the golden amber, the 'horse-back brown' so often praised in Highland burns. When it has any colour at all, it is green, as in the Quoich near its linn. It is a green like the green of winter skies, but lucent, clear like aquamarines, without the vivid brilliance of glacier water. Sometimes the Quoich waterfalls have violet playing through the green, and the pouring water spouts and bubbles in a violet froth. The pools beneath these waterfalls are clear and deep. I have played myself often by pitching into them the tiniest white stones I can find, and watching through the appreciable time they take to sway downwards to the bottom.

Some of the lochs also are green. Four of them bear this quality in their names—Loch an Uaine. They are all small lochs, set high in corries, except for the Ryvoan Loch, the lowest and most decorative. Perhaps I should say, decorated. It lies within the tree level, which none of the others do, and has a lovely frieze of pine trees, an eagle's eyrie in one of them, and ancient fallen trunks visible at its bottom through the clear water. The greenness of the water varies according to the light, now aquamarine, now verdigris, but it is always pure green, metallic rather than vegetable. That one which hangs between a precipice and sloping slabs of naked rock on the face of the great curve of cliffs between Braeriach and Cairntoul, has the sharpest beauty of the four—a stark splendour of line etched and impeccable. Ben MacDhui and Cairngorm of Derry have the other two, less picturesque than the first, less exquisite than the other. The Spey slope of these mountains has the best of it with lochs, but the Dee slope has the lovelier burns—they fall more steeply, with deep still pools below the falls.

Two of the lochs are black by name—the Dubh Loch of Ben a' Bhuird, and the Dubh Loch that lies in the second cleft that cuts the plateau, the Little Lairig; but they are black by place and not by nature, shadowed heavily by rock. That the water has no darkness in it is plain when one remembers that the clear green Quoich runs out of the one loch and the Avon is fed by the other. In winter the ice that covers them has green glints in it, and in April dark streaks run through the glinting ice, showing where the springs are already running strong beneath. In summer I have stood on the high buttress of Ben a' Bhuird above the Dubh Loch, with the sun striking straight downward into its water, and seen from that height through the water the stones upon its floor.

This water from the granite is cold. To drink it at the source makes the throat tingle. A sting of life is in its touch. Yet there are midsummer days when even on the plateau the streams are warm enough to bathe in. In other years on the same date the same streams surge out from caves of snow and snow bridges span not only the Dee on its high plateau but the Etchachan in its low hung corrie; and fording the Allt Druie, which is too swollen to cross dryshod, I have been aware of no sensation at all, not even of the pressure of the current against my legs, but cold.

The sound of all this moving water is as integral to the mountain as pollen to the flower. One hears it without listening as one breathes without thinking. But to a listening ear the sound disintegrates into many different notes—the slow slap of a loch, the high clear trill of a rivulet, the roar of spate. On one short stretch of burn the ear may distinguish a dozen different notes at once.

NAN SHEPHERD

LIGHT

Light in Scotland has a quality I have not met elsewhere. It is luminous without being fierce, penetrating to immense distances with an effortless intensity. So on a clear day one looks without any sense of strain from Morven in Caithness to the Lammermuirs, and out past Ben Nevis to Morar. At midsummer, I have had to be persuaded I was not seeing further even than that. I could have sworn I saw a shape, distinct and blue, very clear and small, further off than any hill the chart recorded. The chart was against me, my companions were against me, I never saw it again. On a day like that, height goes to one's head. Perhaps it was the lost Atlantis focused for a moment out of time.

The streams that fall over the edges of the plateau are clear—Avon indeed has become a by-word for clarity: gazing into its depths, one loses all sense of time, like the monk in the old story who listened to the blackbird.

> Water of A'n, ye rin sae clear,
> 'Twad beguile a man of a hundred year.

Its waters are white, of a clearness so absolute that there is no image for them. Naked birches in April, lighted after heavy rain by the sun, might suggest their brilliance. Yet this is too sensational. The whiteness of these waters is simple. They are elemental transparency. Like roundness, or silence, their quality is natural, but is found so seldom in its absolute state that when we do so find it we are astonished.

NAN SHEPHERD

MAN COMES UPON THE SCENE

In one of the latest geological periods, known as the Ice Age, nature made use of a sculpture-tool no longer to be seen at work in Britain. When the present valleys and hills had been long in existence, the climate gradually became arctic in character, and sheets of snow and ice settled down upon the country. As in Greenland at the present time, an ice-sheet covered the whole of Scotland, and moved seaward in vast icy streams. Creeping over the land for a protracted period, it ground down its surface, removing the angular forms left by the previous sub-aërial waste, and replacing it by the smooth, polished and striated surface so characteristic of glacier-friction. A large amount of detritus was also produced, which was spread over the low grounds and slopes of the hills as boulder-clay. Huge blocks of rock were likewise borne far away from their native mountains, and dropped upon the hill-tops and plains of the lowlands.

Since the ice melted away, the sea, rains, streams, springs, and frosts have renewed their old work of demolition. The smoothed and flowing outline which the ice left behind it is now undergoing a slow destruction, and the rocks are quietly resuming the rugged outlines which they had of old. The sea-coasts are receding before the onward march of the waves. Former ravines have been deepened and widened by the rivers, and new ones have been formed. Man, too, has come upon the scene, and has set his mark upon well-nigh every rood of the land from mountain-top to seashore. He has helped to demolish the ancient forests; he has drained innumerable fens and mosses, and turned them into fertile fields; he has extirpated the wild beasts of the old woods, thus changing both the aspect of the country and the distribution of its plants and animals. He has engraved the land with thousands of roads and railways, strewn it with villages and hamlets, and dotted it with cities and towns. And thus more has been done by him, in altering the aspect of the island, than has been achieved, during the brief period of his sojourn, by all the geological agencies put together.

ARCHIBALD GEIKIE

THE WONDER OF HUMANKIND

I am a jingo patriot of planet earth: 'Humanity right or wrong!'

Particularly in Autumn. At noon I crossed a field off which the last of the stooks had been lifted and led captive away, the gaping stubble heads pushed through the cricks of clay, the long bouts of the binder wound and wheeled around the park, where the foreman had driven his team three weeks before. And each of those minute stubble stalks grew from seed that men had handled and winnowed and selected and ploughed and harrowed the earth to receive, and sown and tended and watched come up in the rains of Springs and the hot Summer suns—each and all of these—and out and beyond their kindred trillions in the other parks, up to the biggings of Upperhill there, and south through all the chave of the Howe to the black lands that start by Brechin and roll down the coast till they come to the richness of Lothian and the orchards of Blairgowrie. . . . This is our power, this the wonder of humankind, our one great victory over nature and time. Three million years hence our descendants out on some tremendous furrowing of the Galaxy, with the Great Bear yoked to The Ploughs and the wastes of space their fields, will remember this little planet, if at all, for the men who conquered the land and wrung sustenance from it by stealth and shrewdness and a savage and surly endurance. Nothing else at all may endure in those overhuman memories: I do not think there is anything else I want to endure.

LEWIS GRASSIC GIBBON

Beginnings

GROWING UP IN LANGHOLM

After journeying over most of Scotland, England and central, southern and eastern Europe, as well as America, Siberia and China, I am of
the opinion that 'my native place'—the Muckle Toon of Langholm, in
Dumfriesshire—is the bonniest place I know: by virtue not of the little
burgh in itself (though that has its treasurable aspects, and on nights
when, as boys, we used to thread its dim streets playing 'Jock, Shine
the Light', and race over the one bridge, past the factory, and over the
other, with the lamp reflections wriggling like eels at intervals in the
racing water, had an indubitable magic of its own), but by virtue of the
wonderful variety and quality of the scenery in which it is set. The
delights of sledging on the Lamb Hill or Murtholm Brae; of gathering
hines in the Langfall; of going through the fields of Baggara hedged in
honeysuckle and wild roses, through knee-deep meadow-sweet to
the Scrog Nut Wood and gathering the nuts or crab-apples there; of
blaeberrying on Warblaw or the Castle Hill; of dookin' and guddlin' or
making islands in the Esk or Ewes or Wauchope and lighting stick fires
on them and cooking potatoes in tin cans—these are only a few of the
joys I knew, in addition to the general ones of hill-climbing and
penetrating the five glens which (each with its distinct character)
converge upon or encircle the town—Eskdale, Wauchopedale, Tar-
rasdale, Ewesdale and, below the town Carlislewards, the Dean
Banks.

As we grew up, too, we learned to savour the particular qualities
and rites of Langholm in comparison with other Border burghs: the
joys of Langholm Common Riding compared with those at Selkirk or
Hawick, for example; the peculiar shibboleths of local pronunciation;
the historical associations of our corner of the 'Ballad-land' rife with its
tales of raidings and reivings and with the remnants of peels; the
wealth of local 'characters' who were still about.

As I grew into my early teens I ranged further afield, and soon all
the Borders were within my ken. Many places had their special
beauties or points of interest and advantage; but none had the variety
of beauty centred round Langholm itself—none seemed so complete a
microcosm of the entire Borderland. I knew where to find not only the
common delights of hill and forest and waterside (and chiefest of all
these to me were the chestnut trees at the sawmill—even now it thrills
me to remember the beautiful chestnuts, large and luxurious as

horses' eyes, which so surprisingly displayed themselves when we cracked open the prickly green shells, and I remember many huge strops of them I strung and many a fierce competition at Conquerors), but also the various kinds of orchises, and butterwort, sundew, and the like; the various nests—including Terrona crags where ravens nested; how to deal with adders and smoke out wasps' 'bikes', and much other lore of that sort. In short, a boyhood full of country sights and sounds—healthy and happy and able to satisfy its hunger with juicy slices of a big yellow neep stolen from an adjoining field.

There were scores upon scores of animals and birds I knew far better than I now know the domestic cat, which is the only specimen of the 'lower animals' of which I see much. My eyes may, perhaps, still seek out and recognise and appreciate a dozen or so wild flowers in the course of a year, but my memory recalls—with a freshness and a fullness of detail with which such living specimens cannot vie at all— hundreds I have not seen for over thirty years. My poetry is full of these memories: of a clump of mimulus 'shining like a dog's eyes with all the world a bone'; of the quick changes in the Esk that in a little stretch would far outrun all the divers thoughts of man since time began; of the way in which, as boys, with bits of looking-glass, we used to make the sun jump round about us. Above all, when I think of my boyhood, my chief impression is of the amazing wealth of colour. A love of colour has been one of the most salient characteristics of Scots poetry down to the best work of our contemporary poets, and I have celebrated it again and again in my own work.

Many great baskets of blaeberries I gathered on the hills round Langholm. Then there were the little hard black cranberries, and— less easy to gather since they grow in swampy places—the speckled craneberries, but above all, in the Langfall and other woods in the extensive policies of the Duke of Buccleuch, there were great stretches of wild raspberry, the fruit of which the public were allowed to pick, and many a splendid 'boiling of jam' I gathered there—gathering more than the raw material of jam, too.

I would come cycling back into Langholm down the Wauchope road with a pillowslipful of crab-apples (as at other times a basket of plovers' eggs) on my carrier; and again there was the Scrog Nut Wood, shaking its bunches of nuts like clenched fists in the windy sunlight. I have nowhere seen loveliness so intense and so diverse crowded into so small a place. Langholm presents the manifold and multiform grandeur and delight of Scotland in miniature—as if quickened and thrown into high relief by the proximity of England.

There is a place at Langholm called the Curly Snake where a winding path coils up through a copse till it reaches the level whence, after passing through a field or two, it runs into the splendid woods of the Langfall. It has always haunted my imagination and has probably constituted itself as the ground-plan of my mind, just as the place called the Nook of the Night Paths in Gribo-Shov, the great forest north of Hillerod, haunted Kierkegaard's.

My boyhood was an incredibly happy one. Langholm was indeed —and presumably still is—a wonderful place to be a boy in. Scotland is not generally regarded as a land flowing with milk and honey. Nevertheless, it can do so more frequently than is commonly understood. It certainly did so in my boyhood—with a bountifulness so inexhaustible that it has supplied all my subsequent poetry with a tremendous wealth of sensuous satisfaction, a teeming gratitude of reminiscence. I still have an immense reservoir to draw upon. My earliest impressions are of an almost tropical luxuriance of nature—of great forests, of honey-scented heather hills, and moorlands infinitely rich in little-appreciated beauties of flowering, of animal and insect life, of subtle relationships of water and light, and of a multitude of rivers, each with its distinct music.

HUGH MACDIARMID

ON HIS BROTHER ROBERT

Letter to Mrs Dunlop

Mount Oliphant, the farm my father possessed in the parish of Ayr, is almost the very poorest soil I know of in a state of cultivation. A stronger proof of this I cannot give than that, notwithstanding the extraordinary rise in the value of lands in Scotland, it was, after a considerable sum laid out in improving it by the proprietor, let a few years ago five pounds per annum lower than the rent paid for it by my father thirty years ago. My father, in consequence of this, soon came into difficulties, which were increased by the loss of several of his cattle by accidents and disease. To the buffettings of misfortune, we could only oppose hard labour and the most rigid economy. We lived very sparingly. For several years butcher's meat was a stranger in the house, while all the members of the family exerted themselves to the utmost of their strength, and rather beyond it, in the labours of the farm. My brother, at the age of thirteen, assisted in threshing the crop of corn, and at fifteen was the principal labourer on the farm, for we had no hired servant, male or female. The anguish of mind we felt at our tender years under these straits and difficulties was very great. To think of our father growing old (for he was now above fifty) broken down with the long continued fatigues of his life, with a wife and five other children, and in a declining state of circumstances, these reflections produced in my brothers' mind and mine sensations of the deepest distress. I doubt not but the hard labour and sorrow of this period of his life, was in a great measure the cause of that depression of spirits, with which Robert was so often afflicted through his whole life afterwards. At this time he was almost constantly afflicted in the evenings with a dull headache, which, at a future period of his life, was exchanged for a palpitation of the heart, and a threatening of fainting and suffocation in his bed, in the night-time.

GILBERT BURNS

ON HIS CHILDHOOD AND YOUTH

Letter to Dr John Moore, 2 August 1787

I was born a very poor man's son.—For the first six or seven years of my life, my father was gardiner to a worthy gentleman of small estate in the neighbourhood of Ayr. Had my father continued in that situation, I must have marched off to be one of the little underlings about a farm-house; but it was his dearest wish and prayer to have it in his power to keep his children under his own eye till they could discern between good and evil; so with the assistance of his generous Master my father ventured on a small farm in his estate.—At these years I was by no means a favorite with any body.—I was a good deal noted for a retentive memory, a stubborn, sturdy something in my disposition, and an enthusiastic, idiot—I say idiot piety, because I was then but a child.—Though I cost the schoolmaster some thrashings, I made an excellent English scholar, and against the years of ten or eleven, I was absolutely a Critic in substantives, verbs and particles.—In my infant and boyish days too, I owed much to an old Maid of my Mother's, remarkable for her ignorance, credulity and superstition.—She had, I suppose, the largest collection in the county of tales and songs concerning devils, ghosts, fairies, brownies, witches, warlocks, spunkies, kelpies, elf candles, dead-lights, wraiths, apparitions, cantraips, giants, inchanted towers, dragons and other trumpery.—This cultivated the latent seeds of Poesy; but had so strong an effect on my imagination, that to this hour, in my nocturnal rambles, I sometimes keep a sharp look-out in suspicious places; and though nobody can be more sceptical in these matters than I, yet it often takes an effort of Philosophy to shake off these idle terrors.—The earliest thing of Composition that I recollect taking pleasure in was, The vision of Mirza and a hymn of Addison's beginning—'How are Thy servants blest, O Lord!' I particularly remember one half-stanza which was music to my boyish ear—

> For though in dreadful whirls we hung,
> High on the broken wave

I met with these pieces in Masson's English Collection, one of my school-books. The two first books I ever read in private, and which gave me more pleasure than any two books I ever read again, were the life of Hannibal and the history of Sir William Wallace. Hannibal gave my young ideas such a turn that I used to strut in raptures up and down after the recruiting drum and bagpipes, and wish myself tall enough to be a soldier; while the story of Wallace poured a Scottish prejudice in my veins which will boil along there till the flood-gates of life shut in eternal rest . . . My father's generous Master died; the farm proved a ruinous bargain; and, to clench the curse, we fell into the hands of a Factor who sat for the picture I have drawn of one in my Tale of two dogs.—My father was advanced in life when he married; I was the eldest of seven children; and he, worn out by early hardship, was unfit for labour.—My father's spirit was soon irritated, but not easily broken.—There was a freedom in his lease in two years more, and to weather these two years we retrenched expences.—We lived very poorly; I was a dextrous Ploughman for my years; and the next eldest to me was a brother, who could drive the plough very well and help me to thrash.—A Novel-Writer might perhaps have viewed these scenes with some satisfaction, but so did not I: My indignation yet boils at the recollection of the scoundrel tyrant's insolent, threatening epistles, which used to set us all in tears.—

This kind of life, the chearless gloom of a hermit with the unceasing moil of a galley-slave, brought me to my sixteenth year; a little before which period I first committed the sin of RHYME.—You know our country custom of coupling a man and woman together as Partners in the labors of Harvest.—In my fifteenth autumn, my Partner was a bewitching creature who just counted an autumn less.—My scarcity of English denies me the power of doing her justice in that language; but you know the Scotch idiom, She was a bonnie, sweet, sonsie lass.—In short, she altogether unwittingly to herself, initiated me in a certain delicious Passion, which in spite of acid Disappointment, gin-horse Prudence and bookworm Philosophy, I hold to be the first of human joys, our dearest pleasure here below.—Among her other love-inspiring qualifications, she sung sweetly; and 'twas her favorite reel to which I attempted giving an embodied vehicle in rhyme—I was not so presumtive as to imagine that I could make verses like printed ones, composed by men who had Greek and Latin; but my girl sung a song which was said to be composed by a small country laird's son, on one of his father's maids, with whom he was in love; and I saw no reason why I might not rhyme as well as he, for excepting smearing sheep and casting peats, his father living in the moors, he had no more Scholarcraft than I had.—

Thus with me began Love and Poesy; which at times have been my only, and till within this last twelvemonth have been my highest enjoyment.—My father struggled on till he reached the freedom in his lease, when he entered on a larger farm about ten miles farther in the country.—The nature of the bargain was such as to throw a little ready money in his hand at the commencement, otherwise the affair would have been impracticible.—For four years we lived comfortably here; but a lawsuit between him and his Landlord commencing, after three years tossing and whirling in the vortex of Litigation, my father was just saved from absorption in a jail by phthisical consumption, which after two years promises, kindly stept in and snatch'd him away—'To where the wicked cease from troubling, and where the weary be at rest.'—

It is during this climacterick that my little story is most eventful.—I was, at the beginning of this period, perhaps the most ungainly, aukward being in the parish.—No Solitaire was less acquainted with the ways of the world.—My knowledge of ancient story was gathered from Salmon's and Guthrie's geographical grammars; my knowledge of modern manners, and of literature and criticism, I got from the Spectator.—These, with Pope's works, some plays of Shakespear, Tull and Dickson on Agriculture, The Pantheon, Locke's Essay on the human understanding, Stackhouse's history of the bible, Justice's British Gardiner's directory, Boyle's lectures, Allan Ramsay's works, Taylor's scripture doctrine of original sin, a select Collection of English songs, and Hervey's meditations had been the extent of my reading.—The Collection of Songs was my vade mecum.—I pored over them, driving my cart or walking to labor, song by song, verse by verse; carefully noting the true tender or sublime from affectation and fustian.—I am convinced I owe much to this for my critic-craft such as it is.

ROBERT BURNS

A BUCHAN WINTER MORNING

Snaa pounced at nicht, sleekit in its ambush. Ye kent in the mornin afore ye waur weel oot o yer bed that the quality o the licht had chynged sin ye crept in amon the oo, the lift had a washed-oot glare an a metallic glint cam sklentin fae the cloods; the bedroom itself wisna the kent place ye were eesed till. Ye could smell snaa afore ye peepit ower the rim o the windae. The parks lay like a clootie dumplin somebody had flattened an dichtit wie sugar; here an there black grun markit the place faar the speen coupin the dazzle had wavered an missed. The mornin air took a haud o ye, made ye notice skin an surface, drave ye quick oot o the sleep raivellin yer noddle. Ye cast aboot for a maazie tae hap yer haill airm, tae ging ticht roon yer neck an smore ye gin it wad only fecht back against the nakitness brocht on bi the caul bite o the bare room. Linoleum jeel't yer taes an the dance for socks an sheen wis the same as gin yer feet had lichtit on a het girdle, nae tae be tholed for lang. Broonies hid a new, shairp edge tae the steadins an hooses; snaa brocht a new rise an faa tae the parks an ye saa palins ye'd seen a thoosan times afore as gin a feverish fairy had tchauved aa nicht tae pit them faar ye saa they waur. Skushlin throwe the fite pooder on the close wis a dance the first mornin; a tramp the second, a tchauve the third. Steps plantit on the grun reclaimed something fae the winter—like a gesture tae deny that the ambush wis a great success. Blin drift kept us back fae the skweel, for fear that roads wad be blockit or we won hame again.

DAVID OGSTON

THE AUL' WAAL

'Come oot o 'at, ye puddlin vratch,'
Skraichs the girnie wife at me.
'Ye'll tummle in an droon yersel,
Ye'll catch yer death o caul'.
Losh, quine, fit div ye get to watch
In 'at aul' waal?'

Fit div I watch? See yon spoot?
Hear the water trinklin oot?
Kep some in yon roosty mull.
Naebody badders gin ye spull,
Doon b' the aul' waal.

I'm feart at yon dark nesty place
Laich ower 'ere, at the back,
Faar green an slivvery tangles dreep
An emmerteens an gollachs creep,
An poddicks lowp an slaters crawl
Roon the eezins o the waal.

Bit I like 'at place faar it's shinin blue,
The colour o the sky;
Faar little pansy-faces teet
Atween the steens, an prood an tall
Pink foxgloves boo to see themsels
In their lookin-gless, the waal.

An fyles on a stull hairst efterneen—
Nae breath o win' to stir
The sma fite deukie's fedder curled
Roun' the dry carl-doddie floo'er—
I see doon 'ere the Muckle Furth twa-faal,
Clood, fleein bird an the toozy heid 'ats me,
The big warl in a little warl, the waal.

'Come oot o 'at, ye puddlin vratch,'
Skraichs the girnie wife at me.
'Come awa fae 'at aul' waal,
'Ere's naething 'ere to see,'
Says she.

FLORA GARRY

OCH AY! THE ORRA LOON!

Och ay!   The orra loon!
Och hon!   The orra loon!
Till a' the warld is deid or gweed,
We'll aye lo'e the orra loon!

Wha weers moleskins lang and ticht?
Ca's the corters oot o' sicht?
Gies his lugs an antrin dicht?
Och ay!   The orra loon!

Wha is't likes te smoke and sweir?
Kens a stirkie fae a steer?
Reads the P'leece News a' the 'ear?
Och ay!   The orra loon!

Wha kicks Blackie wi' his tae?
Blaws up puddocks wi' a strae?
Thinks na o' the Judgement Day?
Och ay!   The orra loon!

Wha wid never blink an ee
Though the Kirk fell in the sea,
And Mains amang the midden-bree?
Och ay!   The orra loon!

Och ay!   The orra loon!
Och hon!   The orra loon!
Till a' the warld is deid or gweed,
We'll aye lo'e the orra loon!

JOHN C MILNE

FIN I CAM' HAME TE NEDDERTON

Fin I cam' hame te Nedderton
Upon a Monday nicht,
Says Mistress Broon, 'Gae milk the kye—
Their aidders will be ticht.'

The first coo that I cam' till
Was lyin in the sta'.
Says I, 'Get up, auld Sweernis!'
Bit she wadna rise ava.

O Blackie is a canny coo,
Wi' mony a bonnie pap!
But a' that I could rug and tug,
She wadna gie a drap!

I gaed up te Sklaverdads,
But wow! she glowered at me!
Says I, 'Gweed faith, my bonnie lass,
I think I'll lat ye be!'

Fin I sat doon by Fitie's side
My hert was like te brak,
And lang ere I had milkit her
I lay upon my back!

Through amang the feeders
A rottan gid a squeal!
I left ahin my milkin-pail,
And a' my wuts as weel!

O faither, faither, tak' me hame!
I carena for my fee!
O faither, faither, tak' me hame,
And a better bairn I'll be!

JOHN C MILNE

THE WHISTLE

He cut a sappy sucker from the muckle rodden-tree,
He trimmed it, an' he wet it, an' he thumped it on his knee;
He never heard the teuchat when the harrow broke her eggs,
He missed the craggit heron nabbin' puddocks in the seggs,
He forgot to hound the collie at the cattle when they strayed,
But you should hae seen the whistle that the wee herd made!

He wheepled on't at mornin' an' he tweetled on't at nicht,
He puffed his freckled cheeks until his nose sank oot o' sicht,
The kye were late for milkin' when he piped them up the closs,
The kitlin's got his supper syne, an' he was beddit boss;
But he cared na doit nor docken what they did or thocht or said,
There was comfort in the whistle that the wee herd made.

For lyin' lang o' mornin's he had clawed the caup for weeks,
But noo he had his bonnet on afore the lave had breeks;
He was whistlin' to the porridge that were hott'rin' on the fire,
He was whistlin' owre the travise to the baillie in the byre;
Nae a blackbird nor a mavis, that hae pipin' for their trade,
Was a marrow for the whistle that the wee herd made.

He played a march to battle, it cam' dirlin' through the mist,
Till the halflin squared his shou'ders an' made up his mind to 'list;
He tried a spring for wooers, though he wistna what it meant,
But the kitchen-lass was lauchin' an' he thocht she maybe kent;
He got ream an' buttered bannocks for the lovin' lilt he played.
Wasna that a cheery whistle that the wee herd made?

He blew them rants sae lively, schottisches, reels, an' jigs,
The foalie flang his muckle legs an' capered ower the rigs,
The grey-tailed futt'rat bobbit oot to hear his ain strathspey,
The bawd cam' loupin' through the corn to 'Clean Pease Strae';
The feet o' ilka man an' beast gat youkie when he played—
Hae ye ever heard o' whistle like the wee herd made?

But the snaw it stopped the herdin' an' the winter brocht him dool,
When in spite o'hacks an' chiblains he was shod again for school;
He couldna sough the catechis nor pipe the rule o' three,
He was keepit in an' lickit when the ither loons got free;
But he aften played the truant—'twas the only thing he played,
For the maister brunt the whistle that the wee herd made!

CHARLES MURRAY

THE GULLION

I can mind the gullion
ayont the midden and the auld Alvis.

I can mind the ducks waddlin oot the gate to dook.
And Peter goose takin oot his wives
through the slap—hissin and streekin his neck.
The gullion for cuttin nettles wi a scythe and whettin-stane
—or bill or heuk noo I mind the words.
And cuttin new gress for pownies owre in the field.
And boontree canes—for bows and airrows.
The gullion for takin oot the powny on a halter
for special grazin when it's dried oot. The gullion
for cuttin fails.

I can mind the gullion wi the swings
and muckle puddles for jumpin. And the stane dyke
for settin up tin cans for shootin at
wi a point two five—I think. And the speugies
and stookies and craws—and blackies e'en.
And waws to sclim to fields for shootin
foxes—yin fox—and maukins and rats. And huntin
oot peeweeps' eggs and stanein wasps' bike
—and rinnin for the gullion.

I can mind the gullion and aw the lans ayont.
I went back   and fund
a wee bit boggy grund.

DUNCAN GLEN

RENEWAL

I

I would return to the magic places o my youth.
Tak you on burnside walk by fithills o Campsies
and the heich hills o innocence. Aa
taen for real without a thocht o leid.

II

I see mysel a youthfu sixteen
walkin alane by the burnside.
Step efter step through the lang gress
and stoopin as needit ablow the trees
hingin owre. The gress bends to my step
and I tak a wey through there
as if a landscape made for me
though pethless and boggy in pairts.

There's the quick rustle o birds aneath the bushes
and mavis's sang shairp frae a branch
heich and daurk agin the blue sky.
And through the cuttin o the burn
suddenly the heich hills
kent in their richtfu place
frae mony lang walks
yet nou moved close in
but a step ayont that nearest linn.

The cheyngin flow o the burn, the quait breeze,
bendin blade o gress and gethered greenness
a diversity o single wunner
shairp and clear. And a warmth aa round
taen as pairt o this weill-kent place.
And silence tae as mavis flees aff,
but soon it, or ither, in full sang frae heicher branch
and juist as naiturally true.

Step efter step and een and ears
and aa that is that youth
in taen perfect harmony as that that is
aa around. Aa perfect to that single youth
and in its richtfu place
as he thocht
and walkt at ane wi it
joyfu in the kennin wunner
—though thinkin aa ayont him
tae.

III

Look back to the stane in mid-stream,
the faaen tree, the fence to be sclimed
and honeysuckle smellt. The hundrit-leggit
beast and the bricht-colourt fungi on the tree.
Look to the face o the heich hill
and white hillside burn flowin owre. The linn
to be stood ahint and rainbows seen.
And rocks to be sclimed to the tap.
The cottage by the burn wi reekin lum,
and ferm set doun low wi shelterin trees
at back. Look to hill-fermer walkin
his mony acres. And his dugs warkin the sheep.

Aa taen then as equal
ayont ony conflict
—and aa circlin round me!

But nou I hae shown it to you
and you to me anew
as real as you
lit by the licht o our luve

—and aa the warld in it . . .

DUNCAN GLEN

JOCK TAMSON'S BAIRNS

When I was a bairn I lived within sight of enemy territory. Only a stones-throw away lay a strange foreign country. England!

I was told the natives were an unfriendly lot. Indeed, they were our bitterest enemies, waiting for an opportunity to slink across the Border, steal our cattle and sheep, and burn down our abbeys.

The very farm on which I lived had been the scene of many a bloodthirsty battle in the past. There were still many scars to prove it, including the ruins of a look-out tower on the hill where the sheep were now peacefully grazing. It was here I played houses, but never forgot to keep a watchful eye on the frontier, ready to fire the beacon and raise the alarm if the dreaded enemy showed face.

> Fee-Fi-Fo-Fum!
> I smell the blood of an Englishman.

I was a trifle disappointed to see nothing more warlike on the horizon than the baker's horse or the postie on his bicycle. My catapults and bows-and-arrows remained unused, for I never even smelt the blood of one Englishman.

The trouble was there was a kind of No-Man's-Land on the Border; nothing but wild rolling hills that were Scottish one moment and English the next, though they looked exactly the same to me on both sides. Could it be that the human beings were alike, too? But how could the English be human?

I was soon to find out.

I met my first foreigner at the village school where I was a Mixed Infant. *She* was much more mixed than I was. Was she not *English*? Had she not cycled over from that dreaded 'other place', and did she not speak with a strange accent? Her ancestors had killed mine, and I wasn't going to let her get away with it.

I fought the battle bravely, but lost. The result: my first black eye, which I richly deserved. I was quite proud of it for a time, and then a strange thing happened. We became firm friends. Me!—fraternising with the English!

From then on, I forgot the bloodthirsty tales of the past, and found out for myself what lay across the divide. The people were people, just like us, though they did speak in a different tongue; but it was only an accent. And, looking at Scotland from the other side, I began to wonder if maybe we were not entirely blameless ourselves. Had we not done *our* share of foraging?

There were scars on both sides, but surely they would heal. My black eye did; and soon my English friend and I were sharing the best of both worlds. We became bilingual. She taught me songs about 'The fishy in the little dishy' and 'Keep your feet still, Geordie hinney'; and in return I introduced her to 'Annie Laurie' and 'The lum hat wantin' a croon'. Soon I forgot she was English. She was just a lassie like myself.

It surprised me to find there was heather growing on her side of the Border, looking every bit as Scottish as it did on mine; and that English sheep had four legs, no different from ours. Ah! But the shepherds were. Ours had his own special way of whistling through his fingers to call the collie dogs to heel, and he counted his flock: 'Ane-twae-three-fower'. The English shepherd, on the other hand, had a queer kind of rigmarole: 'Een-teen-tethera-methera'. But it all added up to the same thing, and he came over the Border to help us at clipping-time. And never spilt a drop of our blood.

Gradually I forgot there was a frontier there at all. I still played houses in the ruined tower, but I never bothered about looking for the enemy or firing the beacon. I watched the horizon instead to see if *she* was coming—my English friend who had taught me we're a' Jock Tamson's bairns, no matter on which side of the Border we live.

LAVINIA DERWENT

LAUGHING TATTIES

It was dark November, and that particular November evening seemed very dark and cold to me as I trudged my way home from school. We were living in little huts at a farm called Arn Bog, halfway between Meigle and Eassie. The huts are still there, down an old road at the corner of a field.

It was about four miles' walk to Meigle school. 'All the other bairns are home long ago,' I thought. 'I wish that teacher wouldn't keep me in every night.'

Children from cotter houses and farms along the way also had to walk home from school. Though they often chanted, 'tinkie, tinkie, torn rags' to me, and didn't walk with me, I could always follow a bit behind them, and I was not so frightened.

I transferred my little school case from my frozen left hand to my right, then put my free hand into my bosom to try to get feeling back into it. Out of the murky darkness a big crow came marching, nearly up to my feet. It was searching for food. 'Are you hungry, too?' I said aloud. I was very hungry myself. They did have a soup kitchen at the school, but it cost a penny a day, and many mornings there was no penny for me to take—nor anything else. So apart from a drink of tea in the morning, I had not yet broken my fast.

Just then, a human figure walked towards me, and my heart was in my mouth for a moment before I recognised it as my mother. Mother was tall for a woman, and in spite of having been pulling turnips all day, walked very straight. She was wearing heavy muddy boots, and I could hear the water squelching in them with every step she took. The front of her dress, too, was all wet and muddy.

'Did that silly teacher keep you in again,' she greeted me.

'Aye Ma,' I answered.

'Instead of trying to fill your head with book learning, better she would go and learn some sense from someone herself. That is if she can find anyone with sense. God pity her, would any woman with sense keep a wean till this time of night, in the dark, dead months of winter. She kens the road you have to come.'

Mother ranted on about the stupidity of the country hantle (non-travellers) for about fifteen minutes, then suddenly the tone of her voice changed. 'Never mind, wean. You've two whole days before you have to go back again. In the morning when I get my coppers from the farmer, I will buy you a pair of warm stockings, and maybe a sweetie.'

I had just reached the age of seven, and had started going to Meigle school in mid October. Before that, I had been potato-picking. Traveller people's children only needed two hundred attendances; then they were free to roam at will. The parents were given a card which stated that a child had attended school for a hundred days, and which could be shown to any policemen or to the 'cruelty'—usually a member of RSSPCC. Sometimes they would be accompanied by a nurse, who would examine the children's heads for vermin, look inside the tents, and check the children's physical appearance, asking numerous questions as they did so. Very often there were few children to examine. At the first wind of these people's presence, the children scattered like rabbits into hiding—up trees, inside harvest stooks, in the middle of whin bushes, or to whatever place they could find. This was not because they were verminous, but because the examination was an insult to their dignity.

Of course, the people sometimes did find children whom they considered to be neglected. These children were forcibly removed from their parents and put into 'homes'. The 'homes' were often founded by people who imagined that they were doing a great service to humanity, and who honestly believed that travelling people were so low in mentality that the loss of their children would put them neither up nor down. Actually, children were loved beyond telling. One seldom sees travelling people without a host of bairns around them. So the suffering of those whose children had been taken was pitiful to see. Especially as they were not allowed to visit them, under threat of prison—a fact which quite a few old travellers will verify.

That night near Meigle, Mother and I arrived at the wee hut very cold and hungry, but we were cheered to find the stove well alight, and a big pot of 'laughing tatties' on top of it—laughing tatties was the name Mother gave to unpeeled potatoes which had burst their skins in the cooking.

BETSY WHYTE

SANDY STEWART AT SCHOOL IN BIRNAM

We mixed up aathegither an played wae yin anither. We wir in wae the bairns o the school. There wes anither tinker bairn richt enough but he shifted away tae Blairgowrie. Higgins ye caad him an he hed a place in Torwood a while. [His fether] hed a motor lorrie an usetae gether scrap—Hughie Higgins. He got his fingers aff in the war Ah think. Ah think the boy was caad efter his fether. The auld school wesnae real finished when Ah left it but we shifted ower tae Burnim an went tae that school intae Torwood. The teacher that teached hus in hit wes Miss Gibb. She usetae bide at the back door o J D Reid's shop, an Miss Stewart, she usetae bide there. The same boy o the shop got married tae Miss Gibb. An thir wir lots come tae Perth tae teach thair but this yins bud in the toon. Thir wes a Miss Munro.

But this auld school wes as ye come oot fae Burnim an thir wes a green den yonder. Well, ye passed hit an thir usetae be a joiner's shoap at the side, an ye come tae twaa or three hooses; ye wid look ower at the side atween the joiner's place an the green, an yed see the old school wi the playgrun. It wes an old stone-made yin. That wes the school we went tae then. Ah can mind the way we dressed when we went tae the school fer sometimes we hed a new suit. When we come hame we changed claes at nichts when we wir bleggartin aboot rubbish an things. We got wirsels washed up an sorted in the moarnin, then away tae school. Ma mither hed lots o claes intae boxes an things, an she kept them back fer us if we made an awfie mess o wirsels. People that kent her usetae gie her big loads o claes, some better than those ye bocht! When we wir intae Burnim, as lang as yer claes wir clean on the inside they wirnae particular. Thir usetae be a nurse went aa ower yer heid. The nurse was ginger-heidit an she bud intae Dunkel. Then thir wes mair come fae Perth an they examined every skull near. Ye wir taen intae a room an aa yer heid wes lookit; yer claes wes lookit—that wes in the new school they done it. They done it in the auld yin tae but they nivver hardly bothered me fer that. Thats the wey they got ye, an no ony me but the rest o the bairns that bud in the toon. They lookit ower every yin that wes thair.

The bairns wes richt enough wae me. We jest bleggard taegether. Thir usetae be a shop at the brig yonder an we'd gaun an get the sweeties an half them wae yin anither. They didnae mind that Ah wes a tinker. Mebbe the odd stranger that come in an dednae ken us micht get a bit rough, but then we micht get a bit rough wae them an they cooled doon. If a drove o them come in that ye never seen, then the ither laddies o the place wid tak yer side. They didnae lea ye oot. Me an the ither laddies usetae dae a lot o devilment. If we seen a puckle hens we stoned them fer fun. We usetae mak four-wheel boaggies fer braes wi pramwheels an a long bourd. Then ye could get a box on the back, nailed fer sittin on. Ye could go doon the brae an guide them wi yer feet an a bit rope. Some exles ye got hed a hole dreelt in them an ye could pit a bolt through fer the bourd in the front. If ye didnae hae a hole, onie smith wid dae it fer ye fer nothin. It wesnae easy fer us dreelin irun but the smith hed a steam thing an could dae it in a minute. He gied ye a bolt tae. We usetae get lots o wheels an thir wir places intae Burnim whaur Ah've seen them gien us whole pram-bulators sometimes.

Thir wir smiths in Burnim an thir wes a seddlers. The seddler's hoose wes doon aneth the War Memorial. Dr Mather's hoose wes at the side an thir wir thae big walnut trees along the hedge. We usetae wallop them doon wi sticks when we wir at the school but ye could never get the same as the shoap yins fer thae wir aye green an wild-taistit. We usetae knock them an chessnuts doon. Ah've seen us knockin them doon fer a whole day an playin conkers. An we usetae play kites an jumpin ower rope tae see how high we could jump. Mair boys usetae come an we usetae aa hae a go at it apiece. Then, when we wir youngur Ah've seen ma fether build us swings fae the tree whaur a big brench come oot. We usetae swing on hit wi a bourd an pass the days that way. Then we made swing-boats wae a great big box an four ropes. Ye could pull yirsel up and doon wi hit. Oh we made some good invenshuns. We usetae get a lot o toys up in Dunkel an Burnim at that

5   Deserted Shieling, Achmore. Photograph by Sam Maynard/Eolas.

6   Hew Ramsay from Garlieston. Buchlyvie Ploughing Match, Stirling.
       Photograph by Peter Davenport.

7   Bowling Green, Port Ellen, Islay. Photograph by Peter Davenport.

8   4th Green, St Fillans Golf Club, Perthshire. Photograph by Peter Davenport.

time. Thir wes a chemist man an he usetae hae a hoose jest at the church yonder, whaur the rest o ma people is buriet. Everytime we come hame fae school we got boxes o aa kinds o toys: motors, railway trains, big wooden horses—all fae this chemist man. When he bocht the new toys we got the rest that the bairns hed.

We usetae get lots o Christmas presents fae people roon aboot the place whaur we wir. We usetae get cakes, sweeties an lots o stuff. At the school a Christmas tree come an we got a lot o guid toys aff it but it come that ye hed tae go tae Perth fer hit. Ye got a line an ye went doon tae St John's Church, hed a good nicht thair an come back up again. When we wir wearied up thair we wir gled tae get doon tae the toon. Ah seen us at Hogmanay at that time, us an a lot o bairns fae the toon, an we usetae run awaa oot guisin. We got lots o pennies an sweeties that nicht by pittin auld wumens frocks on an wir faces black. Ye hed a good time o it at that day. Better than what yer haen noo! Ye wisnae wearied an hed ay plenty o company. But noo when yir sittin yirsel at the camp ye get wearied tae death.

recorded and edited by ROGER LEITCH

BACKGROUND

Frost, I mind, an' snaw,
An' a bairn comin' hame frae the schule
Greetin', nearly, wi' cauld,
But seein', for a' that,
The icicles i' the ditch,
The snaw-ploo's marbled tracks,
An' the print o' the rabbits' feet
At the hole i' the wire.

'Bairn, ye're blue wi' cauld!'
An apron warmed at the fire,
An' frostit fingers rubbed
Till they dirl wi' pain.
Buttered toast an' tea,
The yellow licht o' the lamp,
An' the cat on the clootie rug
Afore the fire.

HELEN CRUICKSHANK

BEECH LEAVES

To-day I leaned on a gate looking into a turnip-field,
And while I was idly comparing
The thin green rows on the ridges of earth
With mustard and cress,
I plucked a glossy new leaf from the old beech-hedge
That ran between the field and the road,
And holding the leaf against my lips
I blew on it, making a noise, half-whistle, half-squeak,
Until the leaf was torn.

And with the sound my mind ran backwards
Fifty years,
And I saw myself, a sturdy lassie of six,
Going to school with my two big brothers,
Down the hill to the village where we were the 'gentry-kids'
Among the rough-spoken children there.
(In Jim's class no one else wore a linen collar, and so
His class-mates called him 'The Laird'.)

I remembered the long beech-hedge at one side of the road,
By the wood that no one entered.
On the other side was a ditch and a high green bank
Topped by the fence of a field of corn.
We used to search for sourocks among the grass, and eat them,
And once the boys found a wasps' byke in the bank
And, gathering other boys from the school, attacked it
With switches of broom,
Sending me first, their protesting sister,
Up the road away out of danger,
For I always wanted to do what the boys did,
And did, too.
But this time I felt on the side of the wasps,
For what had they done, that their house should be harried and torn?
So I went up the road and watched, hoping the boys would get stung,
And hoping, too, that they wouldn't.

HELEN CRUICKSHANK

GUDDLING FOR TROUT

We had a bell in our schoolroom which Miss McArthur rang at 9 o'clock when morning lessons began and *we* rang at 12.30 when we were dismissed. As soon as that bell was put back on her table we tore out of the classroom as if someone had shouted 'Fire!' It was then a race, a wild stampede across the green and down to the bridge, into the almost dried-up bed of the burn, hopping from stone to stone, with incredible speed and agility, till at last we reached our destination—the one deep pool by the waterfall that was all that an unusually sunny June had left of its swift brown waters. Here, all was dark and silent except for the noise of the water. The high cliffs of rock and bracken shut out the sunlight on two sides, and lower down through the bared peat of the crumbling bank you could see the black bones of ancient tree roots. Here there were huge granite boulders and shelves of rock over which we hung for hours at a time—gently feeling for the fat, brown, speckled trout that slept below, nose in, tail outwards, dreaming perhaps of dragon flies and spate waters—gently, gently we felt, our arms plunged deep into the icy water, gently, slowly, till you knew that your delicate searching fingers were touching something more solid than water and your pulse quickened and your heart began pounding so loud that the trout must surely hear it, and your fingers began stroking, gently, gently, till your arm ached like a tooth with the coldness of it, and you slowly began changing the position of your hand, but slowly, gently, stroking and turning until *WOOMF!* You suddenly clutched with all your might, throwing your arm and your whole body back in one fleet movement, and sometimes, not very often, but *sometimes*, there would be a greeny-brown, opaque yet shining little fish with a dark cream belly and red spots on his dappled side, gasping there in the heather beside you—and a distinct strange fishy smell in the air.

VERONICA MACLEAN

MY SCOTLAND

A question most frequently put to me . . . 'Do you ever get homesick for Scotland?'

The answer is simple. . . . No. . . . The reason for it is equally simple, my Scotland, two corners of the North East, in Morayshire and Aberdeenshire, are small enough to be contained both spiritually and emotionally. I carry their climate intact—within myself.

From the age of six it was impressed upon me that I had my roots in the soil of Morayshire—albeit that discovery was made gazing down on the six feet of earth—that ultimate heritage of all men.

Every Sunday, rain or shine, I went with my mother to Elgin Cemetery, 'the dead' she always reminded me, 'are quiet folk', acknowledging in passing the 'quiet folk' she had known in their life-times. But the purpose of her pilgrimage was to the grave of one

> John Grant
> Farmer
> Burnside

to whom she laid claim—first claim! . . . 'My Grandfather'—before allowing me a *lesser* kinship! 'Your Great Grandfather'. She also bequeathed me with his surname as an extension of her own name to atone perhaps for the fact that my natural begetter remained forever . . . nameless!

With maturity and hindsight I realise that our weekly visits to the grave of John Grant were for my mother an affirmation of her own roots—blurred sometimes by what must have been to her an alien way of life in a tenement room in a slum 'close'.

My Grandmother—a farmer's daughter, married a farmer—a Tenant farmer—with 'a Place'. In the North East farms are referred to as 'Places'—Crofts as 'placies'. The right word for them, 'Place' something to which we are all entitled, and which becomes to each his own.

The Landowner, casting a possessive eye on my Grandfather's rented land, decided that he'd like it back for himself, and served an eviction order accusing my Grandfather of being 'A bad Husband-man'. An accusation which greatly distressed my Grandmother, her priorities were concerned with her family, not with their possessions;

so that she kept impressing on her children . . . 'It doesn't mean that your father is a—bad Husband—Husbandman is a different thing'.

My Grandfather fought the case in the Court at Edinburgh, and won it, vindicating his reputation as an Husbandman. A hundred years ago for a small farmer to 'take on' a Landowner needed both courage and conviction. My Grandfather had both.

I share his conviction . . . in that Morayshire seems to me to be *my* Scotland.

My other claim to Scotland, that small part of rural Aberdeenshire on the threshold of the Don, brings to mind the lines of Rupert Brooke:

> Now God be thanked
> Who has matched us with his hour.

Albeit in a different context! For almost a decade that bleak locale matched the bleakness of my spirit in its exile from Morayshire, a land that to *me*, was harsh and austere by comparison. It never had the mellowness of Moray's wooded landscape; the colour of its cottage gardens, in this part of Aberdeenshire gardens became 'Yards'. Planted but for . . . utility.

I missed the Ancient Mariners,—the tellers of tall tales,—who had 'held me with their glittering eyes'— in the close mouth in Elgin.

Sometimes though, rare, heart-stopping times, my two such opposite lands would merge and speak with one voice in an Aberdeenshire school-room—

> Up the airy mountain
> Down the rushy glen
> We dare not go a-hunting.

'But I knew that long, long ago,' I'd claim to myself. 'I learned that in Elgin.'

And yet . . . with the passing of time, I began to realise that words, in their Aberdeenshire brevity, had the merit of truth. A quality insisted on by our Dominie who deplored and detested what he described as 'Padding'.

I was no longer 'conned', maybe manipulated is the better word, by the flattery of grown-ups into running for 'messages' which they themselves disliked to undertake . . . 'My fine quinie just ask Higgins to put it on the slate.' Praise in Aberdeenshire accents was genuine. Blame was fair. And neither had ulterior motives.

'Train up a child in the way it should go', was an oft repeated axiom in the orphanage. 'And when it is old it will not depart from it.' An axiom not much to my liking at the *time*! Nor suited to my temperament. But, when I *did* grow older, it stood me in good stead, both in my 'bread and butter' working life and in my writing life, where discipline had to be all. As indeed did the Dominie's No Padding edict. I pare to the essence.

Both of these small areas of Scotland moulded me, laid claim on me, as I do on them, Morayshire . . . the heart. Aberdeenshire . . . the mind.

JESSIE KESSON

TODD

My father's white uncle became
  Arthritic and testamental in
  Lyrical stages. He held cardinal sin
Was misuse of horses, then any game

Won on the sabbath. A Clydesdale
  To him was not bells and sugar or declension
  From paddock, but primal extension
Of rock and soil. Thundered nail

Turned to sacred bolt. And each night
  In the stable he would slaver and slave
  At cracked hooves, or else save
Bowls of porridge for just the right

Beast. I remember I lied
  To him once, about oats: then I felt
  The brand of his loving tongue, the belt
Of his own horsey breath. But he died,

When the mechanised tractor came to pass.
  Now I think of him neighing to some saint
  In a simple heaven or, beyond complaint,
Leaning across a fence and munching grass.

STEWART CONN

THE HORSES

I was charmed by everything that flew, from the humble bee to the Willie Longlegs. At that stage the novelty of seeing a creature flying outweighed everything else.

My height from the ground determined my response to other things too. When my father and Sutherland brought in the horses from the fields I stood trembling among their legs, seeing only their great, bearded feet and the momentary flash of their crescent-shaped shoes flung up lazily as they passed. When my father stopped with the bridle in his hands to speak to me I stood looking up at the stationary hulks and the tossing heads, which in the winter dusk were lost in the sky. I felt beaten down by an enormous weight and a real terror; yet I did not hate the horses as I hated the insects; my fear turned into something else, for it was infused by a longing to go up to them and touch them and simultaneously checked by the knowledge that their hoofs were dangerous: a combination of emotions which added up to worship in the Old Testament sense. Everything about them, the steam rising from their soft, leathery nostrils, the sweat staining their hides, their ponderous, irresistible motion, the distant rolling of their eyes, which was like the revolution of rock-crystal suns, the waterfall sweep of their manes, the ruthless flick of their cropped tails, the plunge of their iron-shod hoofs striking fire from the flagstones, filled me with a stationary terror and delight for which I could get no relief. One day two of our horses began to fight in the field below the house, rearing at each other like steeds on a shield and flinging out with their hind-legs, until Sutherland rushed out to separate them. A son of our neighbour at the Haa had a crescent mark on his forehead where a horse had kicked him; I stared at it in entrancement, as if it were a sign in the sky. And in a copy of *Gulliver's Travels* which my eldest brother had won as a school prize there was a picture of naked men with hairy, hangdog faces. The horse was sitting on its hindquarters, which had a somewhat mean and inadequate appearance; its front hoofs were upraised and its neck arched as if to strike; and though the picture was strange and frightening, I took it to be the record of some actual occurrence. All this added to my terror of horses, so that I loved and dreaded them as an explorer loves and dreads a strange country which he has not yet entered.

EDWIN MUIR

HORSES

Those lumbering horses in the steady plough,
On the bare field—I wonder why, just now,
They seemed terrible, so wild and strange,
Like magic power on the stony grange.

Perhaps some childish hour has come again,
When I watched fearful, through the blackening rain,
Their hooves like pistons in an ancient mill
Move up and down, yet seem as standing still.

Their conquering hooves which trod the stubble down
Were ritual that turned the field to brown,
And their great hulks were seraphim of gold,
Or mute ecstatic monsters on the mould.

And oh the rapture, when, one furrow done,
They marched broad-breasted to the sinking sun!
The light flowed off their bossy sides in flakes;
The furrows rolled behind like struggling snakes.

But when at dusk with steaming nostrils home
They came, they seemed gigantic in the gloam,
And warm and glowing with mysterious fire
That lit their smouldering bodies in the mire.

Their eyes as brilliant and as wide as night
Gleamed with a cruel apocalyptic light.
Their manes the leaping ire of the wind
Lifted with rage invisible and blind.

Ah, now it fades! it fades! and I must pine
Again for that dread country crystalline,
Where the blank field and the still-standing tree
Were bright and fearful presences to me.

EDWIN MUIR

GROWING UP IN WYRE

When I think of our winters at the Bu they turn into one long winter evening round the stove—it was a black iron stove with scrollwork on the sides, standing well out into the kitchen—playing draughts, or listening to the fiddle or the melodeon, or sitting still while my father told of his witches and fairicks. The winter gathered us into one room as it gathered the cattle into the stable and the byre; the sky came closer; the lamps were lit at three or four in the afternoon, and then the great evening lay before us like a world: an evening filled with talk, stories, games, music, and lamplight.

The passing from this solid winter world into spring was wild, and it took place on the day when the cattle were unchained from their stalls in the six months' darkness of the byre, and my father or Sutherland flung open the byre door and leaped aside. The cattle shot through the opening, blind after half a year's night, maddened by the spring air and the sunshine, and did not stop until they were brought up by the stone dyke at the other end of the field. If anyone had come

4   Ploughing on Orkney. Photograph by Gunnie Moberg. © Owl Productions Ltd.

in their way they would have trampled over him without seeing him. Our dog Prince, who kept a strict watch over them during the summer, shrank before the sight. That was how spring began.

There were other things connected with it, such as the lambing; I think our lambs must have been born late in the season. I have a picture of my mother taking me by the hand one green spring day and leading me to the yard at the back of the house to see two new-born lambs. Some bloody, wet, rag-like stuff was lying on the grass, and a little distance away the two lambs were sprawling with their spindly legs doubled up. Everything looked soft and new—the sky, the sea, the grass, the two lambs, which seemed to have been cast up without warning on the turf; their eyes still had a bruised look, and their hoofs were freshly lacquered. They paid no attention to me when I went up to pat them, but kept turning their heads with sudden gentle movements which belonged to some other place.

Another stage in the spring was the sowing. About that time of the year the world opened, the sky grew higher, the sea deeper, as the summer colours, blue and green and purple, woke in it. The black fields glistened, and a row of meal-coloured sacks, bursting full like the haunches of plough-horses, ran down each one; two neat little lugs, like pricked ears, stuck up from each sack. They were opened; my father filled from the first of them a canvas tray strapped round his middle, and strode along the field casting the dusty grain on either side with regular sweeps, his hands opening and shutting. When the grain was finished he stopped at another sack and went on again. I would sit watching him, my eyes caught now and then by some ship passing so slowly against the black hills that it seemed to be stationary, though when my attention returned to it again I saw with wonder that it had moved. The sun shone, the black field glittered, my father strode on, his arms slowly swinging, the fan-shaped cast of grain gleamed as it fell and fell again; the row of meal-coloured sacks stood like squat monuments on the field. My father took a special delight in the sowing, and we all felt the first day was a special day. But spring was only a few vivid happenings, not a state, and before I knew it the motionless blue summer was there, in which nothing happened.

There are zones of childhood through which we pass, and we live in several of them before we reach our school age, at which a part of our childhood stops for good.

EDWIN MUIR

A ST KILDA CHILDHOOD

We made our own amusements. And we played games with the village children. But not many of the games that children play on the mainland. Their games were mainly concerned with imitating what their elders did in the everyday life of the community. For instance, the playing of dogs and sheep. Dogs catching the sheep. You know, of course, that the dogs caught each sheep individually.

Well, each dog was trained, each working dog was trained to catch a sheep, and its teeth, its canine teeth were filed for that purpose so that it wouldn't damage the sheep. The children used to play at this game—you know, some of us were sheep and the other would be the shepherd with perhaps one or two dogs, and you would whisper into somebody's ear, go and catch so-and-so, and the dogs would run and single out one particular sheep from the flock and drag it to the shepherd's side, and this sort of thing, you know, a childish game, imitating the elders. And we played rounders. We used to have many a riotous game of rounders—in the Springtime especially, when the evenings got long, and the ground was nice and dry. Hide and seek we were very fond of hide-and-seek, and there were lots of places to play. Lots of walls and crannies that we could hide in, and we really had a wonderful time.

The dogs sometimes had to run in very precipitous places, and it did sometimes happen that sheep sometimes went over the cliff. The people themselves wore no shoes. They went bare-foot when they went about that work because it was much safer. They were less likely to slip on the ledges and on the steep places. And I can remember a boy of ten clamouring to be allowed to go down—as his brother, his older brother and his father were doing—and he was lowered down the cliff like the older people and up he came, quite triumphantly, in a few minutes, with a few birds.

They tried to catch the fulmar before it had time to squirt the oil out—that's its means of defence. The oil was very valuable. It was used for lubricating the wool before it was manufactured and I suppose for various other purposes as well. They used it in the old days, before the advent of paraffin lamps, they used it for their cruisies. And I've seen a cruisie burning with fulmar oil in it at a time when paraffin was short. I remember seeing a man weaving by the light of a cruisie.

The St Kildan people were very particular about the keeping of the Sabbath—like many other Highland folk, and they weren't willing to handle cargo on Sunday. And I remember in the summertime when the Glasgow steamers came—that was the occasion on which the Inspector of Schools made his annual visit. On this occasion the ss *Hebrides* arrived on a Sunday, the cargo couldn't be unloaded until after midnight, the captain was very anxious to sail as soon as possible afterwards, so we were all mustered out of our beds shortly after midnight so that we could meet the inspector and answer the necessary questions. But I'm afraid we didn't make a very impressive show but at least the regulations were complied with.

It was the understood thing that everybody went to church. It was unheard of to stay at home, and if you had a newly born baby in the house, well you just took the baby too. And if Mother had to feed the baby in church, well she just fed the baby in church.

MARY CAMERON

Mary Cameron, a daughter of the minister of St Kilda, recorded her memories of the 1920s in an interview with George Bruce for the Scottish Home Service of the BBC.

A CHILDHOOD IN SOUTH UIST
Mrs Cath Wilson of South Uist talks about her childhood

We were about six miles outside Lochboisdale on the West coast; on the Atlantic side as it were.

I was born in one of the thatched houses—they called it a black house. It had two bedrooms and a kitchen cum living room. Six of us were born in the thatched house, but my sister was born in a stone house built for my father in 1923. In these days we had the box bed and another bed for the younger ones. The boys all slept in a bedroom. It was clay flooring. You swept it and went to the shore for fine white sand. You cleaned the floor and then spread the sand over it. It was the fashion in those days and then they started getting concrete floors. We had peat fires. The men cut the peats and we went and turned them till they dried. In Lewis it was the women that cut the peats, but I've never cut peat in my life.

We didn't have a stove in these days. Everything was done on a kind of open fire. That's where you did all your baking. My mother baked with the girdle. She made scones and oatcakes and, in those days, barley bread. My father took barley to the mill and they ground it and we got it back to make the barley bread.

Everything was done from the time it was cut and threshed by hand, not by machine. In the barn we had a round hole and my father spread the corn on sticks with a peat fire underneath to dry it. Then he took it to the mill.

My father and my uncle had a boat between them and they fished for lobsters during the summer. Then he did joinery on the side—he was very good with his hands. He did a lot of things, like mending clocks. He also made coffins. There was another joiner in the village and my father did it for the protestants and he did it for the catholics. South Uist did not have many protestants. In North Boisdale there was our family and three other families. There was a big chest for storing flour. My father had a work bench and a box of tools in the stable which he kept in the boys' room in winter when the horses were in the stable. One night the boys were wakened up by the noise of somebody rumbling in the box—and there were three bags of meal on top of it. When they told my mother she wanted it taken out of the house. That was an omen that there was a coffin to be made, and sure enough a cousin died soon after of pleurisy, and my father made the coffin. Quite a few things like that happened. My father had to shape the wood for the shoulders, and he had to take the kettle and steam it so that the wood could bend. That was when we had one of these American stoves—and the kettle used to jump on the stove before my father made the coffin. And my mother would say: 'Oh I wonder who is going to die next.'

We had to walk to church. It was three miles and back again. We sang psalms. The service was an hour and a half at least. My father was the precentor in Gaelic for a good number of years until he got too old and then my brother took over. It was Church of Scotland. We had to go to Sunday school. It was held in our house since my father was an elder. We had to rush home from church and get our dinner over before the Sunday school started.

We had sheep and our own cows and my father had a garden. We never really were short of anything. We got good wholesome food. My father's croft was 20 acres. We had three horses. They had to do all the work.

We had to walk two and a half miles to school.* Sometimes in the winter my father had to come to meet us, because of the wind and snow. You had to carry your piece in your pocket and sometimes it was eaten before you were half-ways to school, and then you were starving by the time you got home. Teaching was in English and Gaelic. It was an Irish headmaster who had been there long before I went to school. He didn't speak Gaelic. There were two other teachers who were from the Island and they could speak it. We weren't taught Gaelic as it is today. We just spoke Gaelic. We sang in Gaelic at the school.

At Halloween we used to dress up and go round the houses. You had to go in with false faces and the people in the house had to guess who you were. The lady of the house would have a big basin of oatmeal on the table with cream in it, and my mother would put her wedding ring, a button, and a thimble in the basin, and whoever got the wedding ring from the basin would get married first. The button was a bachelor and the thimble was a spinster. We had great fun. If one of the boys got the ring off the spoon they kept it in their mouth while everyone else was digging into the basin to find it. That was my idea of a party. We didn't keep Christmas in those days. It was held by the catholics. They went to mass on Christmas Eve.

At Hogmanay we went round first footing—well the boys did. Girls weren't allowed. The boys knocked on the door. They held a candle and they spoke or sang rhymes, all in Gaelic of course. The boys got scones and tea. They had a bag for small gifts, and they wished the lady of the house a good new year.

We had storms. They were very bad one year. My aunt had a thatched roof and it was lifted right off. Sometimes my father and mother had to go out to secure the corn stacks. Parts of them were found miles away. But we had lovely summers too. We never wore boots from April to September. Our mother wouldn't allow us to leave off our boots until the weather was warm, but we used to take them off and hide them behind a big stone near the schoolhouse, and then we collected them on the way home.

My mother had to make do with what we had. We had hens. My father got an egg but the younger ones just got the top of my father's egg. I would stand and look and wonder if I was going to get the top off the egg. We got porridge and a piece of scone. I hated the taste of barley bread. It was thin. We couldn't grow wheat, the soil was too thin and sandy. We had six or seven cows.

Father got up at four in the morning in the summer to go fishing; the boat was one with oars and sail. They fished for lobsters which were sent to Billingsgate. My father scythed enough corn to keep my mother busy till he got back from the fishing. My mother had a basket with fifteen dozen eggs in it and she would get all the groceries at the shop in exchange for the eggs, only six pence a dozen. She had to walk the two and a half miles with a big basket of eggs. My mother was a weaver. She made all the boys' tweed. She washed the wool, dyed it, then carded and spun it, and wove it. The loom was in a neighbour's house. My mother was up to all hours and then up early to milk the cows. Men didn't milk cows. My mother had to do the churning by hand. She made cheese too. It wasn't stored: it was eaten.

Interview with MRS CATH WILSON
recorded and edited by GEORGE BRUCE

* Garrynamonie school, which Mrs Wilson's parents also attended. Each carried a peat daily to school. Their headmaster (1890–1894) was F G Rea.

BETWEEN SEA AND MOOR

My house lay between the sea and the moor; the moor which was often red with heather, on which one would find larks' nests, where one would gather blaeberries: the moor scarred with peatbanks, spongy underfoot: blown across by the wind (for there is no land barer than Lewis). I am a child again, barefooted, jerseyed, bare-kneed, the daisies are growing, the daffodils are a blaze of yellow. The smoke of the village chimneys is rising into the sky. There is a vague desultory hammering, dogs are barking, there are cows munching clothes on the line.

Days when we played football all day, nights when we played football by the light of the moon, returning home across the moor like sweaty ghosts, the moon a gold football in the sky.

How can one be that boy again? How can one walk home from the well with the two pails brimming with water, on paths that are probably now gone, between the cornfields, and through the long grass.

The moor and the grass and the sea. Throwing stones at telegraph poles, jumping rivers, watching roofs being tarred, hearing the lazy hammering of stones from the quarry.

The high sky of Lewis above the sea, the bleak landscape almost without distraction of colour.

And beyond it all on moonlit nights hearing the music of the accordion and the feet of the dancers from the end of the road, having thoughts of a warm eternity brooded over as by a hen with red feathers.

Later, but in Dumbarton, I would try to write about some of this in a complex of images which I called 'Some Days Were Running Legs':

> Some days were running legs and joy
> and old men telling tomorrow would be
> a fine day surely, for sky was red
> at setting of sun between the hills.

> Some nights were parting at the gates
> with day's companions: and dew falling
> on heads clear of ambitions except light
> returning and throwing stones at sticks.

Some days were rain flooding forever the green
pasture: and horses turning to the wind
bare smooth backs. The toothed rocks rising
sharp and grey out of the ancient sea.

Some nights were shawling mirrors lest the lightning
strike with the eel's speed out of the storm.

IAIN CRICHTON SMITH

A BOY IN THE STRATH

In the Highlands of Scotland a strath is a small glen. For a small
boy—a boy up to ten or twelve years of age—a strath is ideal in size,
because its physical features are not so vast or extensive but they can
be encompassed on foot yet are extensive or 'far off' enough never to
be exhausted in interest or wonder or the unexpected. A glen can be
too big, its mountain sides too high, its cataracts or river too fierce or
deep to cross, its distances too bare and forbidding for a small boy to
know with any intimacy more than his own home part of it. Our Strath
we knew throughout its length—or very nearly. To walk its full length
to the river source—always called the Waterhead—was the ultimate
adventure and the thought of it inhabited the mind with a peculiar
strangeness. Unlike the old lady who did not believe that Jerusalem
was on this earth, we believed the Waterhead was—but only just, so
we could laugh at the old lady very loudly in our appreciation of the
joke. For a small boy three miles up a strath and three miles back, with
loiterings and deviations, was a very long journey, indeed a whole
day's adventure, with a meal missed and a hunger that made a
leanness of the belly that could be felt inside. And outside, too, by
one's own hand, or by the hand of a companion invited to 'have a
feel'. We were given to 'proving' things in this empirical way.
   These first two or three miles were the rich ones. After that the trees
thinned, the strath grew shallower, and glimpses of the moor were
caught. It was a vast moor, austere as a desert, and the farthest rim of
the horizon lit itself on the far edge of the world. Leftward the ridges
of near hills shut off the mountains beyond, and somewhere in that
country where moor and mountains met the river had its source. But
the rich part was so infinitely varied in attraction that only in odd

moments did we think, or dream, of one day setting out for the Waterhead.

It would be difficult even to make a list of individual attractions, for any one item had in the matter of place, quantity and quality a very intricate pattern, so that within a given or general attraction there were particular attractions, and for us, ah! it was the particular that mattered.

Take hazel nuts. Hazel trees grew at haphazard or in congested clumps throughout the whole area, on the river flats and on the steep slopes or braes, not so numerous as the birches, but more numerous than rowans (mountain ash), alders, oaks or other stunted varieties of trees that often seemed to exist singly and did not interest us because we did not need them for any purpose. We hardly even noticed them, until they became particularly striking, like a rowan laden with a heavy crop of blood-red berries.

As there are varieties of apples so, for us, there were varieties in nuts. We could tell them at a glance by size and colour, just as one distinguishes a Cox's Orange Pippin from a Mackintosh Red. The glance, the appearance, told the invisible but all-important thing: the taste, the flavour. I do not know if a description of the taste of an Orange Pippin has ever been caught in a phrase but we had our phrase for the corresponding nut (which was not unlike the pippin in colouring) and it was 'a whisky taste'. That none of us may ever have tasted whisky was no matter. Our elders had, as we so very well knew, and possibly in some backward reach of time one elder, the day being dry, had chewed this particular nut and found within its slipping flavours the memory of a more ardent taste.

But apart from the different varieties or kinds, a knowledge of the places where they grew and the spots where maturity came early, there was always the chance that in this strath of continuous exploration you would come on one particular tree where all the excellences were gathered together. And it happened.

The glance, the wonder, the doubt, the climbing, the cluster. You put your finger on the tip of the nut and it turns over in its sheath. Ripe! You turn it right over and out. Its bottom is dark brown. Not only brown but with a peculiar suggestion of greyness like a bloom. This is it! It must be! . . . *It is!* And the teeth you had all but shoved into your skull in cracking it settle back again.

NEIL GUNN

THE BOY AND THE SALMON

With his head tilted back to keep the water from lapping into his mouth, the boy feels for the bottom of the pool, and the big toe of his right foot comes gently against a surface that yields. As his eyes widen so does his mouth, and the water laps in. Choking and threshing the surface he rolls over, reaches blindly overhand, kicks hard and grounds on the edge of the pool, where his body goes into a slow convulsive squirm in its desperate effort to spew water and suck air at the same time. When it seems everything is coming up, a little breath gets down. As the gasping lessens, he draws out of the pool like an otter and subsides among the stones and gravel.

But the glisten of the incredible in his eyes does not lessen. The choking struggle had hardly interfered with it. Now the glisten holds and he listens. From the hazel tree at the neck of the pool, over on the other side where he has left his clothes, a cock chaffinch gives an angry *spink! spink!* But from the hillside above it a willow wren's song comes tumbling down over leafy branches in sunny ease. Its carefree warmth in that world of its own, which is also the watching world, is reassuring. Letting out the gasp he has held in, he lifts his head slowly and his eyes rove over the willow wren's trees, and round, and down to the river, and up the river to the bend where it disappears two hundred yards away, and still farther round until he is looking over his shoulder across the flat ground that runs back for a short distance to the other wooded slope of the winding Strath. No one. Not a suspicious movement of a branch. Nothing against a skyline. Nothing.

But even if there is an invisible someone, what of it? He has done nothing. They cannot collar him for doing nothing. So he gets up, his naked body clothed in this innocence, and doesn't even swim back the way he had come, but walks up round the edge, stooping and slipping awkwardly, as if his innocence for all the world had made a girl of him, as if the stones really hurt his feet, until he reaches the narrow neck of the pool. Here the gush of water is strong and his difficulty in crossing is laughable. But he gets across and on to the rock ledge beside his clothes under the shadow of the hazel tree, and in an instant his innocence vanishes.

That feel on his big toe, that slippery yielding as the salmon took the caress! He looks at his big toe. On its own it comes apart from the other toes and gives a small crack. The salmon liked the feel of his toe. Its body had given slightly, not lain over but yielded, as a dog to a hand it likes. And his touch had been light as a feather because the buoyant water had bobbed him off.

The size of the fish and its strength are fearsome, but he is watching the pool. A swirl in the shallows at the tail-end where the salmon turns; the wave-swirls die out and all is as before.

The gulps come as if he had run a great race and, fear or no fear, down the pool he goes, wades the shallows at the foot, peering into the water, reaches the other side and comes up on the submerged flagstone with the clear miraculous lie. No fish there. Beneath the ledge, no shadow. Nowhere. So it must be the fourth, black, deep lie.

Within a couple of minutes he is heaving stones over that lie. They hit the surface with whacks that could be heard at horizons. They spout fountains in the air. Let them! A man cannot do something and not do it. Heave them in! That'll shift him! His recklessness is terrible and glorious. For at last he is committed.

How many hours he hunted the salmon on that summer day he could afterwards only guess, his absorption was so utterly complete. The water streaming down his face troubled him no more than it troubled an otter. Fear almost left him, except for the queer primitive fear that the salmon might boil up again between his legs. But even that didn't stop his big toe. And once when he nearly drowned himself the panic quickly passed and he felt all the better for it, more confident.

But inevitably the time came when he could not find the salmon anywhere, when he was beaten. The salmon is having a stormy passage because the river is at summer level, spread out into small shallow pools, with innumerable tails and necks and, everywhere, great boulders and flagstones. In his haste, as though pursued by the father and mother of all otters, the fish runs aground on a sloping flagstone, wallops loudly, and is off; but the boy sees him, comes abreast of him, skipping from one stone to another with a speed that had he gone by the head might well have finished him.

Wading in, he heaves a stone that just misses, but it turns the salmon. The fish can go faster up than down but blind speed is his danger, for if he doesn't take the deepest runnel he will shore up and flounder. The boy turns him again, and loses him, and finds him in a small pool, where they come to close quarters. But as he heaves his large stone he slips, goes headlong in front of the salmon, and the salmon rams him in the navel. He embraces the fish, but the great brute goes out at his chin like a greased thunderbolt. After that the boy goes berserk.

The end comes when he lands his heavy missile fair on the nape where the otter bites, for the salmon, losing all sense of direction now, tears through the shallows to one side and beaches himself a full yard beyond the water's edge, there to wallop the stones with the sounds of two immense butter-clappers. With his body the boy blockades him, and in time wedges his head and kills him, then lies beside him until his gasping lungs ease and he can see properly.

But he doesn't see properly until the fish is lying on mossy grass under a hazel tree. Then realization of what he has done breaks on him. It is a cock fish, deep at the shoulders, marvellously shaped, grace with power, perfect and magnificent. It is the biggest salmon he has ever seen. Wonder is in his adoration. He wipes some fine gravel off the silver. The incredible is true.

NEIL GUNN

A COMPLETE EDUCATION IN A COUNTRY MANSE

The notable scholar William Robertson Smith (Professor at Free Church College, Aberdeen, Editor of the 9th edition of *Encyclopedia Britannica*, Professor of Arabic at Cambridge University—1883), was brought up in the Free Church Manse of Keig, and educated there by his father Rev William Pirie Smith, along with the family and four young boarders. 'The Free Manse of Keig can be seen as a symbol of the older Scottish culture in which clergymen and teachers diffused university influence and intellectual cultivation throughout the rural society in which the university (Aberdeen) had its roots' (RD Anderson). The Rev W S Bruce visited the manse and witnessed how the boy, William, could bring into a single focus the wide ranging education.

One of the things which impressed me in W R Smith was his power of applying old sayings to modern instances. The one that remains with me is the saying of Heraclitus, πάντα ῥεῖ; 'all things are in flux' suited William's scientific tastes, and he would talk to us endlessly in illustration of it—how the clouds came over Bennachie ('Banff Bailies' they were called in Keig), how they filled the streams that fed the Don, which flowed to the sea; how the mist rose from the German Ocean and again formed the clouds and the cycle went on. Then it would be some illustration of the plants capturing air, water, and salts, and with the sun's help building themselves up by vital alchemy into complex substances, then the farmers' cows eating the plants and a new incarnation beginning; then the cows being killed and becoming part of ourselves by the Sunday dinner of beef . . . then man dying and returning to the earth, and the cycle again beginning as the microbes of decay disintegrated the dead, and all returned to water and salts and air, to be again taken up by the grass and clover. All flesh is grass, πάντα ρεῖ; nothing is lost; all things flow on. Willie was most impressive in that kind of talk and delighted greatly in it. We boys listened in stillness as his quick mind scoured over endless fields of illustration of this kind . . . and enforced upon our boyish minds the impermanency of the Cosmos and the wisdom of the old philosophers of Greece for whom he had a great admiration at that time. . . . I dreamt whole nights over πάντα ρεῖ and evolution after my return from the Manse of Keig.

At noon Dr Pirie Smith took his pupils for a walk, which 'it was quite understood to be part of the education of the Manse. Often out of the minister's pocket would come a volume for our delectation—probably Tennyson's *In Memoriam*. At another time it would be fragments of the Poet Laureate in the grand style, such as *Oenone* or *Ulysses*. . . .

Prose too had its place in these rambles and talks; stories about Gibbon, Emerson, Carlyle, and Dr Chalmers would vary the racy chat of the twelve to one o'clock walks. Sometimes, however—to my great delight and Willie's too—Dr Smith would stop at a point on the hill where the huge rocks abutted on the path, and would give us a very graphic description of rock formation, and of the chemical action of percolating water on the stone. We were shown how the Aberdeen granite was clearly of igneous origin, and how big Bennachie across the Don had been consolidated in the cooling of the earth's crust and then shot upwards into its long camel's back and various 'taps' which had become more sharply defined by subsequent denudation. . . . We could scarcely believe all that was said, and hardly knew that we were learning modern science, so pleasantly and jocularly was much of it done. We joked at the tea-table about Bennachie's back, and would take liberties with the hard crusts of loaf to show the girls how, with a little squeezing, it was the easiest possible thing to produce miniature Bennachies and camels' backs and thus make room for descending Dons and their tributary streams.

JOHN SUTHERLAND BLACK and GEORGE CHRYSTAL

Folk

PROLOGUE

Letter from Mendelssohn to Karl Klingemann, Berlin, March 26, 1829

Dear Klingemann,

NEXT AUGUST I AM GOING TO SCOTLAND,
with a rake for folksongs, an ear for the lovely, fragrant countryside,
and a heart for the bare legs of the natives.

Klingemann, you must join me; we may lead a royal life! Demolish
the obstacles and fly to Scotland. We want to take a look at the
Highlanders.

Your distracted, hurried and really weeping

FMB

FELIX MENDELSSOHN-BARTHOLDY

from the EPITHALAMIUM on the occasion of the Marriage of Mary Queen of Scots to the Dauphin of France   *24 April 1558*

Not here will I tell you about the country's acres of fertile land, about
its glens fruitful in cattle, its waters fruitful in fish, its copper and
lead-laden fields, its hills where is found bright gold and hard iron, its
rivers flowing through metalliferous veins—enriching commodities
which other nations besides ours possess. These things let the
numbskull mob admire, and those who despise everything but
wealth. . . .

But the real boast of the quivered Scot is this: to encircle the glens in
the hunting, to cross, by swimming, the rivers, to bear hunger, to
despise the variations of cold and hot weather; not by moat and walls,
but by fighting to defend their native land, and to hold life cheap
when their good name has to be maintained unimpaired; once a
promise has been made, to keep faith; to revere the holy spirit of
friendship; and to love not magnificence but character.

GEORGE BUCHANAN trans by HUGH MACDIARMID

5   The Dance on Dun-Can, From *Picturesque Beauties of Boswell by Rowlandson*. Courtesy of the Trustees of the National Library of Scotland.

DR JOHNSON IS RECEIVED IN RAASAY

Our reception exceeded our expectations. We found nothing but civility, elegance, and plenty. After the usual refreshments, and the usual conversation, the evening came upon us. The carpet was then rolled off the floor; the musician was called, and the whole company was invited to dance, nor did ever fairies trip with greater alacrity. The general air of festivity, which predominated in this place, so far remote from all those regions which the mind has been used to contemplate as the mansions of pleasure, struck the imagination with a delightful surprise, analogous to that which is felt at an unexpected emersion from darkness into light.

When it was time to sup, the dance ceased, and six and thirty persons sat down to two tables in the same room. After supper the ladies sung Erse songs, to which I listened as an English audience to an Italian opera, delighted with the sound of words which I did not understand.

I inquired the subjects of the songs, and was told of one, that it was a love song, and of another, that it was a farewell composed by one of the Islanders that was going, in this epidemical fury of emigration, to seek his fortune in America.

SAMUEL JOHNSON

DOROTHY WORDSWORTH AND PARTY ARE RECEIVED BY MRS MACFARLANE

26 August, 1803. Near the Trossachs

The good woman had provided, according to her promise, a better fire than we had found in the morning; and indeed when I sate down in the chimney-corner of her smoky biggin' I thought I had never been more comfortable in my life. Coleridge had been there long enough to have a pan of coffee boiling for us, and having put our clothes in the way of drying, we all sate down, thankful for a shelter. We could not prevail upon the man of the house to draw near the fire, though he was cold and wet, or to suffer his wife to get him dry clothes till she had served us, which she did, though most willingly, not very expeditiously. A Cumberland man of the same rank would not have had such a notion of what was fit and right in his own house, or if he had, one would have accused him of servility; but in the Highlander it only seemed like politeness, however erroneous and painful to us, naturally growing out of the dependence of the inferiors of the clan upon their laird; he did not, however, refuse to let his wife bring out the whisky-bottle at our request: 'She keeps a dram', as the phrase is; indeed, I believe there is scarcely a lonely house by the wayside in Scotland where travellers may not be accommodated with a dram. We asked for sugar, butter, barley-bread, and milk, and with a smile and a stare more of kindness than wonder, she replied, 'Ye'll get that,' bringing each article separately.

We caroused our cups of coffee, laughing like children at the strange atmosphere in which we were: the smoke came in gusts, and spread along the walls and above our heads in the chimney, where the hens were roosting like light clouds in the sky. We laughed and laughed again, in spite of the smarting of our eyes, yet had a quieter pleasure in observing the beauty of the beams and rafters gleaming between the clouds of smoke. They had been crusted over and varnished by many winters, till, where the firelight fell upon them, they were as glossy as black rocks on a sunny day cased in ice. When we had eaten our supper we sate about half an hour, and I think I had never felt so deeply the blessing of a hospitable welcome and a warm fire.

DOROTHY WORDSWORTH

DESCRIPTION OF THE WESTERN ISLANDS OF SCOTLAND

WOMEN were antiently deny'd the use of Writing in the Islands, to prevent Love-Intrigues: their Parents believ'd, that Nature was too skilful in that matter, and needed not the help of Education; and therefore that Writing would be of dangerous consequence to the weaker Sex.

Lewis

THE Inhabitants of this Island are well proportion'd, free from any bodily Imperfections, and of a good Stature: the Colour of their Hair is commonly a light-brown, or red, but few of them are black. They are a healthful and strong-body'd People, several arrive to a great Age: Mr *Daniel Morison*, late Minister of *Barvas*, one of my Acquaintances, died lately in his 86th Year.

THE Natives are generally ingenious and quick of Apprehension; they have a mechanical Genius, and several of both Sexes have a Gift of Poesy, and are able to form a Satire or Panegyrick *ex tempore*, without the Assistance of any stronger Liquor than Water to raise their Fancy. They are great Lovers of *Musick*; and when I was there they gave an Account of eighteen Men who could play on the Violin pretty well, without being taught: They are still very hospitable, but the late Years of Scarcity brought them very low, and many of the poor People have died by Famine. The Inhabitants are very dextrous in the Exercises of Swimming, Archery, Vaulting, or Leaping, and are very stout and able Seamen; they will tug at the Oar all day long upon Bread and Water, and a Snufh of *Tobacco*.

MARTIN MARTIN

THE CHARACTER OF THE HIGHLANDER

(The original of this letter, which was once in Edinburgh University Library, has been misplaced. We do not know to whom it was addressed or when it was written.)

. . . If I had not been in the Highlands of Scotland, I might be of their mind who think the inhabitants of Paris and Versailles the only polite people in the world. It is truly wonderful to see persons of every sex and age, who never travelled beyond the nearest mountain, possess themselves perfectly, perform acts of kindness with an aspect of dignity, and a perfect discernment of what is proper to oblige. This is seldom to be seen in our cities, or in our capital; but a person among the mountains, who thinks himself nobly born, considers courtesy as the test of his rank. He never saw a superior, and does not know what it is to be embarrassed. He has an ingenuous deference for those who have seen more of the world than himself; but never saw the neglect of others assumed as a mark of superiority . . .

ADAM FERGUSON

VIEWS ON THE SCOTS

The Lowlanders Cool, the Highlanders Fiery

To Dr Lewis

As the soil and climate of the Highlands are but ill adapted to the cultivation of corn, the people apply themselves chiefly to the breeding and feeding of black cattle, which turn to good account. Those animals run wild all the winter, without any shelter or subsistence, but what they can find among the heath. When the snow lies so deep and hard, that they cannot penetrate to the roots of the grass, they make a diurnal progress, guided by a sure instinct, to the sea-side at low water, where they feed on the *algae marina*, and other plants that grow upon the beach.

Perhaps this branch of husbandry, which requires very little attendance and labour, is one of the principal causes of that idleness and want of industry, which distinguishes these mountaineers in their own country—When they come forth into the world, they become as diligent and alert as any people upon earth. They are undoubtedly a very distinct species from their fellow subjects of the Lowlands, against whom they indulge an ancient spirit of animosity; and this difference is very discernible even among persons of family and education. The Lowlanders are generally cool and circumspect, the Highlanders fiery and ferocious: but this violence of their passions serves only to inflame the zeal of their devotion to strangers, which is truly enthusiastic.

Matt Bramble

The Peasantry of Scotland

CARLISLE, *Sep* 12.

To Dr Lewis

DEAR DOCTOR,

The peasantry of Scotland are certainly on a poor footing all over the kingdom; and yet they look better, and are better cloathed than those of the same rank in Burgundy, and many other places of France and Italy; nay, I will venture to say they are better fed, notwithstanding the boasted wine of these foreign countries. The country people of North-Britain live chiefly on oat-meal, and milk, cheese, butter, and some garden-stuff, with now and then a pickled-herring, by way of delicacy; but flesh-meat they seldom or never taste; nor any kind of strong liquor, except two-penny, at times of uncommon festivity— Their breakfast is a kind of hasty pudding, of oat-meal or pease-meal, eaten with milk. They have commonly pottage for dinner, composed of cale or cole, leeks, barley or big, and butter; and this is reinforced with bread and cheese, made of skimmed-milk—At night they sup on sowens or flummery of oat-meal—In a scarcity of oats, they use the meal of barley and pease, which is both nourishing and palatable. Some of them have potatoes; and you find parsnips in every peasant's garden—They are cloathed with a coarse kind of russet of their own making, which is both decent and warm—They dwell in poor huts, built of loose stones and turf, without any mortar, having a fireplace or hearth in the middle, generally made of an old mill-stone, and a hole at top to let out the smoke.

These people, however, are content, and wonderfully sagacious—

All of them read the Bible, and are even qualified to dispute upon the articles of their faith; which in those parts I have seen, is entirely Presbyterian.

Matt Bramble

These opinions may be taken as those of the author of Humphry Clinker, TOBIAS SMOLLETT.

LITERATURE IN THE HEBRIDES

I never was in any house of the Islands, where I did not find books in more languages than one, if I staid long enough to want them, except one from which the family was removed. Literature is not neglected by the higher ranks of the Hebridians.

SAMUEL JOHNSON

LITERACY IN LANARKSHIRE

Dorothy and William Wordsworth and Coleridge at Leadhills

We talked with one of the miners, who informed us that the building which we had supposed to be a school was a library belonging to the village. He said they had got a book into it a few weeks ago, which had cost thirty pounds, and that they had all sorts of books. 'What! have you Shakespeare?' 'Yes, we have that,' and we found, on further inquiry, that they had a large library, of long standing, that Lord Hopetoun had subscribed liberally to it, and that gentlemen who came with him were in the habit of making larger or smaller donations. Each man who had the benefit of it paid a small sum monthly—I think about fourpence.

The man we talked with spoke much of the comfort and quiet in which they lived one among another; he made use of a noticeable expression, saying that they were 'very peaceable people considering they lived so much underground;'—wages were about thirty pounds a year; they had land for potatoes, warm houses, plenty of coals, and only six hours' work each day, so that they had leisure for reading if they chose. He said the place was healthy, that the inhabitants lived to a great age; and indeed we saw no appearance of ill-health in their countenances; but it is not common for people working in lead mines to be healthy; and I have since heard that it is *not* a healthy place.

DOROTHY WORDSWORTH

ROBERT BURNS ENCOURAGES A COMMUNITY LIBRARY

To Sir John Sinclair of Ulbster, Bart

[Ellisland, August or September 1791]

Sir,

The following circumstance has, I believe, been omitted in the Statistical Account, transmitted to you, of the parish of Dunscore, in Nithsdale. I beg leave to send it to you, because it is new, and may be useful. How far it is deserving of a place in your patriotic publication, you are the best judge.

To store the minds of the lower classes with useful knowledge, is certainly of very great consequence, both to them as individuals, and to society at large. Giving them a turn for reading and reflection is giving them a source of innocent and laudable amusement; and besides, raises them to a more dignified degree in the scale of rationality. Impressed with this idea, a gentleman in this parish, ROBERT RIDDELL, Esq; of Glenriddel, set on foot a species of circulating library, on a plan so simple, as to be practicable in any corner of the country; and so useful, as to deserve the notice of every country gentleman, who thinks the improvement of that part of his own species, whom chance has thrown in to the humble walks of the peasant and the artisan, a matter worthy of his attention.

Mr Riddell got a number of his own tenants, and farming neighbours, to form themselves into a society, for the purpose of having a library among themselves. They entered into a legal engagement, to abide by it for 3 years; with a saving clause or two, in cases of removal to a distance, or of death. Each member, at his entry, paid 5s.; and at each of their meetings, which were held every fourth Saturday, 6d. more. With their entry money, and the credit which they took on the faith of their future funds, they laid in a tolerable stock of books at the commencement. What authors they were to purchase, was always to be decided by the majority. At every meeting, all the books, under certain fines and forfeitures, by way of penalty, were to be produced; and the members had their choice of the volumes in rotation. He whose name stood, for that night, first on the list, had his choice of what volume he pleased in the whole collection; the second had his choice after the first; the third after the second, and so on to the last. At the next meeting, he who had been first on the list at the preceding meeting, was last at this; he who had been second, was first; and so on, through the whole 3 years. At the expiration of the engagements, the books were sold by auction, but only among the members themselves; and each man had his share of the common stock, in money or in books, as he chose to be a purchaser or not.

At the breaking up of this little society, which was formed under Mr Riddell's patronage, what with benefactions of books from him, and what with their own purchases, they had collected together upwards of 150 volumes. It will easily be guessed, that a good deal of trash would be bought. Among the books, however, of this little library, were, Blair's Sermons, Robertson's History of Scotland, Hume's History of the Stewarts, the Spectator, Idler, Adventurer, Mirror, Lounger, Observer, Man of Feeling, Man of the World, Chrysal, Don Quixotte, Joseph Andrews, &c. A peasant who can read, and enjoy such books, is certainly a much superior being to his neighbour, who, perhaps, stalks beside his team, very little removed, except in shape, from the brutes he drives.

Wishing your patriotic exertions their so much merited success,

I am, SIR, Your humble servant,

A Peasant

ROBERT BURNS

It was Burns rather than Riddell who instigated the community library.

HOSPITALITY AT LOCH NESS

When we entered, we found an old woman boiling goats-flesh in a kettle. She spoke little English, but we had interpreters at hand; and she was willing enough to display her whole system of economy. She has five children, of which none are yet gone from her. The eldest, a boy of thirteen, and her husband, who is eighty years old, were at work in the wood. Her two next sons were gone to Inverness to buy meal, by which oatmeal is always meant. Meal she considered as expensive food, and told us, that in Spring, when the goats gave milk, the children could live without it. She is a mistress of sixty goats, and I saw many kids in an enclosure at the end of her house. She had also some poultry. By the lake we saw a potatoe-garden, and a small spot of ground on which stood four shucks, containing each twelve sheaves of barley. She has all this from the labour of her own hands, and for what is necessary to be bought, her kids and her chickens are sent to market.

With the true pastoral hospitality, she asked us to sit down and drink whisky. She is religious, and though the kirk is four miles off, probably eight English miles, she goes thither every Sunday. We gave her a shilling, and she begged snuff; for snuff is the luxury of a Highland cottage.

SAMUEL JOHNSON

WORDSWORTH HEARS A GIRL SINGING

On 13 September 1803, Wordsworth saw fields near Loch Katrine being harvested. On his return to England he wrote the poem.

> Behold her single in the field,
> Yon solitary Highland Lass,
> Reaping and singing by herself—
> Stop here, or gently pass.
> Alone she cuts and binds the grain,
> And sings a melancholy strain.
> Oh! listen, for the Vale profound
> Is overflowing with the sound.
>
> No nightingale did ever chaunt
> So sweetly to reposing bands
> Of travellers in some shady haunt
> Among Arabian Sands;
> No sweeter voice was ever heard
> In spring-time from the cuckoo-bird
> Breaking the silence of the seas
> Among the farthest Hebrides.

D

Will no one tell me what she sings?
Perhaps the plaintive numbers flow
For old unhappy far-off things,
And battles long ago;—
Or is it some more humble lay—
Familiar matter of to-day—
Some natural sorrow, loss, or pain
That has been, and may be again?

Whate'er the theme, the Maiden sung
As if her song could have no ending;
I saw her singing at her work,
And o'er the sickle bending;
I listen'd till I had my fill,
And as I mounted up the hill
The music in my heart I bore
Long after it was heard no more.

WILLIAM WORDSWORTH

HIGHLAND OLD AGE

To Harriet Reid, Oban 1773

. . . This is certainly a fine country to grow old in. I could not spare a look to the young people, so much was I engrossed in contemplating their grandmothers.—Stately, erect and self-satisfied, without a trace of the langour or coldness of age, they march up the area [of the Kirk of Kilmore] with gaudy coloured plaids, fastened about their breasts with a silver brooch like the full moon in size and shape.

I was trying to account for the expression in the countenance of these cheerful ancients (many above fourscore) while the pastor, with vehement animation, was holding forth in the native tongue. Now here is the result: people who are forever consecrating the memory of the departed, and hold the virtues, nay the faults of their ancestors, in such blind veneration, see much to love and revere in their parents, that others never think of. They accumulate on these patriarchs all the virtues of their progenitors, and think the united splendour reflects a lustre on themselves. The old people, treated with unvaried tenderness and veneration, feel no diminution of their consequence, no chill in their affections. Strangers to neglect, they are also strangers to suspicion. The young readily give to old age that cordial, by which they hope to be supported when their own almond trees begin to blossom. But fine people do not seem ever to think they shall be old. Now, in their way, I should love my father not merely as such, but because he was the son of the wise and pious Donald, whose memory the whole parish of Craignish venerates, and the grandson of the gallant Archibald, who was the tallest man in the district; who could throw the putting stone farther than any Campbell living, and never held a Christmas without a deer of his own killing, four Fingalian greyhounds at his fireside, and sixteen kinsmen sharing his feast. Shall I not be proud of a father, the son of such fathers, of whose fame he is the living record? Now, what is my case is every other Highlander's; for we all contrive to be wonderfully happy in our ancestry; and by this means the sages here get a good deal of reverence and attention, not usually paid to the 'Struldbruggs' of other countries. Observe, moreover, that they serve for song books and circulating libraries; so faithfully do they preserve, and so accurately detail, 'the tales of the times of old', and the songs of the bards, that now strike the viewless harp on wandering clouds. All this, with their constant cheerfulness, makes them the delight of the *very young*, in the happy period of wonder and simplicity; and their finding themselves so, prevents their being peevish, or querulous. Ossian was never more mistaken than when he said, 'Age is dark and unlovely'; here it appears 'like the setting moon on the western wave', and we bless the brightness of its departure . . .

ANN GRANT

THE GOOD POSTMAN

To Augustus Godby Esq
Secretary of the Post Office in Scotland   *Edinburgh 1 May 1824*

Sir,
Connected with my report of this date on the subject of the West Highland posts I beg to state that the Postmaster of Arrochar has signified his intention of resigning.

As this office only produces £50.0s.8d. gross Revenue, and the amount of the Edinburgh Correspondence is only £7.8s.10d, I propose to make it a Sub Office on Luss, and reduce the Salary from £10 to £5 per Ann., thus diminishing the business along this line, precluding the necessity of a stop, and affording equal Accommodation to the Country.

As a saving of £5 per Ann. will thus be effected, I am induced to bring forward a case for the humane consideration of the Postmaster General, which has been sometime lying by, and repeatedly pressed by Mr Downie MP for Appin, and the other Residents of that part of the Highlands.

The Runner between Bonaw and Appin, a distance of 12 miles, has to cross two ferries, frequently dangerous, and to walk the rest of the distance through Glansalloch (or the dirty glen) the wildest path in the Highlands—so much so, that although the other road is 6 miles round and liable to great delay from the breadth of the ferries (which are crossed by the Runner at the narrowest part) I scarcely met with any Highland gentlemen who had ever been through it, the path being along a stream swelling over it on a fall of rain, which is here abundant.

(I can attest the difficulty of this path from personal inspection, having traversed it during a slight storm.)

The Runner performs this stage *during the night*; and the difficulties he has to encounter during winter must be very great.

His pay is 9s. a week only, the same as is paid for a similar stage along the high road.

The present individual, his father *and Mother*, have performed this Journey with the Mails for above 25 years with zeal and astonishing regularity, and if the Postmaster General should be pleased to devote the sum of £5 to be reduced from the Salary of the Office at Arrochar to encrease the pay of the stage, I think it would be received as a mark of recognition of long and faithful performance of a most laborious duty, and have a good effect in the Service in general.

I am, Sir,
Your obedient Servant,

CHAS F REEVES

CELT AND SAXON

The English emigrant is prosaic; Highland and Irish emigrants are poetical. How is this? The wild-rose lanes of England, one would think, are as bitter to part from, and as worthy to be remembered at the antipodes, as the wild coasts of Skye or the green hills of Ireland. Oddly enough, poet and painter turn a cold shoulder on the English emigrant, while they expend infinite pathos on the emigrants from Erin or the Highlands. The Highlander has his Lochaber-no-more, and the Irishman has the Countess of Gifford's pretty song. The ship in the offing, and the parting of Highland emigrants on the sea-shore, have been made the subject of innumerable paintings; and yet there is a sufficient reason for it all. Young man and maid are continually parting; but unless the young man and maid are lovers, the farewell-taking has no attraction for the singer or the artist. Without the laceration of love, without some tumult of sorrowful emotion, a parting is the most prosaic thing in the world; with these it is perhaps the most affecting. 'Good-bye' serves for the one; the most sorrowful words of the poet are hardly sufficient for the other. Rightly or wrongly, it is popularly understood that the English emigrant is not mightily moved by regret when he beholds the shores that gave him birth withdrawing themselves into the dimness of the far horizon—although, if true, why it should be so? and if false, how it has crept into the common belief? are questions not easy to answer. If the Englishman is obtuse and indifferent in this respect, the Highlander is not. He has a cat-like love for locality. He finds it as difficult to part from the faces of the familiar hills as from the faces of his neighbours. In the land of his adoption he cherishes the language, the games, and the songs of his childhood; and he thinks with a continual sadness of the gray-green slopes of Lochaber, and the thousand leagues of dim, heartbreaking sea tossing between them and him.

The Celt clings to his birthplace, as the ivy nestles lovingly to its wall; the Saxon is like the arrowy seeds of the dandelion, that travel on the wind and strike root afar. This simply means that the one race has a larger imagination than the other, and an intenser feeling of association. Emigration *is* more painful to the Highlander than it is to the Englishman—this poet and painter have instinctively felt—and in wandering up and down Skye you come into contact with this pain, either fresh or in reminiscence, not unfrequently. Although the member of his family be years removed, the Skyeman lives in him imaginatively—just as the man who has endured an operation is for ever conscious of the removed limb. And this horror of emigration— common to the entire Highlands—has been increased by the fact that it has not unfrequently been a forceful matter, that potent landlords have torn down houses and turned out the inhabitants, have authorised evictions, have deported the dwellers of entire glens.

ALEXANDER SMITH

LAIRD AND COTTER

from 'The Twa Dogs'

CAESAR

I've aften wonder'd, honest *Luath*,
What sort o' life poor dogs like you have;
An' when the *gentry*'s life I saw,
What way *poor bodies* liv'd ava.
  Our *Laird* gets in his racked rents,
His coals, his kane, an' a' his stents:
He rises when he likes himsel;
His flunkies answer at the bell;
He ca's his coach; he ca's his horse;
He draws a bonie, silken purse
As lang's my tail, whare thro' the steeks,
The yellow letter'd *Geordie* keeks.
  Frae morn to een it's nought but toiling,
At baking, roasting, frying, boiling;
An' tho' the gentry first are steghan,
Yet ev'n the *ha folk* fill their peghan
Wi' sauce, ragouts, an' sic like trashtrie,
That's little short o' downright wastrie.
Our *Whipper-in*, wee, blastet wonner,
Poor, worthless elf, it eats a dinner,
Better than ony *Tenant-man*
His Honor has in a' the lan';
An' what poor *Cot-folk* pit their painch in,
I own it's past my comprehension.

LUATH

Trowth, Caesar, whyles their fash't enough;
A *Cotter* howkan in a sheugh,
Wi' dirty stanes biggan a dyke,
Bairan a quarry, an' sic like,
Himsel, a wife, he thus sustains,
A smytrie o' wee, duddie weans,
An' nought but his han'-daurk, to keep
Them right an' tight in thack an' raep.
    An' when they meet wi' sair disasters,
Like loss o' health or want o' masters,
Ye maist wad think, a wee touch langer,
An' they maun starve o' cauld and hunger;
But how it comes, I never kent yet,
They're maistly wonderfu' contented;
An' buirdly chiels, and clever hizzies,
Are bred in sic a way as this is.

CAESAR

But then, to see how ye're negleket,
How huff'd, an' cuff'd, an' disrespeket!
L—d man, our gentry care as little
For *delvers, ditchers*, an' sic cattle;
They gang as saucy by poor folk,
As I wad by a stinkan brock.
    I've notic'd, on our Laird's *court-day*,
An' mony a time my heart's been wae,
Poor *tenant bodies*, scant o' cash,
How they maun thole a *factor*'s snash;
He'll stamp an' threaten, curse an' swear,
He'll *apprehend* them, *poind* their gear;
While they maun stan', wi' aspect humble,
An' hear it a', an' fear an' tremble!
    I see how folk live that hae riches;
But surely poor-folk maun be wretches!

LUATH

Ther're no sae wretched's ane wad think;
Tho' constantly on poortith's brink,
They're sae accustom'd wi' the sight,
The view o't gies them little fright

Then chance and fortune are sae guided,
They're ay in less or mair provided;
An' tho' fatigu'd wi' close employment,
A blink o' rest's a sweet enjoyment.
     The dearest comfort o' their lives,
Their grushie weans an' faithfu' wives;
The *prattling things* are just their pride,
That sweetens a' their fire side.
     An' whyles twalpennie-worth o' *nappy*
Can mak the bodies unco happy;
They lay aside their private cares,
To mind the Kirk and State affairs;
They'll talk o' *patronage* an' *priests*,
Wi' kindling fury i' their breasts,
Or tell what new taxation's comin,
An' ferlie at the folk in LON'ON.
     As bleak-fac'd Hallowmass returns,
They get the jovial, rantan *Kirns*,
When *rural life*, of ev'ry station,
Unite in common recreation;
Love blinks, Wit slaps, an' social Mirth
Forgets there's *care* upo' the earth.

                                   ROBERT BURNS

*Robert Burns's favourite dog, Luath, was killed the day before his father's
death. The Luath of the poem represents Burns's point of view, Caesar the
Laird's.*

FARM WOMAN

She left the warmth of her body tucked round her man
before first light, for the byre, where mist and the moist
hot breaths of the beasts half-hid the electric veins
of the milking machines. Later, she'd help to hoist
the heavy cans for the tractor to trundle down
to the farm-road end, while her raw hands scoured the dairy.
By seven o'clock, she'd have breakfast on the table,
her kitchen bright as her apron pin, the whole house airy.
Her men-folk out in the fields, the children off to school,
she'd busy herself with the house and the hens. No reasons
clouded the other side of the way she brought
to her man the generous amplitude of the seasons.

Not much of a life, they'd whisper at church soirées
as they watched her chat, her round face buttered with content,
unable to understand that for her each moment
rubbed out the one before, and simply lent
nothing for words of theirs to touch to argument.

MAURICE LINDSAY

FARM WIDOW

She moved among the sour smell of her hens' droppings,
her cheeks rubbed to a polish, her skirts bustled
with decent pride; alone since the day the tractor
hauled itself up the field on the hill and toppled

her man away from her. Around her feet
her daughter played, the face of innocence puckered
with the solemn self-importance of being alone
in a grown-up world; her friends, the hens that speckled

her mother's allotment. Some of the weekly folk
who came to buy eggs, watched her counting
their change from the money in her purse, and had given her
silent pity, then sensed that she wasn't wanting

anything they could offer; that she seemed
like one whom life had used too soon for writing
some sort of purpose with, her gestures' economies
spelling completeness; gone beyond our waiting

for times and places to happen, behind the will,
to where time and place lie colourless and still.

MAURICE LINDSAY

TRAVELLING FOLK

Cornered in wastes of land, spinnies of old roads
lopped back from the new, where done horses
leant once on starved haunches, battered cars
nuzzle scrunted bushes and caravans.

Copper-breasted women suckle defiance
at schools inspectors. Sanitary men
are met with bronze-age scowls. All to no purpose.
Blown across Europe's centuries, bound only

in piths and withies to settlements not moved
by permanent impermanencies—smokey
violins, dusks gathered from skies
purple as hedge-fruits, or plucked stolen chickens—

these exiles from our human order seed
in the rough, overlooked verges of living,
their stubborn litter filling with vagrancy,
the cracks our need for conformation shows.

MAURICE LINDSAY

6   Travelling Folk, c.1910, West Coast. Courtesy of Scottish Ethnological Archive, National Museums of Scotland.

7   Travelling Folk getting ready for the road, working their way around Galloway painting farmhouses and buildings. Courtesy of Scottish Ethnological Archive, National Museums of Scotland.

ON THE ROADS WITH SANDY STEWART

Sometimes we hed a powny an sometimes we hednae. If we sellt the powny we hed a barrae, an then if we hednae that, ma people wid cairry a bunnle. Auld yins usetae cairry thir camp-sticks on thir shooder wi the sharp ends up. When they got thir shape ye see, they keppit. Hit wes like a bow an arrae tae look at. Ah've seen ma fether when he wes stuck wioot a cairt, makkin two big bunnles an pittin them across the powny's back—whit they caa seckets, same as if ye wir gaun tae the ghillie'n. Onie big cloot that we hed done an ye jest tied them across the powny's back, pit a blanket aneth so as no tae skin the beast's back. Ye just hed tae cairry on till ye got a cairt. Same if ye didnae get the taickle fer tae yoke it on, ye made the britchin wi new rope. Fermers could make it fer workin cairts at wan time. They hed the workin seddle right enough but some just made the britchin the same as we done.

If we hed a cairt we micht tak stuff fer wir tents, stuff fer sleepin, strow or hay fer pittin doon on the grun at nicht afore we pit wir things doon, an strow fer the horse. Thir wir dishes, pots, cans—aa kinds o things. Ma fether wesnae much in fer the scrap but he micht get the odd bit brass an bits o copper, rags an everything like that. Ye hed cairts an floats as big as a wee lorrie at the back. Sometimes we hed a float cairt wi wuiden wheels an ye got square cairts spinnelt wi rails alang the side. If rain come we could pit a cover on the cairt wirsels. Ye could mak a tent ontae hit fer tae keep wir stuff dry an aa us bairns wid be dry on the inside o it. Fae the tap o the rails o yer cairt ye pit boughs ower, an when ye come tae camp at nicht, ye could tak it doon an pit up yer tent. Ye got lamps on cairts at that days that went wi penny caunnles. That caunnle wid tak ye fae Fife tae Aiberdeen.

Noo thir wes a camp they caad the Toll Wuids or the Rattlin Coffin. It was abeen Dundee but the wuids ull be cut doon noo. They wir big wuids at that time they tell me. Ye could come ower in tae Tullybaccart an doon on the tap o Coupar Angus fae them. Thir wes a hill went ower an a tar road, but when ye come tae this wuids it wes a very waste-wuid an they caad hit the Rattlin Coffin. Auld tinkers afore my day said that thir wes an auld wumin an she died in a tent. She wes a tinker wumin an didna belong to this country. Ah think she belonged tae the Muir o Ord or the Black Isle or some place. She wes supposetae dee in a tent thair an the rest o the people wes beside her when she died. When bedtime come she started swearin an she sunk her ain coffin. When she was coffin'd she cursed till mornin. The language that come aff her wes somethin awfie. The rest o the boys hed tae run an report her, an she got shifted oot. They ran away when they heard her fer they thocht the devil wes wae her. They got her pitten intae the mortuary or whaurever she hed tae go. They caad that wuid the Rattlin Coffin efter that, cos she rattled the coffin wae swearin.

An at wan time thir wes an awfie lot o Burkers went roond the country an ye hed tae watch yirsel on the roads wae them. Ye could be traivellin along the road an they could meet ye aboot the back o five o clock in winter, in a waste bit, an they could tak ye awaa tae God knows whaur—colleges or oniething. Ye see, they couldnae get bodies at that time so they had tae tak them—kidnap them, fer tae practise on thae bodies. When ye wir sleepin in a tent it wes dangerous, very dangerous. Thir wir certain camps—whaur camps come up and doon tae a lot—that they hed watched. They kent all the old campin-gruns aboot Arbroath, Dundee an aa roads. Ken, whaur tinkers campit— away by Coupar Angus an up tae the Hielans o Perthshire. They kent every campin mark, even whaur tramps lay. Ye see, tramps usetae go aneth road bridges an pit fires in them, an they tell me ye wid hardly see a tramp bidin aneth them cos the kidnappers were sae thick at that time. They got ye intae waste wuids, hills or onie places.

The Burkers traivelled steady wi horses an this machine. When they went oot at night they kept gaun aa night. Thir wes a college in Logiealmond an they could come fae Dundee, some o thae kidnappers. Ye wid get them mebbe in Edinburgh; whaurever big colleges wes, an they wir learnin tae be doctors an professors. Thats whaur they wir. The machine wes a square, four-wheeled machine wae a dickey fer sittin on at the front o it. Thir wir a thing come on the tap like a big black umbarella but hit wes bigger. It wes covered wi what they caa black douk, like navvies tartan—ken, thon stuff on huts. A drawer pullt oot fae aneth it an thats the way they workit. They wir every nicht on the prowl. They tell me ye could never sleep at that days. An thir wir rubber pads come ower the taps o thir horses feet an the lamps they hed in that days wes awfie dim. It wid be nae good if they kept them too brifht, fer folk wid see them comin. The only thing ye could get notice o wes this four-wheeled thing squeakit on the auld roads. As it wes comin it gien a squeak—'squeak squeak'—like a boot but mair louder. Then they kent it wes comin an that gien them time tae run.

Yince they got an uncle belongin tae ma fether—Donald Whyte. He usetae bide doon Kirriemuir way. Well, they got him years ago at

Dunkel. Ootside Dunkel thirs a brae taks ye up tae the slauchter-hoose. Finnert they caa it. The road gans richt ower tae Butterstoon past the loch. The rest wes gaun oot that wey an this auld yin, he slunk ahun an fell asleep. He wes roarin but it wes nae use, fer they hed him near intae this machine. Then the ithers got big palin refters—ken, thae slack yins in fences—an hed tae breach the doctors tae get the auld yin oot. They lowsed him an taen the machine tae Burnim. It's in Sim's Garage at the back of Burnim an the horses wes pit intae a field an sellt, fer the kidnappers never come back fer them. If ever yer in Sim's Garage, yil see it sittin amongst the scrap but the wheels is aff it.

Ah heard ma fether say that ye wid think thae kidnappers hed jest come oot o a burial. When ye lookit at them they hed swallae-tail coats wi two buttons at the back, stookie ties, an some wi hair on thir face an some bare-shaved. Thir wir aa kinds o them. If they met ye on the road or got ye, they jest stuck a thing like a plaster ower yer mooth an ye couldnae dae nae mair then! Ye forgot everything jest the same as ye wir dead. They wid tak ye, then operate on yer body in a college. That saved them payin fer bodies.

recorded and edited by ROGER LEITCH

MAISIE MORLOCH'S FINAL TALE

In 1946 the father of Stanley Robertson, Master story teller, resumed a contract with a farmer at Alford to gather flax. 'We dwelt', Stanley Robertson writes, 'in the bottom-floor flat of a tenement at 19 Powis Crescent, in Aberdeen, where the majority of the scaldie population had an awful distrust and inbred hatred for the travelling people.' The departure from Aberdeen was a moment of great excitement and release from the burden of mental and sometimes physical assault. At each encampment stories were told and songs sung. The last evening before returning to Aberdeen was a special occasion, in which the whole community of travellers took part. Stanley Robertson gave the tale to be told, which had to be fortifying, to Maisie Morloch. This is a part of Maisie Morloch's Final Tale.

The Last Day at Kingswells and the final Ceilidh

The last day at Kingswells was indeed a memorable occasion.

Though there were mixed feelings amongst all the travellers of sadness, mingled with nostalgia over the end of the summer season—on reflection this was to prove a great day!

The sun had shone so rosy all that final day—and as evening drew nigh a deep red sky overshone the hinterland—so that, young as I was, I could nevertheless feel the strange magic of the moment—one that I never wanted to end!

The ceilidh started quite naturally . . . a group of men sitting around the campfire talking about the wheelings and dealings of the day and, as each of them told of the little happenings and events that had beset them . . . the group began to swell. Now, little children always liked to hear what their fathers were saying . . . My father always had a good tale to tell, and he aye managed to do something of interest each day! And so—as the evening grew cooler and the travellers gathered closer to the communal fire, and rekindled their own special imaginative flame—the stories usually took a supernatural turn, and the story-tellers would enthral the listener.

Gradually, as the wilder side of the event gentled, a peaceful and tranquil serenity prevailed and this atmosphere took a more poignant turn when at last the ancients took their places as 'the Guardians of the Gates of Wisdom'—for now it was their turn to impart their immense knowledge to the younger ones.

Only the pipers, away in the distance, were still resounding—and their music, calling through the night—now blended gently with the melodies of the old women's tales . . . Eventually the pipers' music faded altogether and the two men returned to the gold-lit fold of the camp-fire where a concentration of purpose and meaning arose, for Maisie Morloch was about to gather everyone to her, for she had something of importance to tell us:

'Weel, a'body, I want tae tell ye this taenight for I've hid a very strange but prophetic dream and I'm gan tae share it wi ye aa.

'Last night I dreamt that I wis intae an awfy bonnie place, whar there wis braw green fields and bonnie walks . . . and as I deeked, an auld gadgie appeared wha wis tall an very wise lookin—ye wid jist think he wis the wise auld man o wisdom himsel—and he wis claid intae the bonniest colours o tuggery . . . Noo he wis manging tae a wee chavie, and this wee chavie seemed tae be awfy interested in whit the aulder gadgie wis manging.

'Weel, they whedded and whedded, and then, fin I deeked nearer: Shannish! it wis naebody else but Wullie's wee gadie Stanley—the same wha is stannin intae the shadow o the fire jist noo—though ye cannae see him for the stoor reek blawin intae his maun . . .'

'O Maisie!' says Rab, 'it soons awfy like me masell ye wis seeing!'

'Button yer lip cove! An hud yer wheest . . . noo . . . the two o them wis walking intae a place whar there wis an awfy thunderstorm raging—and yet they were speaking real gently tae each other.

Then, lo and behold whin I deeked the next time—I saw a man intae the scene playing a whistle—like the magic whistle that Jake made (and indeed I believe it must hae bin this very same een!) for he piped oot the bonniest music ever heard so that aa the folks came frae far and near tae listen. Weel, nae only did they listen, but aa they folks gaithered untae this auld man.

Further back I could hear Piper Rab and Chanter tuning up their pipes—Piper Rab had a lovely set of silver-and-ivory mounted pipes, while Chanter had a hummel set (frankly, Chanter with his hummel set was the better player). Anyway, they swung round together, playing 'O Bonnie Ann', followed by a mixture of strathspeys and reels, and then they brought their music to the fireside to be joined by Smilie on the accordion and Lippie on the fiddle:

That was too much to bear for two or three of the lassies, who jumped up and danced a few highland reels, with a number of the older people stamping their feet and clapping their hands to the music and dance!

Alang wi the hantel aa coming—there also came a bonnie doze of animals o aa kinds, with legion aifter legion o birds o aa descriptions flying ower mi tae be wi this auld man . . . O! There wis animals I didnae ken whit species they were (cos I hid never seen them afore an I dinnae think I'll see the likes o again) . . . Whit a braw display o feathers there were! And there were birds wi ither birds ontae their wings . . . and wild animals cairrying wee lambs and deer upon their backs . . . an reely!—Whit a fine sweet feeling wis ower a'thing!

Then a great Ark came alang . . . an there wos waater aa wyes . . . the rain wis jist poorin doon like a burn and aa the folks and animals and birds and a'thing that wis there—they aa followed this music intae the Ark.

The auld man—wha I kent by noo wis faither Noah—bid Stanley fareweel and the bairn waved a cheerio tae a'body and a'thing as it wint awa intae the distance an ower the horizon, wi aa the rain an thunder . . .

Noo, fin dae I ken that this dream wis indeed a prophecy that will come tae pass intae a later time—cos aabody kens that auld Faither Noah wis a traiveller an aa, an ye see he kent whit it wis for folks tae laugh at him—but he aye proved tae them aa—that it's aye better tae tak heed o a warning frae a Higher Power and tae act upon it thus turning yer sense intae wisdom.

STANLEY ROBERTSON

PASTORAL—JOHN TODD, SHEPHERD

When I knew him, his life had fallen in quieter places, and he had no cares beyond the dulness of his dogs and the inroads of pedestrians from town. But for a man of John Todd's propensity to wrath these were enough; he knew neither rest nor peace, except by snatches; in the gray of the summer morning, and already from far up the hill, he would wake the 'toun' with the sound of his shoutings; and in the lambing time, his cries were not yet silenced late at night. This wrathful voice of a man unseen might be said to haunt that quarter of the Pentlands, an audible bogie; and no doubt it added to the fear in which men stood of John a touch of something legendary.

That dread voice of his that shook the hills when he was angry, fell in ordinary talk very pleasantly upon the ear, with a kind of honied, friendly whine, not far off singing, that was eminently Scottish. He laughed not very often, and when he did, with a sudden, loud haw-haw, hearty but somehow joyless, like an echo from a rock. His face was permanently set and coloured; ruddy and stiff with weathering; more like a picture than a face; yet with a certain strain and a threat of latent anger in the expression, like that of a man trained too fine and harassed with perpetual vigilance. He spoke in the richest dialect of Scots I ever heard; the words in themselves were a pleasure and often a surprise to me, so that I often came back from one of our patrols with new acquisitions; and this vocabulary he would handle like a master, stalking a little before me, 'beard on shoulder', the plaid hanging loosely about him, the yellow staff clapped under his arm, and guiding me uphill by that devious, tactical ascent which seems peculiar to men of his trade. I might count him with the best talkers; only that talking Scots and talking English seem incomparable acts. He touched on nothing at least, but he adorned it; when he narrated, the scene was before you; when he spoke (as he did mostly) of his own antique business, the thing took on a colour of romance and curiosity that was surprising. The clans of sheep with their particular territories on the hill, and how, in the yearly killings and purchases, each must be proportionally thinned and strengthened; the midnight busyness of animals, the signs of the weather, the cares of the snowy season, the exquisite stupidity of sheep, the exquisite cunning of dogs; all these he could present so humanly, and with so much old experience and living gusto, that weariness was excluded. And in the midst he would suddenly straighten his bowed back, the stick would fly abroad in demonstration, and the sharp thunder of his voice roll out a long itinerary for the dogs, so that you saw at last the use of that great wealth of names for every knowe and howe upon the hillsides; and the dogs, having hearkened with lowered tails and raised faces, would run up their flags again to the masthead and spread themselves upon the indicated circuit. It used to fill me with wonder how they could follow and retain so long a story. But John denied these creatures all intelligence; they were the constant butt of his passion and contempt; it was just possible to work with the like of them, he said—not more than possible. And then he would expand upon the subject of the really good dogs that he had known, and the one really good dog that he had himself possessed. He had been offered forty pounds for it; but a good collie was worth more than that, more than anything, to a 'herd', he did the herd's work for him. 'As for the likes of them!' he would cry, and scornfully indicate the scouring tails of his assistants.

R L STEVENSON

FUT LIKE FOLK?

Fut like folk in yon braid Buchan lan'?
Folk wha ken their grun like the back o' their han',
Divot and clort and clod, rock, graivel and san'.

Fut like folk in yon gran' Buchan howe?
Folk wha gar their grun near' onything growe,
Neaps and tatties and corn, horse, heifer and yowe.

Fut like folk in yon braw Buchan neuk?
Thrawn-like folk wha ken but the brods o' their Beuk,
And worship the Horseman's Word and the shearin heuk.

Folk wha say their say and speir their speir,
Gedder gey birns o' bairns and gey muckle gear,
And gang their ain gait wi' a lach or a spit or a sweir.

JOHN C MILNE

MAINS O YAWAL'S DOOK

Based on Chapter 5 of Johnny Gibb of Gushetneuk
by William Alexander.

The wark's weel tee, the hey's in cole, the mossin's gey near by,
Ben the midden dyke gwan a bags hing furth to dry.
The bailie an the orra loon's awa to Aikey Fair
An Mains o Yawal's aff to tak his annwal at Tarlair.

Oh, blue's the lift abeen the Firth this bonny Simmer day
An blue's the water reeshlin ower the san's on Deveron Bay.
The win' blaas saft doon Langmanhull an rare's the caller guff
O tar an raips an dilse alang the sea-wynds o Macduff.

Bit Mains is in a bog o swyte, his winkers fite wi styoo.
He's stecht in's wivven draavers an sair hankit in's surtoo.
He's burssen, fool an yokie, an crochlie i the queets.
The vera feet o him's roassen an fair lowpin in his beets.

Wi Mally lows't an stabl't noo, he hyters to the shore,
Skytin upo' knablick steens an slidderin amo' waar.
He's caain for a lippin peel, a lythe an sinny nyook,
For he's dwebble an he's druchtit an he's mangin' for his dook.

Breeks weel rowe't up, his hose an sheen he casts afore his claes.
He picks the strabs an' yaavins oot atween his crunkl't taes.
Syne he tirrs doon tull his middle, hat, surtoo, sark as weel
An, ae fitt syne anidder, he gyangs plype intull the peel.

He raxes for a puckle dilse an scoors his back an front
Wi mony a haach an pyocher wi mony a pech an grunt.
Syne oot he spangs, his sark an cwyte an hat again he seeks
An tirrs up tull his middle, castin wivven draars an breeks.

He's lichtsome as a stirkie that's shakken aff the branks.
A pirl o win' plays hey-ma-nannie roun' his spinnle shanks.
He splyters in the peel again. Oh, rare an caul' an roch's
The gluff o saat sea-water slocknin Mains's gizzent hochs.

Bit dooks, like idder pleesures, come ower seen tull an en'.
Ower seen in draars an breeks the legs are clossacht up again.
An noo, upo' a girssy knowe, he dowps doon, dacent carl,
For this ae oor o a' the year, at peace wi a' the warl.

FLORA GARRY

BUCHAN

Buchan—a land o' plenty,
Peat-bogs and puddock-steels,
Weet and clorty widder,
And contermashious deils!

JOHN C MILNE

DRUMDELGIE

There's a fairmer up in Cairnie,
Wha's kent baith faur and wide,
Tae be the great Drumdelgie
Upon sweet Deveronside.
The fairmer o' yon muckle toon
He is baith hard and sair,
And the cauldest day that ever blaws,
His servants get their share.

At five o'clock we quickly rise
An' hurry doon the stair;
It's there to corn our horses,
Likewise to straik their hair.
Syne, after working half-an-hour,
Each to the kitchen goes,
It's there to get our breakfast,
Which is generally brose.

We've scarcely got our brose weel supt,
And gi'en our pints a tie,
When the foreman cries, 'Hallo my lads!
The hour is drawing nigh.'
At sax o'clock the mull's put on,
To gie us a' strait wark;
It tak's four o' us to mak' to her.
Till ye could wring our sark.

And when the water is put aff,
We hurry doon the stair,
To get some quarters through the fan
Till daylicht does appear.
When daylicht does begin to peep,
And the sky begins to clear,
The foreman cries out, 'My lads!
Ye'll stay nae langer here!'

'There's sax o' you'll gae to the ploo,
And twa will drive the neeps,

And the owsen they'll be after you
Wi strae raips roun' their queets.'
But when that we were gyaun furth,
And turnin' out to yoke,
The snaw dank on sae thick and fast
That we were like to choke.

The frost had been sae very hard,
The ploo she wadna go;
And sae our cairting days commenced
Amang the frost and snaw.
But we will sing our horses' praise,
Though they be young an' sma',
They far outshine the Broadland's anes
That gang sae full and braw.

Ye daurna swear aboot the toon
It is against the law,
An' if ye use profanities
Then ye'll be putten awa'.
O, Drumdelgie keeps a Sunday School
He says it is but richt
Tae preach unto the ignorant
An' send them Gospel licht.

The term time is comin' on
An' we will get our brass
An' we'll gae doon tae Huntly toon
An' get a partin' glass
We'll gae doon tae Huntly toon
An' get upon the spree
An' the fun it will commence
The quinies for tae see.

Sae fare ye weel, Drumdelgie,
For I maun gang awa;
Sae fare ye weel, Drumdelgie,
Your weety weather an' a',
Sae fareweel, Drumdelgie,
I bid ye a' adieu;
I leave ye as I got ye—
A maist unceevil crew.

ANON

JOHNNY GIBB DISCUSSES THE SITUATION

The general belief was that Johnny would flit down to the Broch, buy
half-a-dozen acres of the unfeued land, and settle down in a sort of
permanent attitude as a small laird, cultivating his own land. Johnny
meditated much on the point but said little, until one day, addressing
his wife on the question of their future arrangements, he ran over one
or two points that had come up to him, and, without indicating any
opinion, abruptly finished with the query, 'Fat think ye, 'oman?'

'Hoot, man,' replied Mrs Gibb, 'fat need ye speer at me? I've toitit
aboot wi' you upo' this place naar foorty year noo, an' never tribbl't
my heid the day aboot fat ye micht think it richt to dee the morn; an'
aw sanna begin to mislippen ye noo at the tail o' the day.'

'Weel,' said Johnny, with an air of more than his ordinary gravity,
'I've been think 't owre, a' up an' doon. It's a queer thing fan ye begin
to luik back owre a' the time byegane. The Apos'le speaks o' the life o'
man as a "vawpour that appeareth for a little, and than vainisheth
awa';" an' seerly there cudna be a mair nait'ral resem'lance. Fan we
begood the pilget here thegither, wi' three stirks, an' a bran'it coo't
cam' wi' your providin', the tae side o' the place was ta'en up wi'
breem busses an' heather knaps half doon the faul'ies, and the tither
was feckly a quaakin' bog, growin' little but sprots an' rashes. It luiks
like yesterday fan we hed the new hooses biggit, an' the grun a' oon'er
the pleuch, though that's a gweed therty year syne. I min' as bricht's a
paintet pictur' fat like ilka knablich an' ilka sheugh an' en' rig was.'

'An' ye weel may, man, for there's hardly a cannas breid upo' the
place but's been lawbour't wi' yer nain han's owre an' owre again to
mak' it.'

'That's fat aw was comin' till. Takin 't as it is, there's been grun
made oot o' fat wasna grun ava; an' there it is, growin' craps for the
eese o' man an' beast—Ou ay, aw ken we've made weel aneuch oot
upon't; but it's nae i' the naitur o' man to gang on year aifter year
plewin, an' del'in, an' earin, an' shearin' the bits o' howes an' knowes,
seein' the vera yird, obaidient till's care, takin' shape, an' sen'in' up
the bonny caller blade in its sizzon, an' aifter that the "fu corn i' the
ear," as the Scriptur' says, onbeen a kin' o' thirled to the vera rigs
themsel's.'

WILLIAM ALEXANDER

THE VILLAGE OF BALMAQUHAPPLE

D'ye ken the big village of Balmaquhapple,
The great muckle village of Balmaquhapple?
'Tis steep'd in iniquity up to the thrapple,
An' what's to become o' poor Balmaquhapple?
Fling aff your bannets, an' kneel for your life, fo'ks;
Gar a' the hills yout wi' sheer vociferation,
And thus you may cry on sic needfu' occasion:

'O, blessed St Andrew, if e'er ye could pity fo'k,
Men fo'k or women fo'k, country or city fo'k.
Come for this aince wi' the auld thief to grapple,
An' save the great village of Balmaquhapple
Frae drinking an' leeing, an' flyting an' swearing.
An' sins that ye wad be affrontit at hearing,
An' cheating an' stealing; O, grant them redemption,
All save an' except the few after to mention:

'There's Johnny the elder, wha hopes ne'er to need ye,
Sae pawkie, sae holy, sae gruff, an' sae greedy;
Wha prays every hour as the wayfarer passes,
But aye at a hole where he watches the lasses;
He's cheated a thousand, an' e'en to this day yet,
Can cheat a young lass, or they're leears that say it;
Then gie him his gate; he's sae slee an' sae civil,
Perhaps in the end he may wheedle the devil.

'There's Cappie the cobbler, an' Tammie the tinman,
An' Dickie the brewer, an' Peter the skinman,
An' Geordie our deacon for want of a better,
An' Bess, wha delights in the sins that beset her.
O, worthy St Andrew, we canna compel ye,
But ye ken as weel as a body can tell ye,
If these gang to heaven, we'll a' be sae shockit,
Your garret o' blue will but thinly be stockit.

'But for a' the rest, for the women's sake, have them,
Their bodies at least, an' their sauls, if they have them;
But it puzzles Jock Lesley, an' sma' it avails,
If they dwell in their stamocks, their heads, or their tails.
An' save, without word of confession auricular,
The clerk's bonny daughters, an' Bell in particular;
For ye ken that their beauty's the pride an' the staple
Of the great wicked village of Balmaquhapple!'

                                            JAMES HOGG

The Yield of the Land

THE PRODUCTS OF THE 'SANDS' OF THE UISTS AND BARRA (1811)

A total want of wood and of regular inclosures gives these islands an aspect of gloomy sterility. In winter, and even until the middle of May, the western division, or Machir, is almost a desolate waste of sand; and this sand encroaches rapidly on the next division, namely that of lakes and that of firm arable ground. In autumn, however, these sands produce crops of barley, oats, rye, and potatoes, or of natural grass and wild clover, far beyond what a stranger would expect. They then assume a variegated and beautiful dress, scarcely yielding in colours or perfume to any fields in the kingdom; and, being of great extent, they afford a prospect of riches and plenty equalled by no other of the Western Isles.

JAMES MACDONALD

PEAT IN OSTIG IN SKYE

The only fewel of the Islands is peat. Their wood is all consumed, and coal they have not yet found. Peat is dug out of the marshes, from the depth of one foot to that of six. That is accounted the best which is nearest the surface. It appears to be a mass of black earth held together by vegetable fibres. I know not whether the earth be bituminous, or whether the fibres be not the only combustible part; which, by heating the interposed earth red hot, make a burning mass. The heat is not very strong nor lasting. The ashes are yellowish, and in a large quantity. When they dig peat, they cut it into square pieces, and pile it up to dry beside the house. In some places it has an offensive smell. It is like wood charked for the smith. The common method of making peat fires, is by heaping it on the hearth; but it burns well in grates, and in the best houses is so used.

The common opinion is, that peat grows again where it has been cut; which, as it seems to be chiefly a vegetable substance, is not unlikely to be true, whether known or not to those who relate it.

SAMUEL JOHNSON

THE NEW HEADMASTER FROM BIRMINGHAM LEARNS ABOUT PEAT CUTTING IN SOUTH UIST

Saturday morning came with the sound of men's voices, the clattering of feet, and the ring of metal on stones near the house. My party of peat-cutters had assembled, fourteen of them all told, with Sandy at their head. I led the way into school where a long table improvised from school benches had been set for breakfast. They followed me, leaving their tools outside. My sister and Catriona were busy preparing fried ham and eggs, and strong tea in large pots and jugs. Piles of scones, butter, cheese and jam were already on the table at which the men seated themselves. A hot plate of ham and eggs with a cup of tea was placed before each and to my surprise they all sat solemnly still gazing in front of them without saying a word. I was wondering if they were waiting for me to say 'grace' when Catriona whispered in my ear: 'The whisky!' This was produced and white-haired Sandy passed round the table handing each a brimming wine-glass of whisky, the contents of which were tossed off without a blink or word and with the utmost solemnity. All sat silent till the last man had drained the glass, then first looking round at each other they began to eat heartily of all before them. Before long they were talking to each other in Gaelic and seemed more natural—the effect of the food and perhaps the whisky, thought I. When they had breakfasted to repletion—and I noticed each man said a grace of thanksgiving, signing himself with a cross as he did so—an ounce of tobacco was given to each from which they shaved and rolled a pipeful, then they sat comfortably smoking and talking in low tones. At a word spoken in Gaelic by Sandy, they all rose and, putting on their caps at the school door, took up their tools and started for the peat banks.

I was curious to see this process of peat-cutting, so followed. We arrived on the raised piece of grass-covered ground which was intersected here and there with ditches. Four or five of the men threw off their coats and with spades removed the turf along the top of the bank bordering a ditch, while others with shovels removed the surface soil that lay beneath the turf. A smooth damp-looking close-fibred brown substance was then revealed. The white-haired leader told me that this first process was known as 'skinning the binks'

and the ground was now ready for cutting the peat. Two men now
came forward to the front edge of the raised peat bank and one of them
jumped into the ditch below. The other man carried in his hand a most
strange implement called 'the iron'. The upper part was just like that
of the ordinary spade, but the lower part, made of heavy steel about
fifteen inches long and three inches wide, had a ten-inch keen-looking
knife-blade some eight or nine inches from its end. This man
advanced to the front of the bank and placed the base of 'the iron' on
the peat so that the knife-blade was directly to his front with its point
exactly on the front edge of the bank. He then pressed a foot on a
protuberance on the shank of his implement just above the blade and
the iron part sank into the damp peat to its own depth. With a jerk of
the handle a clean-cut piece of peat fell from the bank into the hands of
the man waiting in the ditch below who immediately threw it with a
sliding motion of the hands on to the bank of the other side of the
ditch. Stepping back the length of the knife-blade the man on the bank
cut another piece, and so on for the whole length of the peat bank, one
man cutting and jerking, the other catching and throwing with such
regularity that the movements appeared to be automatic.

F G REA

8   Peat Cutting, Buchan c.1880s. Courtesy of Scottish Ethnological
Archive, National Museums of Scotland.

HE LEARNS ABOUT LIFTING THE PEATS

The weather had been remarkably dry for some time and Catriona, the Useful, told us that 'the peats should be lifted' now; she suggested that school-children volunteers should do it in the interval between morning and afternoon school sessions. As I was curious to know the process of 'lifting the peats' I accompanied her to my peat banks. When we reached the ground I saw that the damp slabs of peat cut not long before were perfectly dry and crinkled on the upper side which had been exposed to the air. Stooping, Catriona picked up two slabs of peat, leant them against each other on end, dry side inwards, when I saw that the under sides that had lain next the ground were quite wet; against the corners of these two slabs she leant four others dry side inwards, and finally another slab, wet side up, on the top, which steadied the whole small stack of seven peats. So I now saw the meaning of the term 'lifting the peats' which I had heard in school recently as a reason for children's absence from school: 'Please sir, I was lifting the peats.' Catriona told me that if the dry weather continued the peat would be ready for 'carrying home' in two or three weeks after the 'lifting'.

Some days later, after procuring a seven-pound jar of sweets, of which, I had learned, all the people (from the youngest to the oldest) were very fond, I asked for boy volunteers for 'peat-lifting', making no mention of any reward. I was surprised at the eagerness shown, and afterwards learned that they looked upon it as a privilege to be allowed 'to lift the schoolmaster's peats'. Choosing two crews, each consisting of twelve boys, and appointing two of them as captains, I led them to the peat banks and saw them start making the little peat stacks, the two crews working at a distance from each other. Seeing that they thoroughly understood the process I left them at it. At intervals I returned to see how they were getting on and complimented them on their progress. A little before school assembly I visited them, looked around, expressed approval, distributed sweets, and dismissed them from the ground—three such days completed the 'peat-lifting'.

F G REA

DR JOHNSON ENTERS A 'HUT' BY LOCH NESS

The old laws of hospitality still give this licence to a stranger.

A hut is constructed with loose stones, ranged for the most part with some tendency to circularity. It must be placed where the wind cannot act upon it with violence, because it has no cement; and where the water will run easily away, because it has not floor but the naked ground. The wall, which is commonly about six feet high, declines from the perpendicular a little inward. Such rafters as can be procured are then raised for a roof, and covered with heath, which makes a strong and warm thatch, kept from flying off by ropes of twisted heath, of which the ends, reaching from the centre of the thatch to the top of the wall, are held firm by the weight of a large stone. No light is admitted but at the entrance, and through a hole in the thatch, which gives vent to the smoke. This hole is not directly over the fire, lest the rain should extinguish it; and the smoke therefore naturally fills the place before it escapes. Such is the general structure of the houses . . .

SAMUEL JOHNSON

A HOUSE IN THE NORTH EAST

> Rowan tree and reid threid
> Keep the witches frae their speed.

Maybe it had been planted in Old John Gavin's day or even in his grandmother's, for once there had been a time when the rowan tree was a talisman that grew at every croft gable; when, to protect the beasts, a cross of *rodden* twigs was placed above the byre door. Long ago that had been, when superstition had gripped the poor crofter folk and a still-born calf or a cow going unexpectedly dry was a disaster; glad enough the old folk had been of their enchantments, the things that had made them at times bow less to God and more to the Devil.

The *bourtrees* and the rowan brought back the past, so that you would wonder whiles what kind of folk had they been; and what kind of dwelling had they *biggit* there, those folk who had first tilled that land? A squalid hovel, like as not, created from what the countryside yielded, made of turf perhaps, one-roomed certainly, with the cow brought in to one end of it when the days of the year drew in. For folk whom life or the laird might suddenly move on there would be little incentive to build for permanence and it is likely their poor dwellings differed little from those of the century before and so witheringly described, in *The Social Life of Scotland in the Eighteenth Century*, by Henry Grey Graham:

> The hovels of one room were built of stones and turf without mortar, the holes in the wall stuffed with straw or heather or moss to keep out the blasts; the fire, usually in the middle of the house floor, in despair of finding an exit by the smoke-clotted roof, filled the room with malodorous clouds. The cattle at night were tethered at one end of the room while the family lay at the other on heather on the floor. The light came from an opening at either gable which whenever the wind blew in was stuffed with brackens or an old bonnet to keep out the sleet and the blast. The roofs were so low in northern districts that the inmates could not stand upright but sat on stones or three-legged stools that served for chairs, and the huts were entered by doors so low and narrow that to gain an entrance one required almost to creep. Their thatching was of ferns or heather, for the straw was all needed for the cattle.

DAVID KERR CAMERON

AN ENGLISHMAN DISCOVERS A MAD-HOUSE ON BORERA

The latter having landed in the Island, happen'd to come into a House where he found only ten Women, and they were employ'd (as he suppos'd) in a strange manner, *viz* their Arms and Legs were bare, being five on a side; and between them lay a Board, upon which they had laid a piece of Cloth, and were thickning of it with their Hands and Feet, and singing all the while. The *English*-man presently concluded it to be a little *Bedlam*, which he did not expect in so remote a Corner: and this he told to Mr *John Macklean*, who possesses the Island. Mr *Macklean* answerd' he never saw any mad People in those Islands: but this would not satisfy him, till they both went to the place where the Women were at work; and then Mr *Macklean* having told him, that it was their common way of thickning Cloth, he was convinc'd, tho surpriz'd at the manner of it.

MARTIN MARTIN

E

MR REA LOSES HIS WAY AND GETS A SURPRISE

I found my face level with a small lighted window. I had found the source of the strange sound. The window through which I looked must have been high up in the room wall, for I gazed down on to a long table round which were seated a number of women crooning a strange kind of song. Descending to the level and going round to the door, I knocked in order to ask my way. The song ceased, the door was opened by a man who exclaimed in Gaelic 'The Schoolmaster!' and in English welcomed me in. I was shown to a seat by the fireside where two or three men were seated on a bench and who politely rose till I was seated. I explained my difficulty about getting home, but was told to rest a while and someone with a lantern would see me home. Having thanked them I was now at liberty to look around me. A large lamp suspended from a beam above the table cast a good light below. Seated on benches round the table were fourteen or fifteen women with sleeves rolled up to the shoulder, hands on table all grasping what looked like a long coarse blanket. At the head of the table sat one who appeared to be the leader for she sprinkled the portion of cloth before her with some liquid taken from a tub at her side, passed a large bar of soap across it two or three times, then the next woman on her left drew it towards her. This was repeated, the cloth being passed from hand to hand all round till the whole had been sprinkled and soaped. Now the leader commenced a weird slow chanting song in Gaelic raising her portion of the cloth in both hands, and then pounding it on the table in rhythm with her song, all the other women following suit and joining the chorus. Gradually the rhythm of the song and of the pounding on the table increased in pace and volume as the cloth was passed along till the arms were soon moving with bewildering speed, yet in perfect time. Sweat was pouring from brow, face and neck of these women when the pace began to slacken. They slowed down till the movement almost ceased, when another woman commenced another song and they proceeded as before. I could but admire the fine physique of the women and the skill with which they worked. They must have been specially selected by the woman of the house.*

    While this had been going on I had noticed that at intervals a few men had entered, singly or in pairs. Suddenly the singing and the

9 Waulking the cloth, Eriskay. Photograph by Walter Blaikie, from *A School in South Uist* by F G Rea, edited by John Lorne Campbell (Routledge & Kegan Paul, 1964).

dub-a-dub-dub ceased. The cloth and tub were removed from sight and the table moved, leaving the centre of the room clear. I was told that a dance was now to take place; but, as it was late, I asked if it would be convenient for me to leave. The man who had opened the door on my arrival found a man who was leaving, and who lived near the school. All stood as I shook hands with the men and bowed to the women, and left with this new experience behind me. My companion with the lantern could speak no English, but he safely guided me home, leaving me at my gate.

F G REA

*Some of the waulking songs sung in South Uist can be found in *Folksongs and Folklore of South Uist* by Margaret Fay Shaw.

THE FIRST CROFTS AT RACKWICK, ORKNEY

The first crofts were hacked and dug and drained from obdurate virgin soil above the shore. Hard to tell what starved sick months passed, fed with limpets and crabs, till the first corn came and grew and yellowed, a thin harvest. They cut querns from the round stones on the beach. In winter they ate shell-fish till their guts loathed them. Three old people died. Thorkeld went after gulls' eggs in the crag and never came home. Ubi found a way of snaring rabbits. The children were thin and querulous as birds. The people could not have survived that first winter and spring if they had not been driven by some harsh will; who fixed yokes on the shoulders of the women, and plucked a hawk from the hill and hooded it, and directed the gathering of stones for dwellings and barns, and set a man on guard over the bag of sacred corn, and gave a good ration to the fishermen and breeding women, and let the old sick folk die in silence. They could not have survived but for that leader who was half a god and half a beast.

The second harvest was good.

In spring they drained and dug new fields from the western slope. Everybody even the children and the old people, gathered stones for the long hall of their chief. Twice or thrice a year the chief went to the assembly of chiefs, the 'thing', in the Island of Horses. A Celtic priest would stay for a night in the chief's house. He told the chief that people must build a chapel for the offering of Mass and the greater glory of God. The chief considered that his hall should be extended, with a room for guests and a room where brides should lie with him first, before they went to their husbands, and a store-house for ale. But in the end the chapel was built. The Abbot of Eynhallow came and blessed the chapel. flinging holy water about him, and said the first Mass.

Frik, who was the best stone worker in the valley, found a long blue stone in the ebb. He squared one end of the stone so that it stood upright. He carved with chisel and hammer dove eyes in the stone. He carried Our Lady of Rackwick into the chapel. That night the statue of Our Lady stood in a corner of the chapel, her feet dappled with seven candle flames. Next morning she was placed in the open air, on the hill, between fields and sea; it seemed her dove eyes kept watch over the labours of fishermen and ploughmen, our Lady of Furrows.

In spring there was ploughing again. The one black ox was yoked, the large field round the Hall was ploughed before the small rigs on the western hill slope. After the sowing, the valley people saw the longships from more prosperous islands sailing west through the Pentland Firth on the spring cruise. The crofters and shepherds of Orkney were pirates for the rest of the summer. But the chief had no longship; the valley was too poor to go a-viking. The best they could manage was a foray in darkness across the Pentland Firth to get Caithness sheep.

In the month of May they dug peats from the moor. The peats for the Hall fires were dug and wind-dried and stacked before the peasants took their own peats home.

GEORGE MACKAY BROWN

THE SOLITARY CROFTER

It may seem absurd—as it probably is—to say that an intelligent eye could, looking over a crofting community, tell the characters of the crofters from the condition of their crops. But here the hay is cut first, there last; here the fields are clean, there rather choked and dirty; here the crops are in a forward state, there they are late—with all gradations of time and tidiness and carelessness between the extremes. The farthest-away croft is always last in harvesting any crop, and there were times last year when we smiled at what seemed the sheer optimism of the man who works it. He was sowing his turnip seed—the early part of the season had been abnormally dry—so late that he could hardly expect to get results worth bothering about. Occasionally we could see him working all alone on an upland, slowly, in a timeless sort of way, as if the idea of haste had never touched the primeval order of his thought. Then one day, meeting him at the end of a row, near the path, I stopped and we fell into talk. His voice was low and quiet and gentle. Och, something would come of it. There would be turnips all right. Maybe it was a little late, but then . . . He smiled. whatever it was it would be no more than he would expect. And if it wasn't that—then perhaps it wouldn't be. 'I have no one to help me.' He did not sound helpless so much as rather remote and vaguely uncaring. But pleasant. He lived all alone. His eyes once or twice became friendly and alight as if he were privileged by the talk. He sounded simple in the way that land and crops are simple. Nothing at all dark or dour, as some make out the primeval to be. And I knew that however long I stood there, he would stand also.

At the moment his hay is gathered in small ricks over the field. His corn is still green (it is harvested elsewhere) but in due course it will come to maturity and whiten. Then it will be cut. In stook it will stand for many days, accept blatters of rain, and, bedraggled, half-collapse. But the dry wind will blow up, and the sun shine after frosty mornings, and in the fullness of time the old horse that stands by the corner of the little barn, with drooping head and the main weight on one hind leg, will be hitched to the sledge and the harvest brought slowly home.

NEIL GUNN

CROFTING IN ABERDEENSHIRE

The Gavins, whatever else they had been, had been lucky in their lairds. Today the list of entries in the estate's old improvements-and-repairs ledger is a litany of ceaseless wants that tell the story of a fight to better poor ground (500 2½ inch tile pipes in 1904) and, with cryptic 'wood and iron' entries, keep poor *biggings* standing. If the Gavins could not get fat on such a holding, neither could the laird, and there must have been years when his crofts were an accountant's nightmare.

As he got older and more respected in the community, Willie Gavin would more easily get the factor's ear to complain about a rotting door or a leaking roof. Likely the laird's man-of-business had always known that the excuse about a winter lull in the masoning trade was no more than the crofter man's poorly-reasoned rationale for taking over the holding. After all, the same conditions precluded all but the most routine of crofting chores. The mason man had fooled nobody; what he and the other men like him felt, has been aptly summed up by yet another of the numerous royal commissions on crofting:

> Above all they have the feeling that the croft, its land, its houses are their own. They have gathered its stones and reared its buildings and occupied it as their own all their days. They have received it from their ancestors who won it from the wilderness and they cherish the hope they will transmit it to the generations to come . . .

It is a statement worthy of a better home than a bureaucrat's report. Its sentiments were frequently as true of the North-east Lowlands landscape as that of the Western Highlands. Written long after Willie Gavin's day, it captures his creed entirely.

DAVID KERR CAMERON

GRINDING WITH THE QUERN IN SKYE

We stopped at a little hut where we saw one old woman grinding with the quern, the ancient Highland implement which it is said was introduced by the Romans. It consists of two circular whinstones like iron plates, roughened by having holes made in them by a pickaxe. These stones are placed one above another. In the centre of the upper one is an opening in which a frame of wood, which serves as the hopper, is fixed, and into which the grain is thrown. There are four holes in the upper stone by way of uniformity, but only one is necessary, *viz.* that into which a stick is fixed by which the stone is turned about. The upper end of the stick is supported by being placed in a little semi-circular opening formed of straw-rope, fixed to the wattling of the roof. The woman turned about the stick, and the upper stone had a pin of wood near the middle fixed in the under one, on which pin it moved as on an axis. The upper stone is convex, and the under concave, by which the meal falls down on all sides of it from the centre. I cannot draw it. But young Coll has promised to send me one from Mull, as he has set up a mill on his estate there, and is abolishing the quern, which is a very poor and tedious implement. I must try if Mr Johnson can describe it. Generally two women work at it. They can grind a boll in a day, as young Coll told me.

JAMES BOSWELL

DIET IN SKYE

That the sea abounds with Fish, needs not be told, for it supplies a great part of Europe. The Isle of Sky has stags and roebucks, but no hares. They sell very numerous droves of oxen yearly to England, and therefore cannot be supposed to want beef at home. Sheep and goats are in great numbers, and they have the common domestick fowls.

But as here is nothing to be bought, every family must kill its own meat, and roast part of it somewhat sooner than Apicius would prescribe. Every kind of flesh is undoubtedly excelled by the variety and emulation of English markets; but that which is not best may be yet very far from bad, and he that shall complain of his fare in the Hebrides, has improved his delicacy more than his manhood.

Their fowls are not like those plumped for sale by the poulterers of London, but they are as good as other places commonly afford, except that the geese, by feeding in the sea, have universally a fishy rankness.

These geese seem to be of a middle race, between the wild and domestick kinds. They are so tame as to own a home, and so wild as sometimes to fly quite away.

Their native bread is made of oats, or barley. Of oatmeal they spread very thin cakes, coarse and hard, to which unaccustomed palates are not easily reconciled. The barley cakes are thicker and softer; I began to eat them without unwillingness; the blackness of their colour raises some dislike, but the taste is not disagreeable. In most houses there is wheat flower, with which we were sure to be treated, if we staid long enough to have it kneaded and baked. As neither yeast nor leaven are used among them, their bread of every kind is unfermented. They make only cakes, and never mould a loaf.

A man of the Hebrides, for of the women's diet I can give no account, as soon as he appears in the morning, swallows a glass of whisky; yet they are not a drunken race, at least I never was present at much intemperance; but no man is so abstemious as to refuse the morning dram, which they call a skalk.

The word whisky signifies water, and is applied by way of eminence to strong water, or distilled liquor. The spirit drunk in the North is drawn from barley. I never tasted it, except once for experiment at the inn in Inverary, when I thought it preferable to any English malt brandy. It was strong, but not pungent, and was free from the empyreumatick taste or smell. What was the process I had no opportunity of inquiring, nor do I wish to improve the art of making poison pleasant.

SAMUEL JOHNSON

UISGEBEATHA [1]

Whisky comes from the Gaelic *uisge-beatha* meaning 'water of life.' In the curious mind this will at once rouse wonder, perhaps even a contemplative effort to surprise the ancestral thought in its creative moment. For clearly there is nothing haphazard or transitory about the designation. It was not coined for the slang or commerce of any age. Rather is it akin to one of the ultimate elements into which ancient philosophers resolved the universe. It is not a description so much as a simple statement of truth and of mystery.

Is it now possible to conceive by what process some long-dead mouth and tongue were led to breathe out the magic syllables upon the liquor's aftermath?

Down round the southern corner of the *dun* there was a field of barley all ripened by the sun. In a small wind it echoed faintly the sound of the ocean; at night it sighed and rustled as the earth mother thought over things, not without a little anxiety. It was cut and harvested and a sheaf offered in thanksgiving; flailed and winnowed; until the ears of grain remained in a heap of pale gold: the bread of life.

In simple ways the grain was prepared and ground and set to ferment; the fermented liquor was then boiled, and as the steam came off it was by happy chance condensed against some cold surface.

And lo! this condensation of the steam from the greenish-yellow fermented gruel is clear as crystal. It is purer than any water from any well. When cold, it is colder to the fingers than ice.

A marvellous transformation. A perfect water. But in the mouth—what is this? The gums tingle, the throat burns, down into the belly fire passes, and thence outward to the finger-tips, to the feet, and finally to the head.

The man was a bit tired, exasperated a little, for things had been going wrong (how often they must have gone wrong with the primitive experimenter!), and, for the rest—or he wouldn't have been at the job—not a little weary with the dulness of social life, including the looks of women and the ambitions of fools.

And then—and then—the head goes up. The film dissolves from the eyes; they glisten. He abruptly laughs and jumps to his feet; as abruptly pauses to look over himself with a marvelling scrutiny. He tries the muscles of his arms. They are full of such energy that one fist shoots out; then the other. A right and left. His legs have the same energy. He begins to dance with what is called primitive abandon. Clearly it was not water he had drunk: *it was life.*

NEIL GUNN

1   *Pron.* ooshkubeha (ooshku, *whence* whisky).

A HIGHLAND VILLAGE

After travelling three or four days, I beheld on the other side of a long,
blue, river-like loch, the house of the Landlord. From the point at
which I now paused, a boat could have taken me across in half an
hour, but as the road wound round the top of the Loch, I had yet some
eight or ten miles to drive before my journey was accomplished.
Meantime the Loch was at ebb and the sun was setting. On the
hill-side, on my left as I drove, stretched a long street of huts covered
with smoky wreaths, and in front of each a strip of cultivated ground
ran down to the road which skirted the shore. Potatoes grew in one
strip or lot, turnips in a second, corn in a third, and as these crops were
in different stages of advancement, the entire hill-side, from the street
of huts downward, resembled one of those counterpanes which
thrifty housewifes manufacture by sewing together patches of different patterns. Along the road running at the back of the huts a cart
was passing; on the moory hill behind, a flock of sheep, driven by men
and dogs, was contracting and expanding itself like quicksilver. The
women were knitting at the hut doors, the men were at work in the
cultivated patches in front. On all this scene of cheerful and fortunate
industry, on men and women, on turnips, oats, and potatoes, on
cottages set in azure films of peat-reek, the rosy light was
striking—making a pretty spectacle enough. From the whole hill-side
breathed peace, contentment, happiness, and a certain sober beauty
of usefulness. Man and nature seemed in perfect agreement and
harmony—man willing to labour, nature to yield increase. Down to
the head of the Loch the road sloped rapidly, and at the very head a
small village had established itself. It contained an inn, a schoolhouse, in which divine service was held on Sundays; a smithy, a
merchant's shop—all traders are called *merchants* in Skye—and, by
the side of a stream which came brawling down from rocky steep to
steep, stood a corn mill, the big wheel lost in a watery mist of its own
raising, the door and windows dusty with meal. Behind the village lay
a stretch of black moorland intersected by drains and trenches, and
from the black huts which seemed to have grown out of the moor, and
the spaces of sickly green here and there, one could see that the
desolate and forbidding region had its colonists, and that they were
valiantly attempting to wring a sustenance out of it. Who were the
squatters on the black moorland? Had they accepted their hard

conditions as a matter of choice, or had they been banished there by a superior power? Did the dweller in those outlying huts bear the same relation to the villagers, or the flourishing cotters on the hill-side, that the gipsy bears to the English peasant, or the red Indian to the Canadian farmer? I had no one to inform me at the time; meanwhile the sunset fell on these remote dwellings, lending them what beauty and amelioration of colour it could, making a drain sparkle for a moment, turning a far-off pool into gold leaf, and rendering, by contrast of universal warmth and glow, yet more beautiful the smoke which swathed the houses. Yet after all the impression made upon one was cheerless enough. Sunset goes but a little way in obviating human wretchedness. It fires the cottage window, but it cannot call to life the corpse within; it can sparkle on the chain of a prisoner, but with all its sparkling it does not make the chain one whit the lighter. Misery is often picturesque, but the picturesqueness is in the eyes of others, not in her own. The black moorland and the banished huts abode in my mind during the remainder of my drive.

ALEXANDER SMITH

'O HAPPY STATE. O' PARADISE'

I sometimes wish I could live for a little while in the years between 1850 and 1875, when there was confidence, peace of mind and a large ease in the countryside. I may seem to overpraise that time, forgetting the occasional bad harvests, the cattle plagues and the hard life of the labouring men: perhaps not—since a mind at ease can endure casual misfortune and the steady draught of labour. The countryside was a good place for many people eighty years ago. For the lairds a very good place, when their steady rents gave them the means and the leisure to practice conspicuous waste, with their gardens and stables, their shoots and dinners and parties, their seasons in town, their tours abroad, their adventures in politics, and now and then a few years of viceregal state in Dublin, Delhi or Ottawa, with a more than regal magnificence—was ever dung more pleasantly transmuted? For the successful farmers a very good place, when the profits of good years easily stood an occasional misfortune, and they had always a ten-pound roast on the sideboard and bought their whisky by the jar. For the ploughman a good enough place because though the wages were small, they were regular, and an enterprising man could always better himself in the towns. The great work of improvement was finished and it must have seemed very good—the mansion houses now sheltered by the woods; the farms and steadings, all built of stone and lime, secure against wind and water, and at their best unequalled anywhere in the world; the land well drained, enclosed in the miles of drystone dykes, managed with skill on a system that steadily improved it—the labour of the generations had been greatly blessed. The times had matured and their temper in the countryside would have been that proper to a vigorous middle age when everything has been made secure. Trust in the six-course rotation and take your pleasure where you find it. O happy state. O paradise.

JOHN R ALLAN

BURNS AT LOCHLEA

(*Letter to Mrs Dunlop*)

During the whole of the time we lived in the farm of Lochlea with my father, he allowed my brother and me such wages for our labour as he gave to other labourers, as a part of which, every article of our clothing manufactured in the family was regularly accounted for. When my father's affairs grew near a crisis, Robert and I took the farm of Mossgiel, consisting of 118 acres, at the rent of £90 per annum (the farm on which I live at present), from Mr Gavin Hamilton, as an asylum for the family in case of the worst. It was stocked by the property and individual savings of the whole family, and was a joint concern among us. Every member of the family was allowed ordinary wages for the labour he performed on the farm. My brother's allowance and mine was seven pounds per annum each. And during the whole time this family concern lasted, which was four years, as well as during the preceeding period at Lochlea, his expenses never in any one year exceeded his slender income. As I was intrusted with the keeping of the family accounts, it is not possible that there can be any fallacy in this statement in my brother's favour. His temperance and frugality were everything that could be wished.

The farm of Mossgiel lies very high, and mostly on a cold wet bottom. The first two years that we were on the farm were very frosty, and the spring was very late. Our crops in consequence were very unprofitable, and notwithstanding our utmost diligence and economy, we found ourselves obliged to give up our bargain, with the loss of a considerable part of our original stock.

GILBERT BURNS

LEARNING TO BUILD A CORN STACK

During your second harvest on the place Badgie Summers taught you how to build a corn stack. Maybe he was just tired of crawling on the corn rucks and wanted a change. Anyway he took the cart you was driving and put you on the stack and showed you where to lay your sheaves, round by round from the inner circle, with plenty of hearting in the middle and a gentle slope to the outer edge, Badgie forking all the time and directing you right to the topmost pinnacle of the stack, then gave you a hand to rope and secure it against wind and weather, and you came down the ladder gratified, proud of your achievement.

It was quite a feat Badgie had taught you, the beginning of your stack-building career that was to last for thirty odd years, in which time you was to build an average of forty or fifty a year, depending on the size of the various farms you worked on, or the sum total of something like two-thousand corn, wheat and barley stacks, besides an experiment in flax building during the war, until the combines came in during the 'sixties and killed this skilful art. It was one job that gave you a pride in your work over many difficult years; a prestige and reputation with the farmers and sometimes though not often an extra pound or two to your meagre wages, besides a better chance of finding a job.

That was something you had to thank Badgie Summers for, him that was foreman at Kingask; otherwise you can't think how you would have managed it, or even made a start, and because of the art involved (or architecture if you like) it turned out to be a job you became really fond of, in spite of your aversion to farming in general. But when Forbie saw the stack you had built he told Badgie he'd better thrash it first in the season in case it watered. Badgie said there was no fear of that but knowing the old man he had to comply with his wishes.

DAVID TOULMIN

FENCIN, HYOWIN AND SCYTHIN

I watched him wie a haimmer in his neive hittin nails intae wid like he
hated the sicht o them. If a nail buckled he reversed the haimmer-
heid, yarkit it oot wie the claw an straichtened the nail on a flat steen or
a post. I watched him wie the tapner pouin neeps, the arc o't eident fae
the funny-been roon on tae the neep's reets, slicin the clort o earth
awa, birlin the neep for the shaw neist an cuttin throwe the stalk wi a
clean, tidy chop. I tchauved ahin him, ower slow tae keep up wie him,
ower awkward tae rax an sned an haud an slice an throw at the same
lick as he gaed at. The dreel I was in was aye langer than his, aye
coorser tae tackle. Beside, I thocht he was lucky, his back hidna the
same time tae get sair in as mine, for if I look twice as lang as him I was
bound tae get twice as forfochen.

    I watched him fencin though my hert wisna in't. Fencin was finikcy,
bitty, an slow. I was up till't in some wyes, nae in ithers. Faan a post
was driven I was handy for haudin't for the mail, the muckle haimmer
wi the twa heids an the shaft o hardwid, but I hated the shiver that
tingled my fingers faan the dunt came an the post sank an inch or twa
intae the grun. The roch laarick scrattit me the tichter I grippit, but gin
I'd lowsned my haun on't the post wad hae skewed an waur nor that,
the mail mith hae sliddered aff target an that wad hae been that, ye
heard stories o men that had got in the wye o a mail on its wye doon
and it could turn yer stammack juist thinkin aboot it. Efter the posts
were hame the wire was raxed, an the staples were haimmered. Wire
was a torment, roosty an thrawn, barbed wie a double-pinted twist
ilka sax inch or so that could rake the skin aff yer haun if it wisna
haunled richt. The strainer steed at the en o the raa o posts, an extra
stoot post sunk weel down an buttressed wie steens tae get mair
purchase. The wires were wuppit roon an syne raxed; the strainer was
the anchor an the fence was a lang riggin histed fae't. There was a
gadget for tichtenin: a chine an a heuk an a haunle, like a block an
tackle, pocket-size. My father notched the heuk intae the chine an
braced himself an ruggit, the wire rose fae the girss, the notch was
advanced, the tension rippled doon the length o the wire an it rose
again, an so on till the hicht was richt an the staples were nott. Doon
the lang line o posts we gaed, me hannin them tae my father; he put
some in his mou faan he bou'd doon, sklented a glance tae see gin his
level was equal, syne drave them faist an hard. Ilka time I tried it I hit

my thoom, an I thocht foo that could be, Dad's thoom was three times bigger nor mine an he hardly ivver clouted himsel.

We gaed hyowin thegither, Dad an me, but nae for lang: half a dreel an I was faain ahin. I enjoyed it faan I got tae dae't maleen, takkin twenty yairds o the en-rigs an plyin back an fore, parin aff the dreels so's I could see some results. It was a slow, fykie job, a saft-shoe shuffle that gaed on an on. In weet widder faan the grun was clorty the hyowe-blade got fuzzy and heavy, ye chappit the cloupit neck on a handy steen trae clean yer edge an yer back got a rest for a meenit or twa. Heukin the spare neeps awa fae the gweed plants, scrapin the dreel tae the apex-shape, tirrin the hinmaist yaird afore ye gaed forrit, ower an ower again it was a gran job for a puckle laads wie plenty tae newse aboot, it was a sair sentence for twa chiels that werena spikkin, an it was a thankless prospect for a man his leen, for there was nae short-cut an nae respite. Ae day twa fee'd loons fae anither place came ower tae Kiddies tae gie's an afterneen at the hyowe. They drave intae the close and speired faar my faither wis. I ran intae the kitchen an said 'They're here' as though they were men o some rare importance. We got tae the park an yokit at it, but they were haveless breets an breenged on as if their beets were burnin, I caa'd them the Roch Chiels an didna badder foo far awa they got fae's. They bade for their supper an Mam made een o her specialities, macaroni cheese drooned in a rich sauce an toasted on the tap, but the Roch Chiels said they werena ower keen on't, could they have some cheese an an oatcake, that wad dae them.

Faan it cam tae the scythe my father was a dab haun. The blade was a curve gettin nerra till the pint, an syne it was lethal: fouk spak o the coorse meshanters than a bairn could faa intae wi a scythe nae hanled richt. The blade was jined tae a widden frame like a triangle, wi twa grips aboot a couple feet apart, it was a man's implement an made for a man's airm-span. The trick in't was keepin the braid end o the blade laich doon and hard by, an skimmin the grun wie't as close as ye daured withoot snaggin a steen or lairin the pint. It was aa in the airm—foo ye swung fae the shooder, foo ye held in yer funny-been so's the sweep o the blade was ticht an sweet. Deen richt it was a treat to see foo the scythe took a clean sweep o aathing afore't. Afore we got yokit wi binder an twine we had roads tae redd roon the edge o the corn, an that was my father's job, tae cut oot a border for the Fordie tae start in on. Mam came ahin him, gedderin an binnin. The binnin was tricky—for loons an feels, nae for my mither, she'd daent' for her father faan she was a quine. She geddered the cut stalks intae a bunnle, an oxterfou, an laid it doon. A hantle o lang an souple strands was wiled oot an havered intae ilka haun, syne they were crossed at

the heids an knotted thegither wie a blur o wrists an the binnin was
made, nae tow tae faisten't; the shafe was laid oot on tap o the binnin
an the ends were crossed again in a corkscrew knot an doubled aneth
for a siccar haud wi the tips o her fingers. It wisna in beuks, yon quick
an souple twist o the hauns: an the mair I tried it the mair I fand oot foo
weel it wised me.

DAVID OGSTON

10   Hoeing, St Vigeans, by Arbroath. Drawing by Colin Gibson.

FEEIN STRATHALDER

The hiring day was called 'Muckle Friday' and in every market town
the workers gathered who were looking for jobs—and the farmers
seeking to engage them. Sometimes we all congregated in the square
or in a street close-by where the markets were held. In Aberdeen it
was always in the Castlegate. There were all sorts there—shepherds,

horsemen, cattlemen, general labourers (orramen as they used to be called in these parts). Then all the farmers would come along. One might stop in front of you and ask if you were looking for a job. You'd say, 'Aye, that's right.' And from then on you were in business. You told him what you could do—what previous experience you had. He told you how much he was prepared to offer you to do it. Then, as he talked, you thought about it, at the same time trying to weigh-up in your mind what sort of bloke he might be. You quickly learned to be a good judge of character, but even then mistakes could be made. Some farmers wore different faces on hiring days, a wee bit like Robert Louis Stevenson's Dr Jekyll and Mr Hyde. They had one face for 'Muckle Friday' which was all smiles and heartiness. And a week later once you were there on the farm working for them you saw the other side of their nature, always glowering and moaning, greedy and grasping. Yes, you made mistakes, but they got fewer as you got older. I suppose you just got wiser, that's all. Anyhow, when both sides were satisfied and terms were agreed, you shook hands. That hand-clasp sealed the bargain. It was a promise on both sides. No man worth his salt—farmer or worker—would ever have gone back on that.

As I've said, you soon learned to watch out for the good farmers in the district and they often came after you when you got a name for yourself as a responsible worker. And, of course, once having got hold of you they would do all in their power to keep you on their farm. This meant that at the end of the term they would offer you an increase in wages and if you were happy with the work and the new money and could see no point in leaving to seek another job, which, after all, might not be so good, you'd just stay on. But it was always a one-sided business. So much depended on the whims and fancies of the farmer. You were beholden to him for too much of your life. It was worse for a married man because he would be living with his wife and children in one of the farm cottages. Naturally, with family responsibilities he didn't want to be moving around from place to place every summer and winter. And if anything happened that made the boss decide not to hire him again for the new term, there he was, not only having to seek a new job, but without a roof over his head until he found one. At the end of the term he would have to be out of the cottage he lived in in order to make room for the chap who was taking his place. Many the cart load of furniture and belongings, with wee kids sitting on top of them and the crying mother in front sitting beside her grim-faced husband, I've seen disappearing down the road from the farm. . . .

The standard hours of work in my early days were ten hours a day, six days a week, Monday to Saturday, but at times, such as during the harvest, you just had to work on until bed-time, especially if the weather had been bad and the crops were late in being cut. And you got no pay for this extra work. No overtime. It had never been heard of. You just carried on, slogging away until the job was finished. The farmer was keen because he wanted it safely stacked in the yard, the workers because they were damned glad to get rid of it. If you'd had three weeks of 'stook parade,' when we had to gather in all the sheaves, and you were soaking wet up to the armpits many a day when it had been raining heavily, you were bloody glad to see the stooks off the field. That was compensation enough for all the extra hard graft.

It was all hands on deck at harvest time—the 'hairst' as we called it. The farmer would have one eye on the weather and the other on the ripening grain, usually corn. All of a sudden he would announce, 'We're starting on Monday, boys.' So, the first job was to clear a road right around the edge of the field using a scythe. Then the binder could get in. In a way I was lucky. Binders were being used on practically every farm I worked on. But before this, at the time of the reaper, all the cut stalks had to be lifted by hand, bound into sheaves, then stooked so that it could dry off in the sun before being carted away to the farm stackyard. Of course now it's combine harvesters everywhere, but in my day the crops weren't so heavy, though at the end of a long day with your back aching and your fingers full of thistles you thought the crop heavy enough, I can tell you.

R GRANT

UPLAND FARM IN THE GRAMPIANS

Life has not much margin here. Work goes on from dark to dark. The hay is brought in in August, the oats (with luck) in October: but at Christmas they may still stand, sodden and black in the tilted fields. And one night, before you know it, stags may have broken in and ravaged the growing crops. The crofter's wife can't go to her brother's funeral in January, because the cows are beginning to dry and if a stranger milks them they may cease to yield altogether, and there's the income gone and milk to be bought for-by. The water must be carried from the well, through drifted snow or slush, unless the crofter himself has ingenuity and useful hands, and has brought his own water supply from the hill to the house; and even then it must be watched and tended through the rigours of a mountain winter.

Sometimes there is no well—no spring rises within reach of the house, but all the water to be used must be carried from the burn, up steep and toilsome banks. Then the washing is done in the centuries-old fashion, down at the foot of the banks in the burn itself—sometimes on a windy day I have seen smoke rising, and caught the wink of fire, and coming near seen a great cauldron in a sheltered nook beside the burn and figures of women moving around it.

In these crannies of the mountains, the mode of supplying elemental needs is still slow, laborious and personal. To draw your water from the well, not even a pump between you and its sparkling transparency, to break the sticks you have gathered from the wood and build your fire and set your pot upon it—there is a deep and pervasive satisfaction in these simple acts. Whether you give it conscious thought or not, you are touching life, and something within you knows it. A sense of profound contentment floods me as I stoop to dip the pail. But I am aware all the same that by so living I am slowing down the tempo of life; if I had to do these things every day and all the time I should be shutting the door on other activities and interests; and I can understand why the young people resent it.

Not all the young want to run away. Far from it. Some of them love these wild places with devotion and ask nothing better than to spend their lives in them. These inherit their fathers' skills and sometimes enlarge them. Others are restive, they resent the primitive conditions of living, despise the slow ancient ways, and think that praising them is sentimentalism. These clear out. They take, however, the skills with them (or some of them do), and discover in the world outside how to graft new skills of many kinds on to their own good brier roots. An unfortunate proportion want white-collar occupations, and lose their parents' many-sidedness. For the young are like the old, various as human nature has always been, and will go on being, and life up here is full of loves, hates, jealousies, tendernesses, loyalties and betrayals, like anywhere else, and a great deal of plain humdrum happiness.

NAN SHEPHERD

THE PLEASANTNESS OF COWS

The byre was the gentlest and sweetest place about the steading, just as cows are the gentlest and sweetest beasts about a farm. I have wondered for a long time why men chose to make the dog their closest friend, for the dog is neither very beautiful in himself nor is he particularly virtuous. But the cow—there is a thing of beauty. She is simple, sensuous and impassioned, like a poem, and she has the Christian virtues as well. She embodies the maternal impulse magnified to the nth degree. She asks but to give and give and give again. In return for a few turnips and a handful of straw she gives streams of lovely milk, rich and health-giving, the very elixir of life. The dog is faithful, but the cow is no less, nor will she ever bite the hand that feeds her. The dog has soft brown eyes; but so has the cow; and the eyes of a cow shine with a soft enraptured light, like moons in a misty sky. The dog is noisy and demonstrative; the cow has an infinite capacity for silence. The dog is a complete extravert and snaps at every passing fly; the cow lives in a deep philosophic calm; she has long thoughts and keeps them to herself. To sum up: the cow is a contented beast and spreads her contentment about her; she is beautiful in her life and in death she can be yet more beautiful when properly divided. She is kind and gentle; in short, she is a perfect female friend. I have always loved cows so much that I would become a farmer if I could afford it. I can imagine nothing that would more gladden my heart than a byre of forty feeding as one.

JOHN R ALLAN

FRIDAY MART AT KITTYBREWSTER

And richt by the factory waa, the first ferm,
The couthie country fat and fou o ferms
As far as the legend-land o Foggieloan,
Ayont the trees whas line alang the lift
Aince gart a bairn believe the mairch o the warld
Fand endin thonder, aye the warld gaes yokan,
Wi park on park for the plou,
Park on park for the paidle,
Parks for the beasts and parks for the barley
(The meat and the meal and the bree o the barley—
Aye, aye, the haill hypothec),
And aa for the mercat, aa for the Friday mart,
The fermers fat as their ferms,
Braid as their beasts and bauld as their barley-bree,
Come traikan intil the toun to swap their trauchle,
To niffer for nowt at the unco unction,
Yarkan their bids at the yammeran unctioneer,
And syne frae the pens til the pubs whaur business is pleisure,

To slocken the stour frae thrang thrapples
In whacks o whisky an lochans o lowse ale
Whaur aa the clash o the country roun gaes sooman,
Skyrie wi mauts and skinklan-bricht wi beers
That wash the langour awa frae the landwart week,
Their trinkle the toun's freedom for ilka fermer.

ALEXANDER SCOTT

CATTLE AND THE DROVE ROUTES

Cattle used to be driven over the hills to markets at Crieff and Falkirk. There were many drove routes, and you can see remains of old cattle rings or sheep rings at several places in the hills. After Scottish Union with England in 1707, this cattle trade increased, and prices tripled between the 1740s and 1790s (Smout 1969). The Rev Charles Grant (*NSA*, 1842) mentions that the Lairig Ghru, 'with much trouble by the removal of immense blocks of granite', was then fitted for the passage of cattle to southern markets. This made it possible to drive cattle to market by a shorter route 'than the great Highland road presents'. Lairig Ghru was used for the passage of cattle at least until late in the 19th century. In the 1930s, Willie Cruickshank of Drum at Abernethy told Nethersole-Thompson how, as a boy, he went with his father when he took cattle through Lairig Ghru to market in the south. In Deeside, drovers often took cattle over Mount Keen in 1830, and there was even an inn there at Coire Bruach, yet by the late 1850s and 1860s few but estate staff continued to use it (Glen Tanar Right of Way Litigation 1931). Hill droving continued until there were railways and later better roads in the valleys. The profitable new meatier cattle and less hardy breeds of cattle could no longer pad the hundreds of miles of rough hill tracks like the old black cattle.

D NETHERSOLE-THOMSON AND A WATSON

HIGHLAND BONES

The long roads travelled meant that the cattle arrived lean and hungry at their destinations—'Highland bones to be covered with Scottish and English beef'. Whether the itinerant drover bought them on the spot directly from the tenants, or through the tacksman or proprietor, the journey still had to be undertaken. In some cases the Highland cattle, *kyloes* from the West or *norlands* from the North, had to take to the water. Drovers swam cattle from Skye across Kyle Rhea. The old method was to get them to the shore at low water and tie them in groups of five to eight in line ahead, the lower jaw of one being fixed by a twisted withy to the tail of the one in front. The withy of the foremost beast was held by a man at the rear of a four-oared boat. From more distant islands, such as Islay, they were transported in open ferry-boats. A visitor to Port Askaig in 1824 found 'the shore was covered with cattle; and while some were collected in groups under the trees and rocks, crowding to avoid the hot rays of a July evening, others were wading in the sea to shun the flies, some embarking, and another set swimming on shore from the ferry-boats; while the noise of the drovers and the boatmen, and all the bustle and vociferation which whisky did not tend to diminish, were re-echoed from hill to hill, contrasting strangely with the silence and solitude of the surrounding mountains'.

ALEXANDER FENTON

WADE'S ROADS IN SCOTLAND

In choosing the line of his road Wade followed the old Roman military method. He went in a straight line, and did not avoid knolls. When climbing a very steep gradient he constructed traverses. The chief obstacles encountered in the actual bed of the road were boulders. Where these were very large they were raised, with the aid of screw-jacks, purchases and handspikes, and rolled to the side of the road, where they served to mark the way in snowy weather. There was great competition between the subalterns (so Edmund Burt tells us) as to whose detachment could lift the largest stone.

The small rocks were sometimes cleared away by digging holes alongside them into which they were dropped, thus helping to make a good bottom for the road. Burt gives some interesting details of how the roads were made through boggy ground. He writes:

'When one of those Bogs has crossed the Way on a stony Moor, there the loose Ground has been dug out down to the Gravel, or Rock, and the Hollow filled up in the Manner following, viz.:—

First with a Layer of large Stones, then a smaller Size, to fill up the Gaps and raise the Causeway higher; and, lastly, two, three or more

Feet of Gravel, to fill up the Interstices of the smaller Stones, and form a smooth and binding Surface. This part of the Road has a Bank on each Side, to separate it from a Ditch, which is made withoutside to receive the Water from the Bog, and, if the Ground will allow it, to convey it by a Trench to a slope, and thereby in some measure drain it.

In a rocky Way, where no loose Stones were to be found, if a Bog intervened, and Trees could be had at any portable Distance, the Road has been made solid by Timber and Fascines, crowned with Gravel, dug out of the Side of some Hill.

This is durable; for the Faggots and Trees, lying continually in the Moisture of the Bog, will, instead of decaying, become extremely hard, as has been observed of Trees that have been plunged into those Sloughs, and lain there, in all Probability, for many Ages. This Causeway has likewise a Bank and a Ditch for the Purpose above-mentioned.'

Five hundred soldiers from the Highland Companies and other regiments took part in the work. The privates were allowed sixpence a day above their pay, corporals eightpence, sergeants one shilling, and subaltern-officers two shillings and sixpence. Barrack huts were erected, and these in turn were developed into inns or change-houses, which finally became known as King's Houses.

J B SALMOND

11   Corgarth Castle and Old Military Road. Courtesy of Malcolm Gray.

SHEEP

The sheep has scarcely any marked character, save that of natural affection, of which it possesses a very great share. It is otherwise a stupid, indifferent animal, having few wants and fewer expedients. The old black-faced, or Forest breeds, have far more powerful capabilities than any of the finer breeds that have been introduced into Scotland; and therefore the few anecdotes that I have to relate, shall be confined to them.

So strong is the attachment of sheep to the place where they have been bred, that I have heard of their returning from Yorkshire to the Highlands. I was always somewhat inclined to suspect that they might have been lost by the way. But it is certain, however, that when once one, or a few sheep, get away from the rest of their acquaintances, they return homeward with great eagerness and perseverance. I have lived beside a drove-road the better part of my life, and many stragglers have I seen bending their steps northwards in the spring of the year. A Shepherd rarely sees these journeyers twice; if he sees them, and stops them in the morning, they are gone long before night; and if he sees them at night, they will be gone many miles before morning. This strong attachment to the place of their nativity, is much more predominant in our old aboriginal breed, than in any of the other kinds with which I am acquainted.

The most singular instance that I know of, to be quite well authenticated, is that of a black ewe that returned with her lamb from a farm in the head of Glen-Lyon, to the farm of Harehope, in Tweeddale, and accomplished the journey in nine days. She was soon missed by her owner, and a shepherd was dispatched in pursuit of her, who followed her all the way to Crieff, where he turned, and gave her up. He got intelligence of her all the way, and every one told him that she absolutely persisted in travelling on—She would not be turned, regarding neither sheep nor shepherd by the way. Her lamb was often far behind, and she had constantly to urge it on, by impatient bleating. She unluckily came to Stirling on the morning of a great annual fair, about the end of May, and judging it imprudent to venture through the crowd with her lamb, she halted on the north side of the town the whole day, where she was seen by hundreds, lying close by the road-side. But next morning, when all became quiet, a little after the break of day, she was observed stealing quietly through the town, in apparent terror of the dogs that were prowling about the streets. The last time she was seen on the road, was at a toll-bar near St Ninian's; the man stopped her, thinking she was a strayed animal, and that some one would claim her. She tried several times to break through by force when he opened the gate, but he always prevented her, and at length she turned patiently back. She had found some means of eluding him, however, for home she came on a Sabbath morning, 4 June; and she left the farm of Lochs, in Glen-Lyon, either on the Thursday afternoon, or Friday morning, a week and two days before. The farmer of Harehope paid the Highland farmer the price of her, and she remained on her native farm till she died of old age, in her seventeenth year.

JAMES HOGG

MY DOG, MY COMPANION

My dog was always my companion. I conversed with him the whole day—I shared every meal with him, and my plaid in the time of a shower; the consequence was, that I generally had the best dogs in all the country. The first remarkable one that I had was named Sirrah. He was beyond all comparison the best dog I ever saw. He was of a surly unsocial temper—disdained all flattery, and refused to be caressed; but his attention to his master's commands and interests never will again be equalled by any of the canine race. . . .

I was a shepherd for ten years on the same farm, where I had always about 700 lambs put under my charge every year at weaning-time. As they were of the short, or black-faced breed, the breaking of them was a very ticklish and difficult task. I was obliged to watch them night and day for the first four days, during which time I had always a person to assist me. It happened one year, that just about midnight the lambs broke loose, and came up the moor upon us, making a noise with their running louder than thunder. We got up and waved our plaids, and shouted, in hopes to turn them, but we only made matters worse, for in a moment they were all round us, and by our exertions we cut them into three divisions; one of these ran north, another south, and those that came up between us, straight up the moor to the westward. I called out, 'Sirrah, my man, they're a' away;' the word, of all others, that set him most upon the alert, but owing to the darkness of the night, and blackness of the moor, I never saw him at all. As the division of the lambs that ran southward were going straight towards the fold, where they had been that day taken from their dams, I was afraid they would go there, and again mix with them; so I threw off part of my clothes, and pursued them, and by great personal exertion, and the help of another old dog that I had besides Sirrah, I turned them, but in a few minutes afterwards lost them altogether. I ran here and there, not knowing what to do, but always, at intervals, gave a loud whistle to Sirrah, to let him know that I was depending on him. By that whistling, the lad who was assisting me found me out; but he likewise had lost all trace whatsover of the lambs. I asked if he had never seen Sirrah? He said, he had not; but that after I left him, a wing of the lambs had come round with a swirl, and that he supposed Sirrah had then given them a turn, though he could not see him for the darkness. We both concluded, that whatever way the lambs ran at first, they would finally land at the fold where they left their mothers, and without delay we bent our course towards that; but when we came there, there was nothing of them, nor any kind of bleating to be heard, and we discovered with vexation that we had come on a wrong track.

My companion then bent his course towards the farm of Glen on the north, and I ran away westward for several miles, along the wild tract where the lambs had grazed while following their dams. We met after it was day, far up in a place called the Black Cleuch, but neither of us had been able to discover our lambs, nor any traces of them. It was the most extraordinary circumstance that had ever occurred in the annals of the pastoral life! We had nothing for it but to return to our master, and inform him that we had lost his whole flock of lambs, and knew not what was become of one of them.

On our way home, however, we discovered a body of lambs at the bottom of a deep ravine, called the Flesh Cleuch, and the indefatigable Sirrah standing in front of them, looking all around for some relief, but still standing true to his charge. The sun was then up; and when we first came in view of them, we concluded that it was one of the divisions of the lambs, which Sirrah had been unable to manage until he came to that commanding situation, for it was about a mile and a half distant from the place where they first broke and scattered. But what was our astonishment, when we discovered by degrees that not one lamb of the whole flock was wanting! How he had got all the divisions collected in the dark is beyond my comprehension. The charge was left entirely to himself from midnight until the rising of the sun; and if all the shepherds in the Forest had been there to assist him, they could not have effected it with greater propriety. All that I can say farther is, that I never felt so grateful to any creature below the sun as I did to Sirrah that morning.

JAMES HOGG

SHALE MINING WEST LOTHIAN

Some years before the world's first productive oil-well was drilled in Pennsylvania USA, Dr James Young, a Scottish chemist—later to be nicknamed Paraffin Young—was refining and marketing mineral oil. His Bathgate plant, drawing on oil-bearing coal, was the first commercial oil works in the world. By 1864 he was using oil-bearing shale, and his works in West Lothian were to produce solvents, lubricants, lamp oil, detergents, gas for street-lighting, and petrol. At its peak, oil-shale mining employed 13,000 men in West Lothian. By the 1920s the industry had shrunk considerably: the last shale mine was closed in 1962. Left behind were the man-made mountains— 'bings'—of shale waste, which have in recent years been used for road-building, brick manufacture and land reclamation projects.

COLIN MACLEAN

12   Shale mining works, with shale-waste bing in background, West Lothian 1920s. Courtesy of Almond Valley Heritage Centre.

13 Digging: Navigation Coal Seam, Bowhill Colliery, Fife, early
twentieth century. Courtesy Trustees of the National Museums of
Scotland.

THE IMAGE O' GOD

Crawlin' aboot like a snail in the mud,
  Covered wi' clammie blae,
Me, made after the image o' God—
  Jings! but it's laughable, tae.

Howkin' awa' 'neath a mountain o' stane,
  Gaspin' for want o' air,
The sweat makin' streams doon my bare back-bane,
  And my knees a' hauckit and sair.

Strainin' and cursin' the hale shift through,
  Half-starved, half-blin', half-mad,
And the gaffer he says, 'Less dirt in that coal
  Or ye go up the pit, my lad!'

So I gi'e my life to the Nimmo squad,
  For eight and fower a day,
Me! made after the image o' God—
  Jings! but it's laughable, tae.

JOE CORRIE

Change

BELL BARROW

Raise up the deid.
A Bell Barrow wi proper ditch
proper rampart
   a cairn
echteen fute hie
and hunner and twenty aroond the base.
Ablow large dresst flaags wi capstane.
   And toom.
Juist a sma heap o earth
in that impossible chaumer
   and soon
     —flettened.

Fairmers are still walkin the sma hills
some hae stane dykes
some hae New Town for neibour
some hae sons in city streets wi open minds
some hae taen to golf

the Bell Barrow is
the tenth green.

DUNCAN GLEN

WALKING INTO THE PAST

Walking into the interior of Skye is like walking into antiquity; the present is behind you, your face is turned toward Ossian. In the quiet silent wilderness you think of London, Liverpool, Edinburgh, or whatever great city it may be given you to live and work in, as of something of which you were cognisant in a former existence. Not only do you breathe the air of antiquity; but everything about you is a veritable antique. The hut by the road-side, thatched with turfs, smoke issuing from the roof, is a specimen of one of the oldest styles of architecture in the world. The crooked spade with which the crofter turns over the sour ground carries you away into fable. You remove a pile of stones on the moor, and you come to a flagged chamber in which there is a handful of human bones—*whose*, no one can tell. Duntulm and Dunsciach moulder on their crags, but the song the passing milkmaid sings is older than they. You come upon old swords that were once bright and athirst for blood; old brooches that once clasped plaids; old churchyards with carvings of unknown knights on the tombs; and old men who seem to have inherited the years of the eagle or the crow. These human antiques are, in their way, more interesting than any other: they are the most precious objects of *virtu* of which the island can boast. And at times, if you can keep ear and eye open, you stumble on forms of life, relations of master and servant, which are as old as the castle on the crag or the cairn of the chief on the moor. Cash payment is *not* the 'sole nexus between man and man.' In these remote regions your servants' affection for you is hereditary as their family name or their family ornaments; your foster-brother would die willingly for you; and if your nurse had the writing of your epitaph, you would be the bravest, strongest, handsomest man that ever walked in shoe leather or out of it.

ALEXANDER SMITH

IMPROVEMENT, BUT NOT BY MAN ALONE

But nature too has helped him. Those vast forces that are lodged beneath the crust of the earth have slowly upheaved the land, and have converted a large part of the bottom of the old estuary into good, dry ground, covered with the richest soil, and fitted in no common degree for the growth of streets. And hence, where his forefathers floated their rude boats he builds his warehouses, and on tracts that were ever wet with the ooze of river and sea, and bore few other inhabitants than the cockle and mussle, he now plants his country villas and lays out his pleasure-grounds.

The disappearance of the ancient woods deserves more than a mere passing allusion, for it has materially influenced the present scenery of the country, and it has a still further interest from the close way in which it is linked with human history. Duly to appreciate the nature and extent of the change which is traceable to this cause, it is necessary to bear in mind the magnitude of the forests which, when man first set foot in Scotland, swept in long withdrawing glades across its surface—the wide black mosses and moors, the innumerable lakes and fens, dense and stagnant indeed on the lower grounds, but which, in the uplands, were the sources whence streamlets and rivers descended through glen, and valley, and dim woodland, into the encircling sea. Beasts of the chase, and among them some that have been for centuries extinct here, abounded in these ancient forests; birds of many kinds haunted the woods and waters; fish swarmed in lake, river, and bay. Among such primeval landscapes did our aboriginal forefathers excavate their rude earthen dwellings and build their weems of stone; from the stately oaks they hollowed out canoes, which they launched upon the lakes and firths; and through the thick glades of the forest they chased the wild boar, the *urus*, the bear, the wolf, and the red deer. The traces of these old scenes are still in part preserved to us. From the lakes and peat-mosses are sometimes exhumed the canoes, stone celts, and other implements, as well as the ornaments of the early races, along with the trunks of oak and pine that formed the ancient forest, and bones of the animals that roamed through its shades. It is from such records that we know both what used to be the aspect of the country and how it has come to be so wholly changed.

An old dead peat-moss, that is, one where the peat is no longer being formed, sometimes affords an excellent illustration of the fact that nothing on the surface of the land is allowed to remain unchanged. So long as the peat is growing, it can generally resist denudation, but when its growth ceases, it becomes liable to attacks from the denuding agents. This may be well observed along the flat crests of hills and in low cols, where level ground has been afforded for boggy vegetation. No longer growing, or at least not growing vigorously enough to ward off atmospheric disintegration, the peat cracks up and is dried and blown away as dust by wind or washed down by rain. It is to this cause that the singularly rugged surface, known in the south of Scotland as 'moss-hags', is due. Deep gutters and pools are dug out of the crumbling mass by wind and rain—black, soft, and treacherous, which the inexperienced pedestrian can only pass in dry weather, and even then often like the march of the Salian priests, *'cum tripudiis sollennique saltatu.'*

This general desiccation and decay of the higher peatmosses may be noticed all over the Southern Uplands. The black cappings of peat which cover so many of the flat hilltops, and extend down their sides, may now be seen to be shrinking up again towards the top. They have a ragged fringe, some parts running in long tongues down the slope, or in straggling isolated patches. These features are well displayed on the high grounds above Loch Skene. The long, bare, flattened ridges have each their rough scalps of peat, of which the black, broken edges hang down the slops of brown heath and bent, while far below are the green valleys, with their clear winding streams, and their scattered shepherds' hamlets.

The enumeration of the later changes in the scenery of Scotland would be incomplete if it included no reference to those which have been brought about by man. Human agency must be reckoned as a not unimportant factor in the geological mutations which now befall the surface of the land. To some of man's operations in this country I have already alluded, and others may be merely cited. He has uprooted the old forests, drained many of the mosses, and extirpated or thinned many of the wild animals of ancient Caledonia. In place of the woods and bogs, he has planted fields and gardens, and built villages and towns; instead of wild beasts of the chase, he has covered the hills and valleys with flocks of sheep and herds of cattle. The cutting down of the forests and the draining of the mosses has doubtless tended to reduce the rainfall, and generally to lessen the moisture of the atmosphere and improve the climate. Sunlight has been let in upon the waste places of the land, and the latent fertility of the soil has been called forth; so that over the same regions which, in Roman times, were so dark and inhospitable, so steeped in dank mists and vapours,

F

and so infested with beasts of prey, there now stretch the rich
champagne of the Lothians, the cultivated plains of Forfar, Perth, and
Stirling, of Lanark and Ayr, and the mingling fields and gardens and
woodland that fill all the fair valley of the Tweed, from the grey
Muirfoots and Lammermuirs far up into the heart of the Cheviots.

ARCHIBALD GEIKIE

NATURE AS DESTROYER

The lands of Culbin were, in the seventeenth century, watered by the
Findhorn which flowed through them to the sea and by its tributary
the Muckle Burn. There is a medieval reference to 'the rough carse of
Culbin', but in Brodie's time the whole estate was called the 'granary
of Moray'. It was more populous and much more fertile than his
estates. It had sixteen rich farms on it, crofts and labourers' cottages
scattered over it, a fishermen's clachan on the Hill of Findhorn and
many fishermen's bothies on the banks of the river. The land was flat,
easy to plough and in the middle of it, surrounded by the fields of the
home farm stood Culbin House, a stone building with gardens, lawns
and trees about it. There were abundant orchards too. 'A stone-built
doocot—the privilege of a barony—stood on a hillock.' Like other
prosperous lairds, the Kinnairds had a church or family chapel at
which some of their people worshipped with them. It must have been
the church whose spire my father warned us not to trip upon.

Only one of the sixteen farms, Earnhill, which is there to this day,
survived the great sandstorm of 1694. It came suddenly from the west
on an October day that year, a high cloud of sand, two miles in width.
It is described as being like a river flowing at great speed. Men reaping
barley had to run from the field and within a few hours the sheaves
they had made and the standing barley not yet cut were smothered. A
ploughman, almost suffocated by sand, had to leave his plough half
way up a furrow, untackle his horse and lead it away. The Mill of
Dalpottie, to which the Laird and his tenants had always brought their
grain, was buried and the waters of the Muckle Burn which drove its
wheel were shelved away from it to the east together with the greater
waters of the Findhorn, which found a new outlet to the sea.

On the first night people stayed in their houses, believing that the
walls would keep them safe, but the sand as it hit each obstruction
piled up into sloping mounds, such as those I have so often seen in
miniature against pebbles on the beach. Only a few sheltered houses

had doors or windows facing east; most faced the west winds. And in the morning almost everyone woke in darkness. All doors and windows were blocked with sand. They had to break gaps in the back walls of their houses to get out. There was a lull in the storm that morning and they drove their animals inland, hoping, I suppose, to reach common grazing or find charitable neighbours who would share pastures with them, for there was no grass on Culbin now, no greenery of any kind, no yellow corn, only miles of sand and a horrible sandy marsh made by the river Findhorn in the night, when its mouth was choked.

On the marsh, as the water drained away during the next few days, lay the corpses of hens, rabbits, hares and even sheep and when the wind dropped there was a pestilential stench of rotting flesh and vegetation.

During the lull, the people went back to their houses, hoping to rescue some of their things, but the storm began again as roughly as before and with more danger in it, for the huge sandhills it had created during the previous day and night were now shifting; the westerly gale lifted them and blew them along in massive, blinding clouds. The sky darkened. The people, believing this was the end of the world, ran for their lives, taking with them only some small things which they could carry.

Next morning there was nothing to be seen but sand, not even the tops of trees, nor even the chimneys of the laird's big house. The church had been deeply buried. The Culbin Estate looked to its inhabitants then much as it looked to me in 1921, except that the sand dunes and sandhills had long been coloured by bent grass, when I first went there with my sisters and parents.

For two and a half centuries, until the 1930s when newly planted trees grew strong enough to break the wind, the sands kept moving. The desert landscape changed with every storm. Large sandhills were blown away and new ones raised. Dead trees were exposed from time to time, and once the west wind tore the sand off living fruit trees which blossomed and bore fruit until they were smothered again for ever.

About the year 1798, two hundred years after the great sand drift, the old laird's house reappeared like a skeleton, the sandy top of its tomb torn off by the wind. The main chimney was the first part to be seen. A man climbed the sand and shouted down it. A voice which was probably the echo of his own answered him from the hollow room below and he ran away.

The Laird of Moy who then owned what was left of the Culbin Estate sent men and carts to demolish the house and bring away load after load of building stone. The remains were soon buried by sand again and people who knew the district in the 1930s could point to an oddly shaped sandhill which, they said, covered the house.

At times and in flat places, the wind took the sand quite away from the old fields. Ploughed and half-ploughed furrows, the whole shape of the rig could be seen, and on the head rigs, the place where the oxen and horses turned before starting on the next furrow, hoof marks two hundred years old were visible. The plough abandoned on the first day of the Great Sand Drift was also found. Part of it is now in the Elgin Museum. But neither the wind nor any searcher has discovered the most precious treasure known to the Culbin people at the time and, by tradition, to generations of their descendants, to have been hidden one night behind a sandhill near the shore.

Smugglers had landed a cargo at night which included, it was said, silk, tea, wine and brandy, goods much in demand in the north of Scotland but too scarce and highly taxed for anyone to buy from lawful merchants. It was too late to rouse carters and in any other place as remote as the Culbin shore, the cargo would have been safe till daylight. But during the night the west wind blew and when three of the smugglers went back at dawn to divide the goods into cartloads, the sand had shifted; the whole landscape had changed; there was nothing to be seen but sand. For hours they searched and tried to dig trenches but were hampered by flying sand until in the evening the

14   Culbin Sands: Marram Grass on the Culbin Desert, Findhorn. Courtesy of Scottish Ethnological Archive, National Museum of Scotland.

wind dropped. News of the loss spread through the countryside and when the carts arrived they were accompanied by dozens of men who joined in the search, scraping with their hands, digging with spades, plunging their arms up to the armpits into the slopes of the sandhills. The carters probed with the long handles of their whips.

My encounters with Nairnshire sandstorms have been slight and not alarming but they gave me a hint of the terror and physical distress that caught people long ago. I have walked back from the Culbin Sands to Nairn, facing the west wind and sand, when there was no one in sight, nor beast, nor seagull, nor lark, nor insect, no earthly sound or sight, no ground under my feet. The river of dry sand that covered my feet made the solid sand I was walking on invisible, and sometimes even that gave way, clenching me up to the shins until I struggled out of it. The hills of the Black Isle, seven miles away on my right were raised above the sea by mist. There was no sea between me and them. I was aware only of the sky above, the powerful wind before me and the sand flying at me, past me, catching to a halt in my clothes. It was stimulating. It was spiritual. It was cold. Cold and excited, I reached Nairn, crossed the harbour footbridge near the gasworks and walked through the Fishertown, sheltered by low houses into The Brackla, the Fishertown bar, where the world was, where the earth was peopled with men huddled close to each other in the warmth.

DAVID THOMSON

RUN-RIGS

The shaping of a nation's landscape is normally a slow and sporadic process triggered from time to time by a variety of forces. In this sense Scotland's experience is no exception. However in her case there was one relatively short period following the 1715 and 1745 rebellions when the pace of change accelerated astoundingly, eventuating in the rural landscape we know today.

The Scottish scene in that period—roughly the middle and latter half of the eighteenth century—was still dominated by the 'run-rig' system of agriculture, a system in which social, institutional and technological factors were completely intertwined. There are few records of this scene. However one unique map, now lodged in West Register House in Edinburgh, describes in detail the pattern of some 100 acres in Angus as they were under the run-rig system. This map,

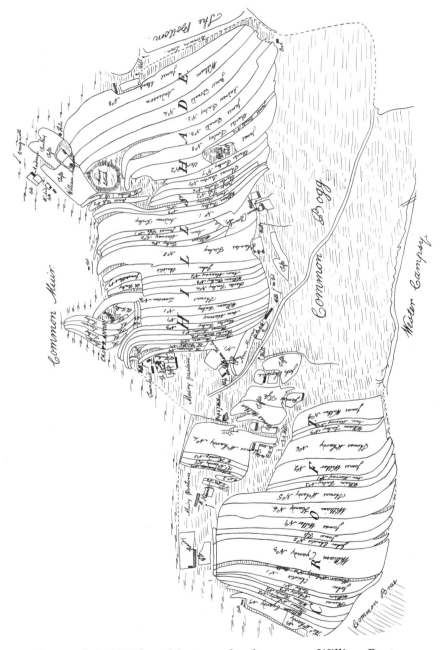

15 Map made in 1773 by a Montrose land surveyor, William Panton, on the ferm toun of Craigyloch in the Parish of Lintrathen, Angus for Airlie estate, from *The Shaping of Scotland*, R J Brien (Aberdeen University Press, 1989).

'Craigyloch in the Parish of Lintrathen' (Figure 1) was drawn by Montrose land surveyor William Panton to facilitate the breaking up and enclosure of the area as it was then and the transfer of parts to larger adjacent farms. It shows in carefully measured detail not only the main types of land we will be discussing and a number of key features of the settlement (houses, yards, tofts, wells, trees, and a kiln) but the individual parcels of land and the names of the people who worked them. This is the only one of about forty of Panton's maps in Register House to show such detail. The surveyors of that age were not so much concerned with the existing land structure as with the new enclosure pattern they were employed to map out.

The subject of this map is a 'ferm toun'—the houses and land of a group of people who cultivated communally the area, using a plough team to draw the old Scots plough. The central feature of the land at that date was the 'inbye' (infield) land, the irregular masses of long, narrow, curving strips of land—the run-rigs produced by the method of cultivation bearing that name.

The rigs themselves were long, sinuous mounds of piled-up soil separated by hollows or 'baulks' of bare wasteland from which the soil had been pared by years of scraping and thrown by the action of the plough towards the centre of the rig (Figure 2). According to writers of these times the landscape so produced was 'like a piece of striped cloth' and 'ridged like the waves of the sea'. In the Craigyloch case the holdings vary from 200 to 400 yards long and from 10 to 25 yards wide. There were no fences, the baulks separated the rigs and the holdings of one man from another's.

These holdings were worked by thirteen families whose tracts were scattered throughout the area, no farmer holding two adjacent strips. The families lived in small irregular clusters of houses, each house being adjoined by a yard and a 'toft' or hand-dug area, the former surrounded by a stone-and-turf wall. In addition to the farmers' families about thirty others, labourers with no claim to land, also lived in the ferm toun.

In many ways this scene was a microcosm of rural Scotland at that time—a small island of cultivated land in a sea of rough, bare,

16   The form of the run-rigs, from *The Shaping of Scotland*, R J Brien (Aberdeen University Press, 1989).

untamed country. In it some thirty families strove without respite to wrest a meagre and tenuous living from the land, which was the source of everything they had—food, clothing and housing. It illustrates some of the main features of the rural landscape—the ferm toun, the division of land, and the run-rigs typical of the inbye area. One significant element is missing—summer shielings, the upland grazing areas to which the women and children of the toun would drive the cattle and stay there with them during the summer months.

This introduces the Scottish rural scene as it was in the middle of the eighteenth century.

R J BRIEN

LETTER FROM ROBERT BURNS TO HIS COUSIN JAMES BURNESS, SOLICITOR, MONTROSE

Lochlee, 21st June 1783

Dear Sir,
My father received your favor of the 10th Current, and as he has been for some months very poorly in health, & is in his own opinion, & indeed in almost ev'ry body's else, in a dying condition; he has only, with great difficulty, wrote a few farewel lines to each of his brothers-in-law; for this melancholy reason I now hold the pen for him to thank you for your kind letter, & to assure you Sir, that it shall not be my fault if my father's correspondence in the North die with him.—My brother writes to John Caird, & to him I must refer you for the news of our family. I shall only trouble you with a few particulars relative to the present wretched state of this country. Our markets are exceedingly high; oatmeal 17 & 18d per peck, & not to be got even at that price. We have indeed been pretty well supplied with quantities of white pease from England & elsewhere, but that resource is likely to fail us; & what will become of us then, particularly the very poorest sort, Heaven only knows—This country, till of late was flourishing incredibly in the Manufacturers of Silk, Lawn & Carpet Weaving, and we are still carrying on a good deal in that way but much reduced from what it was; we had also a fine trade in the Show way, but now entirely ruined & hundreds driven to a starving condition on account of it.—Farming is also at a very low ebb with us. Our lands, generally

speaking, are mountainous & barren; and our Landholders, full of ideas of farming gathered from the English, and the Lothians and other rich soils in Scotland; make no allowance for the odds of the quality of land, and consequently stretched us much beyond what, in the event, we will be found able to pay. We are also much at a loss for want of proper methods in our improvements of farming: necessity compels us to leave our old schemes; & few of us have opportunities of being well informed in a new ones. In short, my dear Sir, since the unfortunate beginning of this American war, & its as unfortunate conclusion, this country has been, & still is decaying very fast.

Even in higher life, a couple of our Ayrshire Noblemen, and the major part of our Knights & squires, are all insolvent. A miserable job of a Douglas, Heron, & Co.'s Bank, which no doubt you have heard of, has undone numbers of them; and imitating English, and French and other foreign luxuries & fopperies, has ruined as many more.—There is great trade of smuggling carried on along our coasts, which, however destructive to the interests of the kingdom at large, certainly enriches this corner of it; but too often indeed at the expence of our Morals; however, it enables individuals to make, at least for a time, a splendid appearance; but Fortune, as is usual with her when she is uncommonly lavish of her favours, is generally even with them at the last; & happy were it for numbers of them if she would leave them no worse than when she found them—

My mother sends you a small present of a cheese, 'tis but a very little one as our last year's stock is sold off; but if you could fix on any correspondent in Edinburgh, or Glasgow, we would send you a proper one in the season. Mrs Black promises to take the cheese under his care so far, and then to send it to you by the Stirling carrier.

I shall conclude this long letter with assuring you that I shall be very happy to hear from you or any of our friends in your country when opportunity serves.—

My Father sends you, probably for the last time in this world, his warmest wishes for your welfare and happiness; and mother & the rest of the family desire to inclose their kind Compliments to you, Mrs Burness and the rest of your family along with

Dear Sir, Your affectionate Cousin,

ROBT BURNESS

AN EARLY NORTH-EAST IMPROVER

It was a simple, obvious system, with the authority of a revealed religion. Oats, turnips, oats, then three years of grass—an harmonious system in which all the parts helped each other and which had as its first principle the steady improvement of the land. It set a pattern on the north which has not changed and few would dare to change without long thought and precaution.

Grant's work at Monymusk took him a lifetime, for progress was slow first. However, he was determined and persistent. Using the lessons he had learned on the Mains, he took other farms into his own hand, improved them and let them to suitable tenants. In some cases he found tenants fit to do the work themselves and encouraged them with long leases at low rents. So the medieval order of the farmlands was redrawn. The new tenant took all the farm into his own hands, levelled and enclosed the fields, and built a house and steading of proper size and comfort. The sub-tenancies disappeared, but many of the sub-tenants became tenants in their own right on smaller farms which they undertook to improve. Some of the smallholdings were only a few acres—insufficient to support a family—but they had a social purpose. The man had the dignity of being his own master as long as he cared to work at home; and the large farmers were glad to employ him whenever he cared to work for a day and a dinner. Most of the large estates were redrawn on those lines—so many big farms; so many small ones; a few crofts for the day men. And then there was the cottar at Platecock who had no door, window or lum—he got no land and had no rights in any thing but his labour. Still, his condition improved. Better cot houses were built on the new farms for the married ploughmen, tied houses they held for the term of their service. They probably slept better; and as meal, milk and potatoes came to be recognised as perquisites, they may have eaten better too. It is impossible to make any social change without leaving a few sore hearts, and no doubt there were some or many who resented the changes, but the improvements left no common feeling of injustice such as followed the Enclosures in England and the Clearances in the Highlands. Both those movements drove people out of the country-side—making in England rich but silent fields, and in the Highland desolate, empty glens. The improvements in the lowland north nourished the land and kept it full of people for more than a hundred years. . . .

How can we assess now the weariness that went to enlarging the stony limits of the fields? Remember the small patches of cultivation, the infield and outfield among the waste. Working outwards from those, year by year and generation by generation, men, women and children dug out the stones, hauled them away on sledges and built them into the dykes that still enclose the fields. It was a monstrous labour. Some of those dykes, hundreds of yards long, twelve feet broad and six feet high, look like things on which a Pharaoh might have tried his 'prentice hand. When the stones were removed the ground was often so rough that it had to be levelled by the spade before the plough could go in. In many cases water was the obstacle, particularly in the old peat mosses where the fuel had been cast, leaving haggs five feet deep, black and dangerous under a cover of moss. The tenants of those unkindly acres dug miles of ditches to run off the water, and again the spade was needed to level out the inequalities for the plough. The man-hours used up on that work would stretch far into eternity. When all that had been done, the result was not always a field in which crops would grow. It might be hungry sand or spouty clay, a dead, inert mass with nothing in it to feed a plant; or peat too acid and unsubstantial for cultivation. The hungry sand had to be fed with dung or turf, and the sodden clay aerated. The moss was consolidated with hundreds of loads of clay to every acre. All the land needed lime that had to be carried long distances over abominable roads. The sum of it all is beyond reckoning. When you travel through the north and see how the cultivation has been carried right over the brow of the little hills, and remember that the work was done with the spade and the mattock, you must surely realise that there were once great men in the land.

The momentum of improvement carried people to fantastic things. When all the likely land had been taken up, young men were driven by a sort of land hunger beyond the reasonable limits of cultivation. For a long time, men with no capital except their own strength, had squatted on some rough moor, had cleared a few fields and built a house and steading. Then the laird agreed to give a lease—at a rent which made certain the poor man would work hard all his life to retain what he had created. So far, the land had been good enough to make that injustice tolerable. Now the squatters were forced up the hillsides, further and further up, till it seemed that the Mither Tap o Bennachie and the Tap o Noth would come under a six-course rotation. But there is a limit to human endurance. As you walk across the lower slopes of the hills you may find a heap of stones that was once a house, and trace among the bracken the rectangle that was once a field. They are melancholy things, witnessing that courage, determination and all the ancient virtues are not enough to bring life out of a stone. A hunger for land drove the people there, and the insatiable hunger of the soil drove them away again. Those ruins are at the stony limit where a human tide spent itselt before it began to ebb away.

After the fields came the steading and the houses. There were two periods of building on the farms. When the land was improved, the old thatched buildings were replaced by modest new ones. Then in the good times which ended in the late 1870s there was a considerable rebuilding. Little was done in the next seventy years; and nothing that changed the plan made a hundred and fifty years ago. The northern farm steading, infinitely repeated with small variations, is in the form of a rectangle, with one side removed. One side is a byre; the second a byre and barn; the third is a stable and cartshed. In the middle is the midden, the storehouse of fertility. Other accommodations had to be found: a turnip shed, for instance, which may be at the angle where the two byres meet. That is where it should be, for convenience in barrowing the turnips to the cattle—fifty feeding bullocks will eat 1 cwt. of turnips a day each, which means the cattleman has to roll 50 cwt. in his barrow, and every yard saved will lengthen his life by a little so much. However, people did not worry very much about saving life or labour at a time when both were so plentiful; the turnip shed might be tucked away in some curious corner and on a lower elevation. The barn usually had a threshing mill driven by a water wheel to which the water came from a mill-dam fed by a stream, if there was one, or by drains from the surrounding fields. If there was no water—and many parts of the north east are very dry, having a rainfall of thirty inches—the mill was driven by horses pulling on levers round a circular course outside the barn. That turned a shaft connected to a driving wheel inside the barn which turned the mill. The barn itself was on two floors. The sheaves were pitched in through a door on the top floor and fed into the drum. The straw was delivered below at one end and the grain at the other. Then there was a granary, usually on the top floor, beside the place where the sheaves came in. Therefore, all the grain had to be carried up a ladder in four-bushel sacks weighing a hundredweight and a half. That also was a certain waste of labour, especially when the rats got into the granary, which was always.

JOHN R ALLAN

TROUBLED FIELDS

After Auchnagatt

We'll try another year again
The seed is in the ground
Harvest will be here again
The season's coming round
And if the rains don't wash away
All we ever had
We'll try another year and stay
Upon this troubled land

What do we have for trouble?
What do we have for toil?
And generation's struggle
Working in the soil
But if the rains don't wash away
The harvest and the yield
We'll try another year and stay
Upon this troubled field

What do we have tomorrow?
What do we have today?
Empty hands and sorrow
And land that's into clay
But if the rains don't wash away
The harvest and the yield
We'll try another year and stay
Upon this troubled field

FRIEDA MORRISON

Auchnagatt is a small village in rural Aberdeenshire. In autumn 1987 over two hundred farmers from that area converged in the local hall to express their worries and concern about their future. As a 'farming journalist' I knew that a series of 'wet' harvests had meant little or no profit. In the early hours of the morning it became clear how serious things were—most of that gathering would have to sell their farms within the year.

17   Highland Clearances, North Uist 1985. Courtesy of Scottish Ethnological Archive, National Museums of Scotland.

THE COST OF NEGLECT

As their zeal for improved farming grew apace, estate managers tried to control the agricultural techniques of their tenants. For example Stobhall Estate near Perth, backward in many ways, abhorred weeds, and this led to the singular practice there of 'Riding the Guild'. The object of the exercise was to eliminate the corn marigold (chrysanthemum segetum), a conspicuous and gregarious arable weed. Certain farms in the area were administered by a Guild and on a specified day in August the Guild members patrolled the fields of the farmers under their control. For every stalk of the corn marigold they found, the negligent farmer was fined one penny. Ironically, this practice meant that while the Guild lands were free of this plant the nearby fields were infested.

But these were only the pinpricks. As farms were being formed and enclosed 'poor cultivators were being expelled', sub-letting was forbidden, and rural areas once thronging with people were being emptied. 'Sub-letting in the past had caused much oppression of the poor and weak by the strong.' As a further instance of this policy, no tenant in the Loch Tayside area could hold more than one farm, which meant that the landlord could get rid of all the odd bits of land held by his followers in adjacent 'farms'. In this case forty notices to quit were served in 1795 and 'many of those who were removed ultimately found their way to Canada'. That there was progress and improvement—as seen on a broader canvas and in a long perspective—is undeniable but the immediate human cost was immense and largely unrecorded.

R J BRIEN

TREES

The biggest effect man has exerted on the history of the Highlands has been in the destruction of the ancient forest—the great wood of Caledon. This has happened within historic time, partly between AD 800 and 1100 and then from the fifteenth and sixteenth centuries till the end of the eighteenth. Even our own day cannot be exempt from this vast tale of almost wanton destruction, for the calls of the two German wars have been ruthless. Much of this priceless remnant in Strath Spey and Rothiemurchus has been felled for ammunition boxes and the old pines of Locheil Old Forest went up in smoke during Commando training. These facts should never be forgotten as one of the *consequences* of war, and if nature reserves ever become a reality in the Scottish Highlands (as something distinct from National Parks, which are lungs for the people and playgrounds), the authorities should go to a great deal of trouble to bring about regeneration of the true Scots pine which is a tree different in many ways from the sombre article commonly grown in plantations as Scots. The true Scots pine of the old forest is a very beautiful tree: its bottle-green is distinctive, and so is the redness of its boughs; the needles are very short and the shape of the mature tree is often much more like that of an unhindered hardwood than the commonly accepted notion of a pine. A long clean stem is not necessarily typical. The true Scots pine is not easy to grow now, and when it is suggested that the authorities should be prepared to go to a lot of trouble to bring about its regeneration, it is because care and patience will be needed in addition to willingness.

The old forest consisted of oak at the lower levels, with alders along the rivers and in soft places, and pines and birches elsewhere. Pines clothed the drier portions and birch the higher and the damper faces of the western hills. The true Scots pine is a relic in the ecological sense, and where fire or the hand of man swept away an expanse of the old pine it was birch which within a year or two provided the new growth. An excellent example of this opportunism of the birch is to be seen at Rhidorroch, above Ullapool, Ross-shire, where the early felling line is clearly marked, pines above and birch below, the opposite arrangement to what would be found in nature. The oak forest has nearly all gone, Argyll and southern Inverness-shire being the main parts where it is to be seen today in any quantity. Scarcely anywhere is it being taken care of, or regeneration active.

F F DARLING

'BLACK AND BARREN MULL'

It is natural, in traversing this gloom of desolation, to inquire, whether something may not be done to give nature a more cheerful face, and whether those hills and moors that afford heath cannot with a little care and labour bear something better? The first thought that occurs is to cover them with trees, for that in many of these naked regions trees will grow, is evident, because stumps and roots are yet remaining; and the speculatist hastily proceeds to censure that negligence and laziness that has omitted for so long a time so easy an improvement.

To drop seeds into the ground, and attend their growth, requires little labour and no skill. He who remembers that all the woods, by which the wants of man have been supplied from the Deluge till now, were self-sown, will not easily be persuaded to think all the art and preparation necessary, which the Georgick writers prescribe to planters. Trees certainly have covered the earth with very little culture. They wave their tops among the rocks of *Norway*, and might thrive as well in the Highlands and *Hebrides*.

But there is a frightful interval between the seed and timber. He that calculates the growth of trees, has the unwelcome remembrance of the shortness of life driven hard upon him. He knows that he is doing what will never benefit himself; and when he rejoices to see the stem rise, is disposed to repine that another shall cut it down.

SAMUEL JOHNSON

VIEWS

. . . On Arboriculture

Trees, therefore, remain the proper and most manageable material of picturesque improvement; and as trees and bushes can be raised almost anywhere—as by their presence they not only delight the eye, with their various forms and colours, but benefit the soil by their falling leaves, and improve the climate by their shelter, there is scarcely any property fitted for human habitation so utterly hopeless, as not to be rendered agreeable by extensive and judicious plantations.

18   Abbotsford, the garden front. Reproduced with permission from the George Washington Wilson collection in Aberdeen University Library.

. . . *On the Art of Landscape Gardening*

There has been for these thirty years past—a considerable and marked improvement in laying out of pleasure-grounds—the spade and shovel have been less in use—the strait-waistcoating of brooks has been less rigorously enforced—and improvers, while talking of Nature, have not so remorselessly shut her out of doors. We believe most landscape-gardeners of the present day would take a pride in preserving scenery, which their masters of the last age would have made conscience to destroy.

The importance of this art, in its more elegant branches, ranks so high in our opinion, that we would willingly see its profession (and certainly it contains persons worthy of such honour) more closely united with the fine arts than it can now be esteemed.

SIR WALTER SCOTT

EMIGRATION AND THE CLEARANCES

DR JOHNSON'S JUDGEMENT

Whether the mischiefs of emigration were immediately perceived, may be justly questioned. They who went first, were probably such as could best be spared; but the accounts sent by the earliest adventurers, whether true or false, inclined many to follow them; and whole neighbourhoods formed parties for removal; so that departure from their native country is no longer exile. He that goes thus accompanied, carries with him all that makes life pleasant. He sits down in a better climate, surrounded by his kindred and his friends: they carry with them their language, their opinions, their popular songs, and hereditary merriment: they change nothing but the place of their abode; and of that change they perceive the benefit.

This is the real effect of emigration, if those that go away together settle on the same spot, and preserve their ancient union. But some relate that these adventurous visitants of unknown regions, after a voyage passed in dreams of plenty and felicity, are dispersed at last upon a sylvan wilderness, where their first years must be spent in toil, to clear the ground which is afterwards to be tilled, and that the whole effect of their undertakings is only more fatigue and equal scarcity.

Both accounts may be suspected. Those who are gone will endeavour by every art to draw others after them; for as their numbers are greater, they will provide better for themselves. When Nova Scotia was first peopled, I remember a letter, published under the character of a New Planter, who related how much the climate put him in mind of Italy. Such intelligence the Hebridians probably receive from their transmarine correspondents. But with equal temptations of interest, and perhaps with no greater niceness of veracity, the owners of the Islands spread stories of American hardships to keep their people content at home.

Some method to stop this epidemick desire of wandering, which spreads its contagion from valley to valley, deserves to be sought with great diligence. In more fruitful countries, the removal of one only makes room for the succession of another: but in the Hebrides, the loss of an inhabitant leaves a lasting vacuity; for nobody born in any other parts of the world will choose this country for his residence, and an Island once depopulated will remain a desert, as long as the present facility of travel gives every one, who is discontented and unsettled, the choice of his abode.

Let it be inquired, whether the first intention of those who are fluttering on the wing, and collecting a flock that they may take their flight, be to attain good, or to avoid evil. If they are dissatisfied with that part of the globe, which their birth has allotted them, and resolve not to live without the pleasures of happier climates; if they long for bright suns, and calm skies, and flowery fields, and fragrant gardens, I know not by what eloquence they can be persuaded, or by what offers they can be hired to stay.

But if they are driven from their native country by postive evils, and disgusted by ill-treatment, real or imaginary, it were fit to remove their grievances, and quiet their resentment; since, if they have been hitherto undutiful subjects, they will not much mend their principles by American conversation.

SAMUEL JOHNSON

THE MORALITY OF FORCED EMIGRATION

There is at this time a considerable ferment in the country concerning the management of the M[arquis] of Stafford's estates: they comprize nearly 2/5ths of the county of Sutherland, and the process of converting them into extensive sheep-farms is being carried on. A political economist has no hesitation concerning the fitness of the land in view, and little scruple as to the means. Leave the bleak regions, he says, for the cattle to breed in, and let men remove to situations where they can exert themselves and thrive. The traveller who looks only at the outside of things, might easily assent to this reasoning. I have never—not even in Galicia—seen any human habitations so bad as the Highland *black-houses*; by that name the people of the country call them, in distinction from such as are built with stone and lime. The worst of the black houses are the *bothies*—made of very large turfs, from 4 to 6 feet long, fastened with wooden pins to a rude wooden frame. The Irish cabin, I suppose, must be such a heap of peat with or without stones, according to the facility of collecting them, or the humour of the maker. But these men-sties are not inhabited, as in Ireland, by a race of ignorant and ferocious barbarians, who can never be civilized till they are regenerated—till their very nature is changed. Here you have a quiet, thoughtful, contented, religious people, susceptible of improvement, and willing to be improved. To transplant these people from their native mountain glens to the sea coast, and require them to become some cultivators, others fishermen, occupations to which they have never been accustomed—to expect a sudden and total change of habits in the existing generation, instead of gradually producing it in their children; to expel them by process of law from their black houses, and if they demur in obeying the ejectment, to oust them by setting fire to these combustible tenements—this surely is as little defensible on the score of policy as of morals.

ROBERT SOUTHEY

LETTER FROM FLORA MACDONALD TO MACKENZIE OF DELVINE

To Mr Mackenzie   *Flodigarry, Trotternish, Sky*
                                         17 August 1772

Dear Sir,
This goes by my Son Johnie who thank God who I am misfortunat in other respects is happy in his having so good a friend as you are to take him under his protection, he seemed when here to be a good natured bidable Boy, without any kind of Vices, make of him what you please and may the Blessing of the almighty attend you along with him which is all the return I am able to make for your many and repeated freindships shown to me and this family; of which there will soon be no remembrance in this poor miserable Island, the best of its inhabitants are making ready to follow their freinds to America, while they have anything to bring there, and among the rest we are to go, especially as we cannot promise ourselves but poverty and oppression, haveing last Spring and this time two years lost almost our whole Stock of Cattle and horses; we lost within these three years, three hundred and twenty-seven heads, so that we have hardly what will pay our Creditors which we are to let them have and begin the world again, anewe, in anothere Corner of it. Allen was to write you but he is not well with a pain in his Side these ten days past. Sir I beg of you if you see anything amiss in the Boys conduct to let me know of it as some Children will stand in awe of their parents more than any body Else.
    I am with my respects to you and Mrs. MacKenzie,

Sir with esteem
Your most obedient
humble servant
FLORA MACDONALD

CANADIAN BOAT SONG

Fair these broad meads—these hoary woods are
  grand;
But we are exiles from our fathers' land.
Listen to me, as when you heard our father
  Sing long ago the song of other shores—
Listen to me, and then in chorus gather
  All your deep voices, as ye pull your oars.

From the lone sheiling of the misty island
  Mountains divide us, and the waste of seas—
Yet still the blood is strong, the heart is Highland,
  And we in dreams behold the Hebrides.

We ne'er shall tread the fancy-haunted valley,
  Where 'tween the dark hills creeps the small clear
    stream,
In arms around the patriarch banner rally,
  Nor see the moon on royal tombstones gleam.

When the bold kindred, in the time long vanish'd,
  Conquered the soil and fortified the keep,—
No seer foretold the children would be banish'd
  That a degenerate lord might boast his sheep.

Come foreign rage—let Discord burst in slaughter!
  O then for clansmen true, and stern claymore—
The hearts that would have given their blood like
    water,
  Beat heavily beyond the Atlantic roar.

ANON

MRS MACFARLANE AND FAMILY EXPRESS THEIR VIEWS TO THE WORDSWORTHS AND COLERIDGE

In talking of the French and the present times, their language was what most people would call Jacobinical. They spoke much of the oppressions endured by the Highlanders further up, of the absolute impossibility of their living in any comfort, and of the cruelty of laying so many restraints on emigration. Then they spoke with animation of the attachment of the clans to their lairds: 'The laird of this place, Glengyle, where we live, could have commanded so many men who would have followed him to death; and now there are none left.' It appeared that Mr Macfarlane, and his wife's brother, Mr Macalpine, farmed the place, inclusive of the whole vale upwards to the mountains, and the mountains themselves, under the lady of Glengyle, the mother of the young laird, a minor. It was a sheep-farm.

Speaking of another neighbouring laird, they said he had gone, like the rest of them, to Edinburgh, left his lands and his own people, spending his money where it brought him not any esteem, so that he was of no value either at home or abroad. We mentioned Rob Roy, and the eyes of all glistened; even the lady of the house, who was very diffident, and no great talker, exclaimed, 'He was a good man, Rob Roy! he had been dead only about eighty years, had lived in the next farm, which belonged to him, and there his bones were laid.'

DOROTHY WORDSWORTH

GLOOMY MEMORIES

To these scenes I was an eye-witness, and am ready to substantiate the truth of my statements, not only by my own testimony, but by that of many others who were present at the time. In such a scene of general devastation, it is almost useless to particularise the cases of individuals; the suffering was great and universal. I shall, however, notice a very few of the extreme cases of which I was myself an eye-witness. John Mackay's wife, Ravigill, in attempting to pull down her house, in the absence of her husband, to preserve the timber, fell through the roof. She was in consequence taken in premature labour, and in that state was exposed to the open air and to the view of all the by-standers. Donald Munro, Garvott, lying in a fever, was turned out of his house and exposed to the elements. Donald Macbeath, an infirm and bedridden old man, had the house unroofed over him, and was in that state exposed to the wind and rain until death put a period to his sufferings. I was present at the pulling down and burning of the house of William Chisholm, Badinloskin, in which was lying his wife's mother, an old bed-ridden woman of nearly 100 years of age, none of the family being present. I informed the persons about to set fire to the house of this circumstance, and prevailed on them to wait until Mr Sellar came. On his arrival, I told him of the poor old woman being in a condition unfit for removal, when he replied, Damn her, the old witch, she has lived too long—let her burn. Fire was immediately set to the house, and the blankets in which she was carried out were in flames before she could be got out. She was placed in a little shed and it was with great difficulty they were prevented from firing it also. The old woman's daughter arrived while the house was on fire, and assisted the neighbours in removing her mother out of the flames and smoke, presenting a picture of horror which I shall never forget, but cannot attempt to describe.

Patrick Sellar was subsequently charged with culpable homicide before the Court of Justiciary at Inverness and was 'honourably' acquitted. But the Clearances continued. In one month parts of the parishes of Golspie, Rogart, Farr and the whole of Kildonan were ruthlessly consigned to the flames.

The consternation and confusion were extreme; little or no time was given for the removal of persons or property; the people striving to remove the sick and the helpless before the fire should reach them; next struggling to save the most valuable of their effects. The cries of the women and children, the roaring of the affrighted cattle, hunted at the same time by the yelling dogs of the shepherds amid the smoke and fire, altogether presented a scene that completely baffles description—it required to be seen to be believed. A dense cloud of smoke enveloped the whole country by day, and even extended far out to sea; at night an awfully grand but terrific scene presented itself—all the houses in an extensive district in flames at once. I myself ascended a height about eleven o'clock in the evening and counted two hundred and fifty blazing houses, many of the owners of which were my relations, and all of whom I knew personally, but whose present condition—whether in or out of the flames—I could not tell. The conflagration lasted six days, till the whole of the dwellings were reduced to ashes or smoking ruins. During one of these days a boat actually lost her way in the dense smoke as she approached the shore, but at night was enabled to reach a landing-place by the lurid light of the flames.

REV DONALD MACLEOD

SUNNY MEMORIES

As to those ridiculous stories about the Duchess of Sutherland, which have found their way into many of the prints in America, one has only to be here, moving in society, to see how excessively absurd they are.

All my way through Scotland, and through England, I was associating, from day to day, with people of every religious denomination, and every rank of life. I have been with dissenters and with churchmen; with the national Presbyterian church and the free Presbyterian; with Quakers and Baptists.

In all these circles I have heard the great and noble of the land freely spoken of and canvassed, and if there had been the least shadow of a foundation for any such accusations, I certainly should have heard it recognized in some manner. If in no other, such warm friends as I have heard speak would have alluded to the subject in the way of defence; but I have actually never heard any allusion of any sort, as if there was anything to be explained or accounted for.

As I have before intimated, the Howard family, to which the duchess belongs, is one which has always been on the side of popular rights and popular reform. Lord Carlisle, her brother, has been a leader of the people, particularly during the time of the corn-law reformation, and *she* has been known to take a wide and generous interest in all these subjects. Everywhere that I have moved through Scotland and England I have heard her kindness of heart, her affability of manner, and her attention to the feelings of others spoken of as marked characteristics.

Imagine, then, what people must think when they find in respectable American prints the absurd story of her turning her tenants out into the snow, and ordering the cottages to be set on fire over their heads because they would not go out.

But, if you ask how such an absurd story could ever have been made up, whether there is the least foundation to make it on, I answer that it is the exaggerated report of a movement made by the present Duke of

Sutherland's father, in the year 1811, and which was part of a great movement that passed through the Highlands of Scotland, when the advancing progress of civilisation began to make it necessary to change the estates from military to agricultural establishment.

HARRIET BEECHER STOWE

AUNTY KATE'S CABIN

Having heard Harriet Beecher Stowe was a guest of the Duchess of Sutherland, Donald Ross, a Glasgow lawyer, wrote to the editor of the Northern Ensign. *(Aunty Kate was Catherine Mackinnon, age 50)*

Glasgow 1854

. . . On 18th Feb last I found poor 'Aunty Kate' under the bush and blankets covering her 'cabin' at Inverie . . . After reaching the spot where I was told it stood I was surprised I could not see it. I went on a little further and then I observed a little mound, like some huge molehill, with some smoke issuing from the end of it. Approaching nearer I was satisfied it was the abode of a human being, for I heard through the openings a hard coughing inside. My friend now came up and we both went to the door of the cabin, and Mr Macdonald (*Father Coll*) asked how Aunty Kate was. At first he got no answer, for the door, which consisted of empty sacks thrown double across a rope, was fast closed down, and two branches were thrown across from the outside, signifying that one of the two inmates was out. Mr Macdonald then went to the other side and having cleared away the snow with his staff, he lifted an old divot and cried—'*A'Cheat, coid an coir a tha airbh an duibh?**' Immediately the poor creature turned round in her bed and putting a little, withered hand out through the hole in the roof, she grasped her friend's hand firmly, telling him at the same time that she felt no better, but worse. I put my eyes to the little opening in the roof . . .

Aunty Kate has a very miserable look, her face is pale, her eyes black, and as she peaks from underneath the blankets at me the place puts me in mind of where I kept my pet rabbits as a boy. The cabin was in two divisions, one for sleeping, the other for cooking. The sleeping division I already noticed, the other is a small place about four and one half feet long, by four feet broad. The height is two feet nine inches. A small partition of staves and pieces of cloth divides the apartments,

and the entrance to the sleeping apartment is just about the size of a
door in an ordinary dog kennel . . .

* 'Catherine, how are you feeling this day?'

*Having heard Mrs Stowe intended to make a comment on the Clearances in a
book,* Sunny Memories, *where she defended the part the Duchess of
Sutherland played in the evictions. Donald Ross wrote to Mrs Stowe but failed
to get a reply. He then sent a second letter care of the Duchess of Argyll.*

To the Duchess of Argyll   *Glasgow 1856*

. . . You are ill-prepared to write anything worthy of being read
regarding the clearances and the cruelties to which the Highland
people are subjected. At Dunrobin Castle you are in a manner tied to
the Duchess of Sutherland's apron strings. You are shown all the glory
and grandeur of the Ducal residence. You are brought to see extensive
gardens, aviaries, pleasure-groves, waterfalls and all that is beautiful
and attractive, and you are occasionally treated to a drive along the
coast road for some miles, through rich farms and beautiful cornfields, and to finish all you are asked to be present at an exhibition of
stockings, plaids, winceys, and tartans made up by poor females from
a distant part of the country. But you have not visited Strathnaver,
you have not penetrated into Kildonan, you have not been up
Strathbrora, you have not seen the ruins of hundreds and hundreds of
houses of the burnt-out tenants . . .

DONALD ROSS

THE CLEARANCES—A SENSE OF SHAME

When I was a boy I saw the sheep by the ruined cottages and
somehow or other I do not recollect asking my parents how they came
to be like that. I wrote one novel about the Clearances—BUTCHERS
BROOM. But my parents never talked about the driving of people
from their homes so that the land could be cleared so that sheep could
be bred. I think there was still a sense of shame at home about those
events. I did not write about the events for the sake of the drama of the
violence, but to let people know about the kind of people who lived in
the houses that were destroyed. It's terrible enough to get burnt out of

your homes and even more terrible to get burnt out in order to make way for sheep, but if you had a kind of way of life that was rich and full of humanity then the violence appears to be more terrible than if you just described the violence alone. Some of the wisdom of that life I embodied in Dark Mairi. Before her death at the end of the book as she wanders. I described her as 'the human mother carrying on her ancient solitary business with the earth, talking good and familiar sense with the boulder and flower and rock.

NEIL GUNN

THE GHOSTS OF THE STRATH

Three ghosts of old communicants
sitting at the table of the manse:
      with no people, a minister;
      with no pupils, a dominie;
and Muckle Donuil the minister's man.

Three ghosts of three old griefs
shuffling through the fallen evening:
Three ghosts of three old comrades
swallowing their doubts of Providence:

These alone came strange to the strath.
These alone remained in the strath:
      the minister and
      the dominie and
Muckle Donuil the minister's man.

JOSEPH MACLEOD ('ADAM DRINAN')

The dominie was an ancestor of Joseph Macleod

A' GHAIDHEALTACHD

Nuair a bhios an taigh fàs,
a' chagailt tais 's an tughadh a' dol air ais
'na thalamh, 's na leapannan a' breothadh,
na plaideachan 's na h-aodaichean a' lobhadh,
creididh sinn an uair sin gun d'fhuair an teaghlach bàs.

Ged a bhiodh clann
an ath dhorais aig mullach an sonais
a' cluiche le pristealan 's a' leum air na cathraichean
a chùm taca uair ri cuideachd an athraichean,
faodaidh sinn a ràdh le fìrinn nach eil beatha ann.

Bidh mi fo sprochd
a' faicinn a-nis uiread de cheanglaichean ris,
ag ionndrain an teine a b'aoidheile lasraichean;
's i a' ghealach a tha a' dèanamh soillse troimh asnaichean
an taighe Ghall-Ghaidhealaich seo na-nochd.

RUARAIDH MACTHÒMAIS

THE HIGHLANDS

When the house is deserted,
the hearth moist and the thatch reverting
to earth, the beds rotting,
the blankets and covers decaying,
we will believe then that the family is dead.

Though the next-door children
were enjoying themselves to the full
playing with shards, and jumping on the chairs
that once supported their forebears' friends,
we may say truthfully there is no life there.

I am depressed,
seeing now so many rafters bared,
missing the fire with its welcoming flames;
the moon sheds light through the ribs
of this Highland-Lowland house tonight.

DERICK THOMSON

TO S R CROCKETT

Blows the wind to-day, and the sun and the rain
          are flying,
Blows the wind on the moors to-day and now,
Where about the graves of the martyrs the whaups
          are crying,
  My heart remembers how!

Grey recumbent tombs of the dead in desert places.
  Standing stones on the vacant wine-red moor,
Hills of sheep, and the homes of the silent
          vanquished races,
And winds, austere and pure:

Be it granted me to behold you again in dying,
  Hills of home! and to hear again the call;
Hear about the graves of the martyrs the peewees
          crying,
  And hear no more at all.

                        R L STEVENSON

THE GREAT POTATO BLIGHT

The great potato blight of the 1840s brought famine or near famine to the people crowded on poor plots by the sea-shore, to which their fathers or grandfathers had been forced in order to provide the cheapest of labours for the exploiters of kelp, and in order to leave the better pasture lands to the big sheep farmers. The 1850s were a time of many Clearances and they continued into the 1860s and even into the 1870s. By 1850 people were being cleared to create or to enlarge deer forests as well as to create sheep farms. Sometimes, without clearing crofts, landlords curtailed the pastures necessary to crofters. In 1865 there was a famous instance of this when Lord MacDonald and his factor took most of Ben Lee from the people of Braes in Skye and let it to one sheep farmer. Braes then was a congested area full of people cleared from Sgoirebreac, Torra-Micheig and even Kilmuir and Staffin. In 1882 the sheep farmer of Ben Lee's lease came to an end and he did not wish to have it renewed; he told the Braes people of this in a friendly way before the end of 1881. It was the determination of the people of Braes to recover Ben Lee that led to the Battle of the Braes in April 1882.

SORLEY MACLEAN
trans from the Gaelic

Customs and Traditions

MR REA LEARNS HOW TO EAT PORRIDGE IN SOUTH UIST

Breakfast next morning consisted of oatmeal porridge and milk, salted herring, newly made scones, oatcake, butter and weak tea. The porridge in soup plates was served first, each plate being accompanied with a large basin of cold milk. This, being new in my experience of taking porridge, caused me considerable diffidence; but Father Allan, tactfully ignoring my hesitancy, commenced his portion, while I followed suit, imitating him as well as I could. We had our basins of milk before us, the plate of porridge on the right; a little of the hot porridge was taken in a large spoon which was then dipped into the cold milk, and porridge and milk then placed in the mouth. I am afraid that I was rather clumsy at first, letting the porridge slip from the spoon into the basin of milk, and having to fish about for it, or taking too large a portion of hot porridge to be cooled quickly and consequently burning my mouth; but I attained greater dexterity before finishing.

F G REA

HOW TO EAT PORRIDGE IN ABERDEENSHIRE

Dod wad be in at the tap en o the table, in the neuk atween the windae an the fire-place. He poored his milk straicht on till his parritch, ontae the same plate, like a milk puddin, faat a slaiger yon wis sweemin aboot. We put a bowl doon tae sit aside the parritch plate an caa'd the speen fae een tae the ither so's the milk was caul tae the boddom o the meal an the parritch kept its firmness an wisna dribbled tae bitties. But the Dawsons aa ett it the same wye, an sugared it ana, a thing we nivver did because oor parritch lay for a meenit faan it was ladled oot an syne a haunfu o dry meal wis cassen on tap o't tae gie't a fine murly taste.

DAVID OGSTON

A STRANGE CUSTOM IN THE WESTERN ISLANDS

The antient way of dressing Corn, which is yet us'd in several Isles, is call'd *Graddan*, from the *Irish* word *Grad*; which signifies quick. A Woman sitting down, takes a handful of Corn, holding it by the Stalks in her left hand, and then sets fire to the Ears, which are presently in a flame: she has a Stick in her right hand, which she manages very dextrously, beating off the Grain at the very instant, when the Husk is quite burnt; for if she miss of that, she must use the Kiln, but Experience has taught them this Art to perfection. The Corn may be so dressed, winnowed, ground, and baked, within an Hour after reaping from the Ground. The Oat-bread dressed as above is loosening, and that dress'd in the Kiln astringent, and of greater strength for Labourers: But they love the *Graddan*, as being more agreeable to their Taste. This barbarous Custom is much laid aside, since the number of their Mills encreas'd. Captain *Fairweather*, Master of an *English* Vessel, having dropt Anchor at *Bernera* of *Glenelg* over against *Skie*, saw two Women at this Imployment, and wondring to see so much Flame and Smoak, he came near, and finding that it was Corn they burnt, he run away in great haste, telling the Natives that he had seen two mad Women very busy burning Corn: the People came to see what the matter was, and laugh'd at the Captain's Mistake, tho he was not a little surpriz'd at the Strangeness of a Custom that he had never seen or heard of before.

MARTIN MARTIN

REV MR BALWHIDDER REPORTS ON NEW SOCIAL CUSTOMS

Before this year, the drinking of tea was little known in the parish, saving among a few of the heritors' houses on a Sabbath evening; but now it became very rife: yet the commoner sort did not like to let it be known that they were taking to the new luxury, especially the elderly women, who, for that reason, had their ploys in out-houses and by-places, just as the witches lang syne had their sinful possets and galravitchings; and they made their tea for common in the pint-stoup, and drank it out of caps and luggies, for there were but few among them that had cups and saucers. Well do I remember one night in harvest, in this very year, as I was taking my twilight dauner aneath the hedge along the back side of Thomas Thorl's yard, meditating on the goodness of Providence, and looking at the sheaves of victual on the field, that I heard his wife, and two three other carlins, with their Bohea in the inside of the hedge, and no doubt but it had a lacing of the conek, for they were all cracking like pen-guns. But I gave them a sign, by a loud host, that Providence sees all, and it skailed the bike; for I heard them, like guilty creatures, whispering and gathering up their truck-pots and trenchers, and cowering away home. . . .

I should not, in my notations, forget to mark a new luxury that got in among the commonality at this time. By the opening of new roads, and the traffic thereon with carts and carriers, and by our young men that were sailors going to the Clyde, and sailing to Jamaica and the West Indies, heaps of sugar and coffee-beans were brought home, while many, among the kail-stocks and cabbages in their yards, had planted groset and berry bushes; which two things happening together, the fashion to make jam and jelly, which hitherto had only been known in the kitchens and confectionaries of the gentry, came to be introduced into the clachan. All this, however, was not without a plausible pretext; for it was found that jelly was an excellent medicine for a sore throat, and jam a remedy as good as London candy for a cough, or a cold, or a shortness of breath. I could not, however, say that they gave me so much concern as the smuggling trade, only it occasioned a great fasherie to Mrs Balwhidder; for, in the berry time, there was no end to the borrowing of her brass-pan to make jelly and jam, till Mrs Toddy of the Cross-Keys bought one, which, in its turn, came into request, and saved ours.

JOHN GALT

THE LIFE OF THE PLOUGHMEN

There was a community on the farm who had little chance of grace and desired less. I mean the ploughmen. They lived in the bothy, a one-roomed house across the yard from the cart-shed. Unlike most of its kind this bothy was pleasant enough, for its back window looked west to the valley and the hills. The furniture was of the simplest—

two big double beds filled with chaff, a wide open fireplace for burning peats, a tin basin to wash in and a roller towel behind the door, and a spotty mirror in one of the windows. Pitch-pine walls and a cement floor looked almost as cold as they were, but they had the necessary merit of being clean. Cold and clean but never a home, you might have said if you had seen it at Whitsunday weekend when the old men had left and the new ones were not yet home, and after Sally had spent a day in scrubbing it out with soap, soda and ammonia. If you had seen it a fortnight later, when the new boys had moved in, you would have found it neither cold nor clean nor any more like home. The farm servant in those days—and I suppose there has been little change—had only two possessions—a kist and a bicycle. So, if you had looked into the bothy, you would have seen the kists set out against the walls and the bicycles in a recess at the foot of the bed. Sunday suits, shirts and long woollen drawers hung from nails on either side of the windows, each man having a bit of the wall for wardrobe. Boots, ranging from stylish browns for Sunday to great tacketty boots all glaur and dung, huddled beneath the beds where they had been lightly thrown off their owners' feet. A strange collection of things littered every shelf—bits and pieces mostly broken, collar studs, screw nails, jews' harps, cogs, flints, gas burners, ball bearings, old knives, corkscrews, cartridges, bicycle clips—everything for which you might find a use if you kept it seven years. Anything they really valued they kept locked in their kists. But you must not think that they left only rubbish about or that they made no attempt at decoration. Most of them had photographs nailed up beside their beds—photographs of relations, very self-conscious in Sunday blacks or white elbow-length cotton gloves; photographs of horses in gala trim on the way to a show or a ploughing match; or photographs of ample ladies in a state of frilly *déshabillé* who must have been left over from the Gay Nineties. These last were real art and treasured as such. Sometimes the reverent owners enclosed them in wreaths of strawplaiting, such as they used in horses' tails, and I suppose the Gaiety Girls must have looked strangely bucolic enclosed in 'long and short' and peeping coyly from under a head of corn. Still I thought they were lovely ladies and so, I am sure, did their owners.

The etiquette of the bothy and stable was equalled in rigidity only by that of the Court of Louis XIV. Each man had his place and was taught to keep it. For the second horseman to have gone in to supper before the first horseman would have created as much indignation as an infringement of precedence at Versailles. The foreman was always the first to wash his face in the bothy at night; it was he who wound the alarm clock and set it for the morning, and so on and so on. The order

of seniority was as strictly observed between the second horseman
and the third, while the halflin always got the tarry end of the stick.
The cattleman's status was indeterminate; I rather think he was on his
own; but, as he tended cows while the others worked that noble beast
the horse, he was always regarded as inferior, whether he admitted it
or not. But the foreman had pride of place in everything. He slept at
the front of the first bed—that is, nearest the fire; he sat at the top of
the table in the kitchen; he worked the best pair of horses; and he had
the right to make the first pass at the kitchen maid. His character had a
considerable influence on the work of the farm; if he was a good-
tempered fellow he kept the others sweet, and if he could set a fast
pace at the hoeing he could save pounds for his master.

The ploughmen usually rose at five in summer and half-past five in
winter. They went to the stable at once, fed their horses and then came
into the kitchen for breakfast. Yoking time was six from March
onwards, and from daylight in winter. They stopped for dinner at
eleven, then yoked at one and lowsed for the day at six, or dark. In
harvest they might work on till ten or eleven, if the dew did not fall
heavily, and I remember two autumns at least when the binder
worked till midnight under the great red harvest moon. As soon as
they had fed their horses they came into the kitchen for supper and in
winter used to remain at the fireside till nine o'clock, telling stories or
playing cards, when they looked to their horses and retired to the
bothy for the night.

Sometimes a few of the boys from the neighbouring farms came to
see them. We would all go out to the bothy then and lie on the beds
while somebody played the melodion and we sang the traditional
songs of the countryside with variations to suit our mood. I enjoyed
those parties. The peat fire glowed with an intense smouldering heat;
the paraffin lamps burned dimly, for there was always a black comet
on the glass; the bothy was warm and smelled of hard soap and
human kind. I lay on the foreman's half of the bed, three parts asleep,
and listened to the melodion, or joined in leisurely songs where the
beat was held up interminably for romantic effect. But, no matter how
hard I tried to keep awake, the sleep overcame me, and I sank down
into the deeps of bliss, troubled only by the gales of laughter that
saluted some hardy tale. Then the foreman carried me into the
house—and morning came in a long moment.

JOHN R ALLAN

A HIGHLAND FUNERAL

Yesterday we were invited to the funeral of an old lady, the grandmother of a gentleman in this neighbourhood, and found ourselves in the midst of fifty people, who were regaled with a sumptuous feast, accompanied by the music of a dozen pipers. In short, this meeting had all the air of a grand festival; and the guests did such honour to the entertainment, that many of them could not stand when we were reminded of the business on which we had met. The company forthwith taking horse, rode in a very irregular cavalcade to the place of interment, a church at the distance of two long miles from the castle. On our arrival, however, we found we had committed a small oversight, in leaving the corpse behind; so we were obliged to wheel about, and met the old gentle-woman half way, being carried upon poles by the nearest relations of her family, and attended by the *coronach*, composed of a multitude of old hags, who tore their hair, beat their breasts, and howled most hideously. At the grave, the orator, or *senachie*, pronounced the panegyric of the defunct, every period being confirmed by a yell of the *coronach*. The body was committed to the earth, the pipers playing a pibroch all the time; and all the company standing uncovered. The ceremony was closed with the discharge of pistols; then we returned to the castle, resumed the bottle, and by midnight there was not a sober person in the family, the females excepted.

TOBIAS SMOLLETT

A LOWLAND FUNERAL

Mrs Smith grew nae weel an it was in the skweel holidays, an Mam put me up tae Kiddies noo an again tae see foo she was deein. As I caad up by Cadger's on the bike this day Dod cam doon fae Kiddies in his Austin Seven, an faan he was level wi'es he rowed doon his windae and stuck his heid oot an said tae me 'She's awa.' I thocht maybe Mrs Smith was in a hospital or maybe even aff tae New Deer for the day so I said tae Dod 'Faur till?' an he said 'She's deid'. The men roon aboot an a puckle weemin gaed up tae Kiddies for the funeral, an

the minister read fae a book on the front doorstep aboot the peace
Jesus left ahin, not as the warld gave but as He gave, it was His peace
an in His Father's hoose waur mony mansions. Men steed in the
gairden, glowerin at their sheen. Faan a drap o rain startit in the
prayer they liftit their hats or their bonnets at an angle fae their bare
heids. The lang kist was taen oot wi a man at ilka neuk, their airms
raxed oot tae the shooders o the man pairin them. They sattlet the
wecht faan they waur aa on level grun an they cairriet the coffin tae the
hearse, their heids held at an angle like the hats in the gairden. They
lookit at neen o's but stracht on, intae naething, as gin they waur seein
deep intae themsels. The fowk won intae their cars an they set aff tae
the cemetery, lichtin their pipes again an newsin a bittie, aboot foo
lang they'd kent her, an foo faur they waur ahin wi the craps, an faan
wad the widder slacken.

DAVID OGSTON

A SCHOOL PICNIC

The skweel picnic aye gaed tae Cullen or Macduff; it wis een o the
fyowe times we wis on a bus, so we waved at aabody, wagging
hankies oot o the windaes at men hyowin in the parks, or gin there
wisna fowk tae wave at, we saluted stirks an yowes as gin they kent
we wis aff on the ran-dan. A peer breet on a push-bike wid get sic a
flappin o hankies he wid winner faa it wis that kent him, an he wid
maybe lift his haun till's afore we waur oot o sicht. Doon on the het
saan the mithers spread their rugs an plunkit doon their bags an yokit
intae wyvin, tull een wid dare the lave tae ging an try the watter wie
her, an they wid hyst their frocks up an styter doon tae the caul waves
tae get their taes weet. We ran races on faativver livvel grun we got a
haud o: the egg-an-speen race wie a Golden Wonder or a Majestic
instead o an egg, the seck race, the three-leggit race an the wheel-barra
race. We played fitbaa or rounders, syne the baker's van appeared an
aa the pyocks wis laid oot on a table for's—aye the same pyock ilka
eer, wie a bridie an a cream-bun an maybe a fly-cemetery. We got
ice-cream later on, bit we gaed an bocht wir ain tee, we drank fizzy ale
oot o wee bottles an sookit ice-lollies. Faan it wis hame-time there wis
aye somebody that wis tint an somebody that thocht the bus wis
coming at half-seiven, nae half-sax, an of coorse they waur bound tae
be awa roon the shops maybe or they'd cried in at their man's sister's
hoose for a fly-cup an naebody kent the address so we couldna ging an

get em. Faan we got roadit, though, the big eens at the back for a caper tae themsels an the little eens at the front, ready fir the time faan they started spewin, we waved an waved an we waggit wir hankies again. We hid saan inside wir pooches, in wir lugs an in wir hair, atween wir taes and even in aneth wir teeth.

DAVID OGSTON

LATHA NA DROBH—A FAIR IN STORNOWAY

On latha na drobh the country folk came to town, but not as fishermen returning to resume their week's work in the vessels which had lain in the harbour even in their absence. They came as crofters, driving flocks of sheep, or herds of cattle. Or riding in little red and blue carts, or brown varnished pony traps. Or leading shaggy horses to the sale ring.

They came from a world that was quite unlike my own, even although at that time many Stornoway families kept a cow or two, as my grannie did, and cultivated an allotment at the back of the town.

And they came in such numbers that Cromwell Street looked as if it might burst apart with the pressure of slow-moving humanity, in the evening, when the market was over and the day's earnings were being liberally spent in the pubs, and we youngsters were reluctant to go to bed, lingering on the streets late into the night in the hope of seeing a fight, which we very often did.

I suppose the girls from the country districts came to the market too, but if they did I have no recollection of them.

It is the boys who march vividly before me as I write. Tall gangling youths with a lumbering athleticism in their gait. The product not of organised games or work in a gymnasium, but of tramping broken moorland, scrambling on cliffs, and jumping in and out of restless boats, launched from rocky geos or open beaches.

All of them wore caps. Huge cloth caps that seemed many times too big for them. Their floppy brims were generally supported by a willowy withy frame so that they stood out like sunhats or sombreros without a crown.

And corduroy knickerbockers unfastened at the knee so that they hung half way down the leg, looking as inadequate and untidy as the caps were excessive but kempt.

Many of them carried walking sticks, or if they didn't, the purchase of one was the first priority when they got to the fairground, with its stalls and its circus, and its coconut shies.

I can hear as I write the lowing of cattle, the baaing of sheep, and neighing of horses. I can feel myself slithering on the sodden, muddy, churned up turf, for it was almost always raining. I can see Sime's toy stall. Taste Finlay's ice cream.

May and June are the loveliest months of the year in Lewis—apart from September. The twilight lingers so that there is almost no night and a steady east wind brings long spells of bracing sunshine. It seemed stupid, almost to the point of perversity, to hold the annual cattle market, one of the great social and commercial occasions of the year, in the month of July when the sultry rain storms were so predictable that they came to be known as 'tuiltean na drobh,'—'the market downpours'.

For us town children, who could not show, by sporting a staff or a shepherd's crook, that we had come to man's estate, and were used to handling sheep at the fank or on the moor, the great prizes of the market, apart from a visit to the circus, were the coconuts and 'aran cridhe'.

How is it possible to make the affluent Lewis child of today understand a world in which a piece of gingerbread was an unusual and sought-for treat? Or that a dance at the road end, under a canopy of stars, with a solitary melodeon for accompaniment, or no instrumental music at all, can give more undiluted enjoyment than evenings spent in a sophisticated dance hall with a famous band, an open bar, and all the money you can spend?

JAMES SHAW GRANT

ABERDEENSHIRE CATTLE SHOW

What an excitement there was about the show when I was a boy, say thirty years ago. I used to live part of the summer with a farmer who always entered horses, cattle and sheep at his local show; and we must have spent the evenings of a week, and some of the days, in preparing the animals. It was an extensive beauty treatment. We brushed and combed the horses until we were afraid to touch them, in case electricity came out of their hair. We washed their feet and dried them with clean sawdust, then brushed and combed the fetlocks until they shone, long and silky, like a girl's tresses. Finally we took new halters and whitened them with blanco so that nothing common should detract from the bloom of the animals. Cows, being inferior creatures, got less attention: as I remember, their tails were washed and brushed out and their hooves dressed, but that was all.

The sheep, however, got the most lavish treatment. To begin with, we washed them in a deep pool in the burn. Being Border Leicesters, they were big, heavy and obstinate. It took a strong man to throw them into the pool and an agile one to avoid going in with them. When they were thoroughly soaked they were allowed to come out and shake themselves, which they did in a way that threw cold water in all directions. Then we caught them and washed their fleeces with soap and water, even the little tracks of dust and tears that ran down from the neuk of each eye, which took time, patience and cunning, for they were always ready to jump away from, or over, us. Then we threw them in the pool again, and kept ducking them there with a long pole until the soap was rinsed from their fleeces. Next day we began again, to dye them. After they had been soaked in the pool we worked yellow dip very thoroughly into the fleeces until they looked like melting butter, and then let them run in the sun to dry themselves.

So far it had been apprentice work: now the artist took them in hand with the shears. Slowly and with many pauses to observe them from all angles, he clipped them into an ideal shape for a Border Leicester, hoping thus to hide small defects from the eyes of the judge and also to bring out the good points, if any. When we had done with them, the beasts were curious rectangular objects of a remarkable yellow colour, still sheep, but sheep stylised, the products of *haute couture*. Schiaparelli could not have improved on them and only Dali could have gone on where we left off.

The ground was suited by nature to the occasion. It was at the foot of a steep slope from the town to the river, so there was a high bank on the north side that made a natural grandstand. On the south, trains ran slowly behind a screen of young beeches and, beyond, the river glinted through the leaves while it swished and rumbled among the silvery stones. To the east there were old beechwoods that clattered with contending rooks. The ground was thus a small, enclosed and shady place, warm when the sun shone, but frequented by the river breezes, cool with a touch of spray. The animals were held in temporary pens all round it while the attendants worked hard with brushes and sawdust and mysterious small bottles of oil to give the touch that might win the last deciding point. The middle of the field was roped off into several rings for judging the various sorts of animals, by far the largest being the horses. Along the railway side there were two big marquees, one for the dairy and baking and the other for the refreshments. Two small tents, one labelled *Secretary* and the other *Judges*, stood side by side under a wide elm tree and looked somehow both official and conniving. In the far corner, out of the way, there were a few ploughs, rakes and carts, maybe a dozen in all, put there by local merchants in the hope of trade, but little regarded in the festival of living things. At five to eleven in the morning the spectators were disposed around the stalls and pens, giving advice to their friends, depreciating with silent contempt the property of their enemies, and taking up postures of immobile obstruction while they discussed the weakness of a hock or the uncertainty of the weather.

When the clock struck eleven from the parish kirk, all the attendants doubled their efforts, making the sawdust fly like snow round the horses' feet. Spectators looked at their watches, then at the two tents, official and conniving under the elm tree. They saw a man with a very large badge in his lapel passing from the one to the other several times with bottles and glasses. It was a sign that the judges were being loaded and the battle would soon begin. Stewards, wearing badges of silver cardboard, ran about waving catalogues, calling on competitors to get ready, and urging the spectators towards the rings so that the animals might have room to move. After a monstrous deal of shouting, attention was fixed in the middle of the field. The judges came from beneath the elm tree in pairs. Sometimes there might be only one judge, but it was considered better there should be two, on the principle that two heads were better than one and each judge could keep an eye on the other. As they stepped into the ring I used to think they had awful majesty. They came from a distance. They were so famous you could sometimes read their names in the paper. And on that day, when the best of the countryside had been gathered together, they were the arbiters of judgement. They were, I thought, in a wonderful position and maybe they thought so too; for, although they were quite ordinary bodies, they took on a remote, impartial air for the occasion. During the next two hours their word was law, beyond all question.

Whatever the animals, the judging was a time of almost intolerable suspense; as a spectacle, the judging of the horses was supreme. Perhaps a dozen, or even twenty, mares would be led round the ring, first at a walk, and then at a trot. They frisked, they bounded, had moments of pretended fright and real panic in the walk while the attendants tried to make them hold up and show their points. But when the walk became a trot, the more rapid movement filled them with pride and joy. The great beasts, shining with health and care, pounded over the hollow turf, throwing back their hairy hooves till their bright shoes caught the sunlight.

JOHN R ALLAN

KELSO HORSE SHOW

Morning discovers it, sprawled in a loop the river
swings itself through the meadow on. Already
horse-boxes, floats and cars have runnellled the edge
of the field to a slush of muddy grass. A steady
straggle of people thickens the booths and the ring.
April neighs coldness. White clouds scud
last winter off the skies. The show-ground shakes
to life as buyers, catalogued with hunches, thud
incautious canters, swerved by the boundary hedge.
Ponies nudge stakes, or rub a child's hand,
soft as their noses. Shouldering knotted halters
the sellers wait their turn behind the stand
where the auctioneer patters, hoarse with loss or profit.
Hunters and hacks parade reluctant paces,
plodding a clomped-up circle. The bidding sways
among five hands, then swings between two faces—
a fighting man whom enemy winds have leathered
smooth as a saddle; and in from the lean hills,
a Border farmer—both of them aware
their urge for satisfaction is the will's
ability to knock down for a song
whatever each has sent his heart upon,
though couldn't care for less as soon as got.
Down goes the Colonel's arrogance; down, down,
before a folly richer than his own.
Hard on the hunter's hooves, a gelding bears
reflections of so many hopeful selves
that most must be unbridled small despairs.
But sold or bought, the time and the place are the horses;
the sweet smell of their sweat, the strung hay
they munch their breath on, the patient stable darkness
rippling their flanks, commotions the livelong day
till it breaks away from its minute-by-minute grazing,
from Countified calls and bawdy Irish curses;
an image riding its own reality
to a sense of recognition no one rehearses;
and for all the human dressage, the play of purses,
something out of the past in me rejoices.

MAURICE LINDSAY

THE HOLY FAIR

In Scotland, they run from kirk to kirk, and flock to see a sacrament, and make the same use of it that the papists do of their pilgrimages and processions; that is, indulge themselves in drunkenness, folly, and idleness. . . . At the time of the administration of the Lord's Supper upon the Thursday, Saturday, and Monday, we have preaching in the fields near the church. At first, you find a great number of men and women lying together upon the grass; here they are sleeping and snoring, some with their faces towards heaven, others with their faces turned downwards, or covered with their bonnets; there you find a knot of young fellows and girls making assignations to go home together in the evening, or to meet in some ale-house; in another place you see a pious circle sitting round an ale-barrel, many of which stand ready upon carts for the refreshment of the saints . . . in this sacred assembly there is an odd mixture of religion, sleep, drinking, courtship, and a confusion of sexes, ages, and characters. When you get a little nearer the speaker, so as to be within the reach of the sound, though not of the sense of the words, for that can only reach a small circle, you will find some weeping and others laughing, some pressing to get nearer the tent or tub in which the parson is sweating, bawling, jumping, and beating the desk; others fainting with the stifling heat, or wrestling to extricate themselves from the crowd: one seems very devout and serious, and the next moment is scolding and cursing his neighbour for squeezing or treading on him; in an instant after, his countenance is composed to the religious gloom, and he is groaning, sighing and weeping for his sins: in a word, there is such an absurd mixture of the serious and comic, that were we convened for any other purpose than that of worshipping the God and Governor of Nature, the scene would exceed all *power of face*.

LETTER FROM A BLACKSMITH TO THE MINISTERS AND ELDERS
OF THE CHURCH OF SCOTLAND (1759)

COUNTRY DANCE

The fiddles tuned up, the smoky wall-lamps were forgotten as the Master of Ceremonies made his opening announcement . . . 'Gentlemen, take your partners for a Highland Schottische!' At once there was a sound like a stampede of cattle on a Western ranch; skidding across the intervening space, each man made a dash to secure the partner he had marked when looking the girls over. He crooked his arm, offered it to her with a bow and mumbled 'May-I-have-pleshur-of-this-dance?' At once, she took it and they joined the Grand March, conversing politely as they moved round the room. When there was enough couples in the parade the signal was given for the dance to begin, and when it ended the lady was escorted back to her seat, her partner bowed low and left her. Soon the dance was in full swing, the piper with one foot thrust forward tapping in time with his music, and the toes of seated folk tapping in appreciation. There were reels, waltzes, quadrilles, and lancers, when the men delighted in whirling their partners off their feet. There were 'The Flowers o' Edinburgh', 'Petronella', 'The Triumph', and 'Rory o' More', besides the Circassian Circle and the Waltz-Country-Dance, a restful slow dance for four to the tune of 'Come o'er the stream, Charlie'. There was gaiety and friendly chaff. The strident music, provided in turn by fiddles, bagpipes, melodeons, and mouth-organs, the odour of sweat and paraffin, the smoke from many pipes of Bogie Roll, the stamping of heavy boots that made dust rise from cracks in the floorboards, the clapping in the lancers and the hooching in the reels . . . all contributed to an atmosphere of abandonment and enjoyment; even the elderly birled on the floor, the old men hooching as loud as any, while all laughed and twirled to Kafoozalum, Cawdor Fair and Tullochgorum.

Fizzy lemonade in green glass bottles, and ginger ale in stone bottles were available, and conversation lozenges. Jock could buy his Jenny a tuppeny poke of sweeties that cost sixpence a pound. From time to time it would be announced that Miss J or Mr B would 'favour the company with a song'. A lass would produce the sang-book she had in readiness, or a big farm-lad would consent to render a bothy ballad. Sitting on the end of the big desk, with arms folded and feet swinging in the true tradition of the corn-kisters (who drummed their heels on the corn-kist in time to the music) the lad would sing in a nasal, indifferent tone, quite unlike his usual robust voice, one of the songs of the land . . . of ploughing matches, of feeing markets, harvesting, courting, and all the other occupations that made up the life of the countryside. One I remember well was the ballad of Johnny Raw, a guileless loon up from the country for a day in town, who was left literally holding the baby. All joined in the jeering refrain, 'And I wish ma Granny saw ye'. We had a different version at school which said:

> Johnny Raw shot a craw
> Took it hame tae his Ma-maw,
> His Ma-maw ate it aw
> An' left the banes for Johnny Raw.

AMY STEWART FRASER

COUNTRY DANCE

The room whirled and coloured
and figured itself with dancers.
Another gaiety seemed born of theirs
and flew like streamers
between their heads and the ceiling.

I gazed, coloured and figured,
down the tunnel of streamers—
and there, in the band, an old fiddler
sawing away in the privacy
of music. He bowed lefthanded and his right hand
was the wrong way round. Impossible.
But the jig bounced, the gracenotes
sparkled on the surface of the tune.
The odd man out, when it came to music,
was the odd man in.

There's a lesson here, I thought, climbing
into the pulpit I keep in my mind.
But before I'd said Firstly brethren, the tune
ended, the dancers parted, the old fiddler
took a cigarette from the pianist, stripped off
the paper and ate the tobacco.

NORMAN MACCAIG

19   Cornkisters. Courtesy of Scottish Ethnological Museum, National
Museums of Scotland.

CORNKISTERS

The cornkist had an important place in rural tradition, for the old
country songs are so closely associated with it as to be known as
cornkisters. You see, the boys sat on the top of the kist and kept time to
their songs by thumping their tacketty boots against the front of it. If
you had been passing the stable door of a summer evening when the
sun was going down and the west wind was blowing softly over the
young corn, you would have heard the mournful words of 'The Dying
Ploughboy' sung with tremendous pathos by a deep baritone, while
half a dozen heels beat time against the kist, like distant thunder, or
the insistent beat of fate's winged chariot hurrying near.

> It's jist *thump* a week *thump* ago *thump* the morn *thump*
> Sin I *thump* wis weel *thump* an hairst—*thump* in corn *thump*;
> Bit some-(*thump*)thing in *thump* my heart *thump* gaed wrang *thump*,
> A ves-(*thump*)sel burst *thump*; the bluid *thump* ootsprang.

And so on through as many verses as the singer could remember or
improvise. The cornkisters are not all as mournful as 'The Dying
Ploughboy'. They express the whole life of the farm servant—the
ecstasies of love, the miseries of marriage, the meanness of masters,
the greed of mistresses, and above all the pride in the plough. Some of
them reach the heights of Rabelaisian humour; others sound great

depths of bathos; but many of them are true and lovely songs. The finest of them all used to be sung by a foreman we once had who combined ruthlessness in pursuit of his pleasures with a romantic taste in song. You did not know what lyrical feeling was until you had heard him sing:

> Braid up your gowden hair,
> Pretty Peggy my dear;
> Braid up your gowden hair,
> Pretty Peggy-o;
> Oor Captain's name was Shaw,
> But alas he wede awa;
> He died for the love of a lady-o.

By the exquisite melody in his voice you knew that he felt deeply the romantic fate of Captain Shaw. Perhaps he thought: 'There, but for the grace of God, go I'; but I am sure that, if there had been any dying to be done for love, he would have left his ladies to do it. The truest of the cornkisters is 'Drumdelgie', which tells of the hard service at 'a fairmtoon up in Cairney'. After a recital of all the miseries suffered there, the singer concludes with the excellent and typical valediction:

> So fare ye weel, Drumdelgie,
> I'll bid ye a' adieu
> An' leave ye as I found ye—
> *A maist onceevil crew.*

JOHN R ALLAN

A PICTURE OF THE CALEDONIAN HUNT

Over their fences with superb aplomb
these claret-blooded hunting gentry soar,
their leathering women, mistresshood confirmed
by hourglass stays and half their years to pour

unquestioned dominance down, curbed in and held
above the silence of their last halloo,
kept from oblivion by the picture's edge
that scuffed their breathless quarry out of view.

Why did they ride to hounds? Some need to assert
the blood's uncertainty, their rulership
of field and ditch? Or, like the pounding fox,
hopeful they'd give their warmest fears the slip?

Or did they straddle stallions to exult
and stretch those instincts men and horses share,
the satisfaction straining thews and sinews
relax into the sense of use and wear?

Did movement threaten from behind scrubbed hedges,
the spring of winter coiled in frosted mould
mock at their privilege, or seem to trap them
nearer the thicket of their growing old?

Still they survive, these lonely, frozen gestures;
the life they leaped at and were ground to, thawed
beneath them, gone with all they thought they stood for.
Yet were they further from whatever flowed

as clarity around their consciousness,
wearing away what living seemed to mean,
but somehow never did, than we are who
catch half-familiar glimpses of it, seen

as landscape flowing from a plane is; clean
in its detachment, of itself complete?
What we are left with here are the blanched stains
imprinting lineaments of a defeat

not different from ours, but doubly separated;
by the unexplorable geography
of time, each of us on our island of it
misted about in our own difficulty.

MAURICE LINDSAY

THE RHYTHM OF THE BLACKSMITH

The custom of beating in time on the anvil's heel is a very ancient one
. . . Firstly, as the blacksmith, the muscles of his brawny arms in full
play, beats the iron into shape his brain is also functioning at full
speed. Sometimes, however, he must think twice before he hits the
iron again, so to mark time he musically taps the anvil once, or twice or
thrice as the case requires . . . As the job or piece of hot iron is being
turned, it is necessary to miss a stroke or so, and every smith with any
sense of rhythm must perforce beat in the time on the anvil; this
operation, if the sledge is being used, can be done very beautifully if
the smith possesses the soul of music . . . The light rhythmic taps on
the anvil are a positive relief to the arms of the smith, who, although
his muscles are 'like iron bands' cannot strike the iron continuously
with herculean strokes without the relief given by the practically
effortless tap, tap, tap on the anvil . . .

JAMES C FORBES

DUNCAN OF KNOCK'S 'ROUGH AND ROUND DINNER'

The requisites for 'a rough and round dinner' were always at Duncan
of Knock's command. There was the beef and mutton on the braes,
the fresh and salt-water fish in the lochs, the brooks, and firth; game of
every kind, from the deer to the leveret, were to be had for the killing,
in the Duke's forests, moors, heaths, and mosses; and for liquor,
home-brewed ale flowed as freely as water; brandy and usquebaugh
both were had in those happy times without duty; even white wine
and claret were got for nothing, since the Duke's extensive rights of
admiralty gave him a title to all the wine in cask which is drifted ashore
on the western coast and isles of Scotland, when shipping have
suffered by severe weather. In short, as Duncan boasted, the
entertainment did not cost MacCallummore a plack out of his sporran,
and was nevertheless not only liberal, but overflowing.

SIR WALTER SCOTT

A WELCOME AT LOCH MAREE

Our barrack fairly fitted up, I set out with my comrade, whose knowledge of Gaelic enabled him to act as my interpreter, to a neighbouring group of cottages, to secure a labourer for the work of the morrow. . . .

The fire was placed in the middle of the floor: the master of the mansion, a red-haired, strongly-built Highlander, of the middle size and age, with his son, a boy of twelve, sat on the one side; his wife, who, though not much turned of thirty, had the haggard, drooping cheeks, hollow eyes, and pale, sallow complexion of old age, sat on the other. We broke our business to the Highlander through my companion—for, save a few words caught up at school by the boy, there was no English in the household—and found him disposed to entertain it favourably. A large pot of potatoes hung suspended over the fire, under a dense ceiling of smoke; and he hospitably invited us to wait supper, which, as our dinner had consisted of but a piece of dry oaten cake, we willingly did. As the conversation went on, I became conscious that it turned upon myself, and that I was an object of profound commiseration to the inmates of the cottage. 'What,' I inquired of my companion, 'are these kind people pitying me so very much for?' 'For your want of Gaelic, to be sure. How can a man get on in the world that wants Gaelic?' 'But do not they themselves,' I asked, 'want English?' 'O yes,' he said, 'but what does that signify? What is the use of English in Gairloch?' The potatoes with a little ground salt, and much unbroken hunger as sauce, ate remarkably well. Our host regretted that he had no fish to offer us; but a tract of rough weather had kept him from sea, and he had just exhausted his previous supply; and as for bread he had used up the last of his grain crop a little after Christmas, and had been living, with his family, on potatoes, with fish when he could get them, ever since.

HUGH MILLER

THE MIDWINTER MUSIC

In the northern islands December is a dark month. The lamps are burning when people go to their work. Light thickens again in the early afternoon. The weather, more often than not, is cold and stormy. There are also calm clear nights when the hemisphere of sky is hung with stars and in the north the Aurora Borealis rustles like curtains of heavy yellow silk.

It is the season of The Nativity. It is also the time of trows.

To the islanders the earth they tilled was an element of dark dangerous contending energies. The good energy of the earth raised their crops into the sun and rain and wind; but there were other earth energies bent on famine, sickness, death. These energies were active always; especially in the dark cold time of the year when nothing grew, the earth seemed to belong to them entirely. The island farmers knew this evil brood as trows, and the trows were more than vague abstract energies, they had shape and substance; they could dance, they could speak, they could travel between the hill and the ploughed field, they were often seen (but only by people who had the gift). The trows belonged to the underworld, to the kingdom of night. Hideous shapes, they represented all the curses of unredeemed nature. The best way to contain the kingdom of winter and death was to lead a decent life, for the trows were among other things embodiments of the seven deadly sins; and it was best to observe duly the rituals of Christianity as well as other rituals that were old when the negalithic people built the stones at Brodgar.

The corn and the animals had to be protected. The trows grew strong and bold in winter in proportion as the creatures of light paled and dwindled. Straws in the form of a cross were fixed to the lintels of barn and byre. So these places were 'sained', made holy. The most precious creatures in a croft, and the most liable to corruption, were the children. A special care was taken of them on Helya's Night, the twentieth of December. In Shetland, the old grandmother went round each bed and cradled and committed the young ones to the care of the Virgin Mary.

> Mary Midder, had de haund
> Ower aboot for sleeping-baund,
> Had da lass and had da wife,
> Had da bairn a' its life.

> Mary Midder, had de haund
> Roond da infants o' oor laund.

This beautiful poem was being uttered in the north three and a half centuries after the Reformation.

If the children were not protected it was easy for the trows to steal them. What happened was this: the trows left their own off-spring in the cradle, and these winter children generally grew up sick and deformed. So the people say of someone who looks permanently ill that he is 'trowie'.

A great peace and silence fell on the islands on Thomasmas, twenty-first of December, and continued till after Christmas. No work was done, except what was absolutely essential.

> The very babe unborn
> Cries O dul! dul!
> For the breaking o'
>   Thammasmas Night
> Five nights afore Yule.

They called December the twenty-third Modra Night. It was the longest night of the year and so the mother of all other nights. And possibly it was the night when the Mother of God, heavy with her burden, set out on the road to Bethlehem.

December the twenty-fourth was a night specially holy and terrible. The trows, in dark hordes, lingered outside every croft. The crofter removed the upper quernstone from the lower. All through the year the women had ground the corn, turning the quernstones in fruitful sunwise circles. It was certain that the trows, given the chance, would secretly turn the quern widdershins, against the sun, so that the stones would be rendered barren and the family would starve during the following year.

The terror of darkness was held in check by a strictly-observed ritual. The mother brought out a basin and filled it with water. The man of the house, priest-like, took three live embers from the fire and dropped them in the water. So, in midwinter, the elements of fire and water were true to the tryst of purification. They would meet and mell in their other dance, fecundity, in spring-time. Let the shrunken earth abide the lustful embraces of sun and rain in the time of seed; tonight all three met in a trance of purity.

In this condensed drama all nature—light and darkness, the four elements, plant and beast and man—were seen as part of a divine festival. The creatures of nature kept their trysts in season, they could not behave otherwise. Man, with his scattered and distracted energies, the flesh tugging for ever against the spirit, 'born under one law, to another bound', moving between the trow-infested earth and the angel-fretted sky, proclaimed his allegiance to the kingdom of light (of which he was the whining wayward heir) in the form of a willed and strictly-observed ritual; as now, when the priest-like crofter, his dwindled fields all around him, mingled the elements of fire and water; for a purification, that his winter-beleaguered household might be worthy to eat bread, a mingling of his own harrow-sweat with heaven's grace. . . . One by one, each member of the family washed himself all over in the fire-kissed water and put on clean clothes. The rooms had been swept already; everything dirty had been bundled away; the dishes on the dresser glinted in the lamplight. The children were put to bed. Midnight was approaching. The other members of the family retired one by one, until only the parents were left. They made then an act of great faith. Though the night outside was thick with trows, they unfastened the door and left the lamp burning and went to bed. It was possible that Our Lady and Saint Joseph with their as-yet-hidden treasure would come to their croft that night, seeking shelter.

Early on Christmas morning the man of the house rose before daybreak, while the others were still asleep. He lit a candle in the skull of a cow, carefully fixing it in the eye-socket. He went into the byre, carrying this lantern. He fed the beasts by its light, giving them more to eat than usual. It was a re-enaction of the scene in the byre at Bethlehem; the animals had also been present at Christ's nativity. The flame in the skull was a reminder to them that they shared both in mortality and in this blessed time, the kindling of the one true light in the world's darkness.

GEORGE MACKAY BROWN

PROVISION IN A SHEILING HUT

On skelfs a' round the wa's the cogs were set,
Ready to ream, an' for the cheese be het;
A hake was frae the rigging hinging fu'
Of quarter kebbocks, tightly made an' new.
Behind the door, a calour heather bed,
Flat o' the floor, of stanes an' fail was made.

ALEXANDER ROSS

LIFE AT THE BU—A FARM IN ORKNEY

We always returned from church to a good dinner of soup with a chicken, or, as we called it, more honestly, a hen, cooked in it, followed by 'spotted dog'. Now that my sailor suit has come back again I find it is associated with these Sunday dinners and the shining spoons and knives and forks laid out on the white tablecloth. During the week we did not bother much about knives and forks and tablecloths. A big plate of herring or other fish was set in the middle of the table, along with a dish of potatoes, and we simply stretched out our hands. The traditional Orkney invitation to a visitor was, 'Put in thee hand,' though when a visitor appeared knives and forks were usually laid out. We hardly ever ate meat or fowl more than once a week. It was the same at all the other farms, and nobody seemed to be the worse for it. Our supper was porridge. The porridge-pot was set down in the middle of the floor, and we all sat round it with great bowls of milk and ladled the porridge into the milk.

Our diet was a curious one by town standards. We went without many necessaries, or what are considered necessaries—beef, for instance—and had a great number of luxuries which we did not know to be luxuries, such as plovers' eggs, trout, crab, and lobster: I ate so much crab and lobster as a boy that I have never been able to enjoy them since. Our staples were home-made oat bannocks and barley bannocks, butter, eggs, and home-made cheese, which we had in abundance; white bread, bought at the Wyre shop, was looked upon as a luxury.

Our life at the Bu was virtually self-supporting. The pig, after being slaughtered each year, was cut up and salted, and the pork stored away in a barrel. I helped with the salting when I was quite small, and got a sense of pleased importance from rubbing the raw slices of meat on coarse salt strewn on a wooden board: these neat cubes did not seem to have any connection with the butchered pig. We had fish almost as often as we wanted it, and crabs when Sutherland went to lift his creels; and Aunt Maggie was often down on the beach gathering whelks. The oat bannocks and barley bannocks, the milk, butter, cheese, and eggs, were our own produce. We sent part of the wool after the sheep-shearing down to a Border town, and it came back as blankets and cloth. We bought at the shop such things as white bread, sugar, tea, treacle, currants and raisins, and paraffin oil for the lamps.

EDWIN MUIR

WONT AND CUSTOM ON A SELKIRK FARM

Some idea of the etiquette in farm-kitchens of the period may be got from a later account of a Selkirkshire farm. When the farmer died in 1745, the goods listed in his testamentary inventory included four beds, two fitgangs (long foot stools before the beds), three big and four small chests, one aumrie (small cupboard), two cupboards, a wool wheel, a lint wheel, a clack reel, a big table, an oval table, a long settle, six chairs, four stools, two meal arks, three tubs, a flesh boat, four butter kits, three cogs, six milk bowies, two stoups, two kail pots and a kettle, a brass pan, a salt fatt (vat), a brander, a girdle, a ladle, a sowens sieve, a babrick (probably the same as *baw breid*, baking board), a meal skep (straw container), two basins, a pewter stoup and jug, six pewter plates, three trenchers and a dish of earthenware, eleven wooden trenchers, six plates, six wooden caups (bowls), twelve horn spoons, eight pewter spoons, six dozen bottles, a crook and clips for hanging pots above the fire, a pair of tongs, and a flesh hook. At this date, the farmer had three ploughs and employed three male and three female servants.

This range covers sleeping, sitting, and the storage, preparation and eating of food. These were the important things. In a later description of the same farm-kitchen, it was said that the *goodman*, the head of the household, sat at the head of a long, stout table that was placed near the window. Possibly this is the one referred to in the inventory. Next to him were his wife and family, with the servants at the lower end. At dinner, two or three large wooden bowls of broth were served, and supped with short horn spoons or *cutties*. Next some wooden trenchers were put on the table and a piece of boiled meat put before the goodman, who carved it with a clasped knife and fork that he always carried. Knives and forks were at this time still exceptions rather than rules, and the meat that was distributed was eaten with the fingers. This lack of cutlery is a point to be considered in looking at the range of everyday food made in earlier days. After the meat had been eaten, the broth was replaced on the table and supped along with barley bannocks. On other days, cheese, butter, milk, salt herrings, or oatmeal dumplings might replace the meat. As yet, potatoes were no more than a garden dainty, and played no part in the daily diet.

On this Selkirk farm, the farmer's family and the unmarried

servants had their meals together, though they kept their separate places at the table. Even in the 1840s in Berwickshire, several remembered how the master shared out butcher meat for the rest to eat with their fingers. But agricultural improvements gradually led to increased segregation of masters and men, and the economy of the farm-house began to be organised, as in Fife about 1800, to 'put an end to that indiscriminate intercourse in respect of sitting and eating, which was common in former times'. Some of the parish ministers regretted the move away from the family board with the goodman presiding, for 'his presence and conversation produced the most beneficial effects on the manners and morals of the domestics'. In Peebles-shire, old habits die hard, for though in general farmers and men ceased to eat together after about 1750, one small laird who died about 1830 always dined with his servants until after his second marriage. His new wife was more fashion-conscious, and he had to compromise by taking tea for breakfast with his wife in the parlour, and eating his porridge afterwards with the servants in the kitchen.

The increase in social differentiation was also accompanied by differentiation in eating when the men who had formerly been in the house were moved into *bothies*, where they slept and ate by themselves. For this reason, in lieu of the food and board they would formerly have got in the house, they now had to have a proportion of their wages in kind, usually in the form of oatmeal and milk, with an allowance of fuel for the fire, though it was still not uncommon on farms in the 1790s that the farmers' wives prepared the servants' food with their own. Increasingly, however, they came to have an allowance of victuals instead. The situation in the Carse of Gowrie, the heart of the bothy area, in 1794, was characteristic: that the men got an English pint of sweet milk daily, or two pints of buttermilk, for breakfast, dinner and supper, with an allowance of thirty-six ounces of oatmeal per man, along with salt or 1s. in lieu. The result of this was that the unmarried ploughmen and farm lads came to eat oatmeal in one form or another three times a day. *Brose* was a preferred dish because it was easily prepared by pouring boiling water on to oatmeal, with a little salt, in a wooden bowl, to be eaten with milk over it.

ALEXANDER FENTON

A FLITTING

On the eve of the flitting it rained. Helen had everything packed and the floors scrubbed out, the pictures down from the walls and the curtains from the windows. The iron bedstead with the brass knobs had been dismantled in the room and laid against the wall, the blankets and sheets folded and bundled into Audie's chaumer kist and meal girnal. The bedding had also been removed from the box-bed and laid out on the floor as a shakie-doon, where Audie and Helen slept the night, with Ruth at their feet, ready to jump at the first cock-crow, or the sound of horses' hooves in the morning. The fireside had been cleaned for the last time and the ash removed. A few kindlers to boil the kettle in the morning was all that was required. Everything had been packed but the tea caddy, a few cups, a teaspoon, a butterknife and a jar of jam. Sugar could be spooned out of a paper bag and the loaf and biscuits were in a tin. Audie had even

20 A Flitting, c.1990, Lochmaddy, North Uist. Courtesy of Scottish Ethnological Museum, National Museums of Scotland.

buried Napoleon deep in the gairden for the last time, which was the cottar's way of saying he had emptied the privy pail in a deep hole, and covered it up with earth, so that the new tenant couldn't say they weren't respectable.

When morning came it was still raining, streaming down from the thatch and running into puddles in the close. Two horse-carts arrived out of the cold grey mist at Millbrae, two mighty Clydesdales with the smell of polished harness about them and harvest frames on the carts, a bundle of straw to pack the furniture, old sacks and ropes. Everything was carried out in the rain and Audie handed up chairs and the iron bed-ends to the foreman on the cart, who was biding on at Sauchieburn and wouldn't have to flit this Term. It took both of them to lift the heavier stuff on to the carts, the massive mahogany sideboard, the dresser and the chest of drawers, the wardrobe and the gate-legged table, Audie's kist and the meal girnal. Helen carried out pots and pans and crammed them into every space she could find among the furniture, and all the time nagging at the foreman about the placing of this and that on the carts; and the man could see that she wore the breeks, and he wouldn't have stood half so much from his own wife.

'My pot flooers are in the washtubs,' she cried up to the man, 'put them on the back of the second cairt; if ye put them on the first cairt the second horse will eat them.' Her face was wet with the rain and it hung about her hair in liquid beads of morning silver.

The man said, 'Oh aye, gin he has a fancy for geraniums,' but felt like telling Helen it wasn't the first flitting he'd done and that he knew his job fine without her telling him.

The hens had been fastened into coops the night before, bedraggled and miserable looking, with an egg or two rolling about their dirty feet, seeing there wasn't a nest to lay in. The cat had a small coop all to herself, where she crouched with large scared eyes, ready to spring for freedom at the first opportunity.

'The hens wad scare the second horse if ye put them on the first cairt,' Helen cried to the foreman, while Audie twisted the rain out of his cap.

'Oh aye,' the foreman said, trying to humour her, 'he's fear't at his ain shadaw as it is. He wunna see his shadaw the day, for want o' the sun, but I suppose he wad be scared tae death o' a clockin' hen. Gweed kens what'll happen gin we meet ane o' Jammie Salter's traction engines—Lord help yer furniture, lass; it wad a' be knocked tae bits.'

Long Dod's wife came running down the close with a towel over her head, splashing through the rain in unlaced shoes. She put a sixpence in Ruth's little palm and said that would be something for her Turra Coo bank.

'Ta ta,' she cried, 'Ta ta, Mrs Foubister, ye're gettin' a terrible day tae flit. Ta ta,' she cried again, this time to Audie, who bore her no ill-will, no more than Helen did, for she had been good enough as a neighbour. The woman closed the towel over her face again and ran up the close, splashing through the muddy pools.

When everything had been loaded and roped on to the carts the foreman and Audie took a horse each by the reins and walked beside the carts. It was too wet and cold to sit on the carts so Helen walked behind with Ruth by the hand. Her little face was chilled blue with the cold and her shoes sapped through. By the time the flitting reached Sauchieburn everything was soaked; the chaff mattresses sodden, the bread in the baskets all gone to sops. But the foreman's wife had lit a fire in the empty house and Ruth stood by it and warmed her hands and steamed herself dry. When all the furniture had been carried inside Audie had to go to the farm steading for four sacks of dry chaff to fill the mattresses, and he had to yoke a horse-cart to drive them down to the house. The rain ceased in the evening and a red sky closed the day. A lorry driver stopped for water to put in his radiator and he left a fry of kippers. Audie thought this was great, for you never got kippers at Millbrae, and the house smelled strongly of frying kippers for tea. Ruth had to get on a chair to climb on to the new-filled chaff bed, and they all slept together again for there was no box-bed at Sauchieburn.

DAVID TOULMIN

THE LIFE OF MANSIE WAUCH, TAILOR

Halloween no longer terrifies old or young, but the customs Mansie Wauch, the tailor, enjoyed, continue.

I never, in the whole course of my life, was fond of lending the sanction of my countenance to anything that was not canny; and, even when I was a wee smout of a callant, with my jacket and trowsers buttoned all in one, I never would play, on Hallo'een nights, at anything else but douking for apples, burning nuts, pulling kail-runts, foul water and clean, drapping the egg, or trying who was to be your sweetheart out of the lucky-bag.

D M MOIR

LIEUTENANT SWABY IS INTRODUCED TO THE DANGERS OF HALLOWEEN

'I counsel you, sir,' said the pawkie auld carl as they were separating, 'no to gang far afield this night, for this is a night that there is na the like o' in a' the year round. It's Hallowe'en, sir, so be counselled by me, and seek your hame betimes; for mony a ane has met with things on Hallowe'en that they never after forgot.'

Considering the exploit on which the cavalier was then bowne, it's no to be thought that this was very heartening music; but, for all that, he said blithely, as Mungo told me himself, 'Nay, not so fast, governor, tell us what you mean by Hallowe'en!'

'Hallowe'en!' cried Mungo Affleck, with a sound o' serious sincerity; 'Do ye no ken Hallowe'en? But I need na say that. Ye'll excuse me, captain—what can you Englishers, that are brought up in the darkness o' human ordinances in gospel things, and who live in the thraldom of episcopalian ignorance, ken of Hallowe'en, or o' any other solemn day set apart for an occasion.—O, sir, Hallowe'en among us is a dreadful night! witches and warlocks, and a' lang-nebbit things, hae a power and a dominion unspeakable on Hallowe'en. The de'il at other times gi'es, it's said, his agents a mutchkin o' mischief, but on this night it's thought they hae a chappin; and one thing most demonstrable is;—but, sir, the sun's down—the blessed light o' day is ayont the hill, and it's no safe to be subjek to the whisking o' the mildew frae the tails o' the benweed ponies that are saddled for yon awfu' carnavaulings, where Cluty plays on the pipes! so I wis you, sir, gude night and weel hame.—O, sir, an ye could be persuaded!—Tak an auld man's advice, and rather read a chapter of THE BOOK, an it should even be the unedifying tenth of Nehemiah, than be seen at the gloaming in this gait, about the dyke-sides, like a wolf yearning for some tender lamb of a defenceless fold.'

Mungo, having thus delivered himself, went away, leaving Swaby as it were in a swither; for, on looking back, the old man saw him standing half turned round as if he was minded to go home. The power of the sin was however strong upon him, and shortly after the dusk had closed in, when the angels had lighted their candles at their windows in the sky to watch over the world in the hours of sleep, Swaby, with stealthy steps, came to Mysie Gilmour's door, and softly tirling at the pin was admitted; for all within was ready for his reception.

JOHN GALT

HOGMANAY

New Year, Gaelic *Caliuinn* (from Kalends), and its eve *Hogmanay* (whose derivation is still disputed, but mostly likely is from the French; at any rate it was originally a cry raised on this night) took over most Christmas customs in different places, as well as those associated with Hallowe'en and other festivals, bonfires, divination and even tricks. Far the most important and general custom was guising or its modern derivative, first-footing. As at Hallowe'en this was done by men, especially younger men, and in this case the tradition has been carried on: perhaps women and children do less first-footing because of the association of the custom with drink, but it is also generally considered lucky for the real first foot, the first person to cross the threshold in the New Year, to be a man, preferably one with dark hair. First-footers nowadays bring a bottle, sometimes food and a lump of coal or something black: this seems to be new, but peats are mentioned among first-foot gifts in earlier times.

Traditional guising at New Year normally involved singing as well as collecting food for consumption on the spot or later. This might happen either on Hogmanay or New Year's Day, and in some places has survived apart from first-footing as a children's custom. A popular rhyme to chant was:

> Rise up, guidwife, and shak yir feathers:
> Dinna think that we are beggars:
> We're only bairnies come to play:
> Rise up and gie's oor Hogmanay.

Earlier versions had 'guid folks' instead of 'bairnies'. The usual 'God bless the master of this house' lines associated with carols and wassailing songs in England, or others, might be added to this.

The Gaelic New Year Rhymes (*Duain Challuinn*) are much more varied: in many places several were known, ranging from ancient Ossianic lays to newly improvised farragos with satirical verses about local people and a good deal of pure nonsense. These were normally recited, not sung, though one or two convivial songs also have special associations with New Year. A *Duan* could be recited by a single first-footer; bands of young men also went round in Gaelic-speaking districts up to the beginning of this century using cowhides and sheepskin, apparently to scare away any evil spirits. This was done both by beating the cowhide, which in earlier times at least was worn by the leader of the band, with shinty-sticks, fire-tongs or primitive whips, and by singeing a strip of skin from a sheep's breast (*caisean-uchd*) to make an evil smell around the houses, where it was held under the nose of each member of the household. A chant accompanied and referred to the beating of the hide. The shinty-sticks link this with the other Highland custom on New Year's Day itself, which was a game of shinty on a beach or some piece of flat open ground between two sides of no fixed number representing different villages, townships or estates, with little regard for rules or even necessarily fixed goals. The similar football games in Shetland were held several times in the Yule season; in Orkney however they were at New Year, or at least that is the occasion of the surviving Kirkwall Ball Game, played between 'Uppies' and 'Doonies' through a main street with well-barricaded shop windows, with one goal at the harbour and the other at the inland end of the town.

A J BRUFORD

ANOTHER VIEW

Thorleif Gudmundson Repp, a Danish scholar, suggested to the Society of Antiquaries of Scotland in 1831 that the words were more likely to be Scandinavian than French, and he interpreted them as meaning:

> Good fairies, approach!
> Trolls, go away!

His theory seems to be borne out by the fact in Orkney Norn (a form of Norse), there is a word *Haugbond* for a fairy, dweller in a *haug* or fairy mound; and of course there are still plenty of stories of trolls or 'trows' as they are called in Shetland, in our Northern Isles. If we assume a word 'Hogman' meaning a fairy in older Scots, we get the sentences '*Hogman, hay! Troll a-laigh!*' (Fairy, come here! Troll below!) without having to go far into any Scandinavian tongue. Many Lowland words—such as *fremmit* for stranger, *stour* for dust and *ettercap* for spider—are either of Scandinavian origin or at least cognate with Scandinavian words, which is not surprising when we consider that we live so near Norway and Denmark.

Many of the ritualistic acts at Hogmanay bear out this theory that the festivity has something to do with the idea of a flitting of the fairies, such as has been seen by students of our folklore in the festivities of Hallowe'en. If you postulate that at Hogmanay the old trolls who have infested the house throughout the year, bringing all sorts of bad luck, might well move out and find some other berth, and that a new set of fairies will come in, possibly bringing a change of luck, you can readily understand all the gestures that are made by Hogmanay celebrants. The new fairies are coming, whether we want them or no; good or bad. It is a well-known practice towards fairies that we never miscall them when they might do us harm, so we are going out of our way to be polite to these stranger fairies coming in from outside. We call the old ones 'trolls', which is a dirty word, but we call the new ones just mound-dwellers, which is being extremely non-committal. We hope they are good, but we shall certainly do nothing to offend them. The first-foot is welcomed with open arms. That is the first man across the threshold. He symbolises the new influences coming into the house, and he brings gifts—sometimes a piece of coal and some salt, signifying fire and food to keep the house warm and prosperous; usually nowadays some drink and some cake, fruit-bun (black bun or currant dodie) or shortbread. The housewife prepares a feast to welcome him, and drinks are exchanged.

That the first-foot is preferably dark suggests the fairy origin, for the ancients regarded the mound-dwellers as being dark, and there may indeed have been an older darker race inhabiting caves and coming out largely at night to be unobserved. Old Scottish legends refer to brownies who came into houses at night and did various tasks for the inhabitants. They could be left food—usually a bowl of cream—and would take it in good grace, but the one thing the householder must not leave out for the brownie was a suit of clothes. If you did that, the brownie would stamp off in a temper and never come back. It may have been that when the fairer invaders took possession of Scotland, some survivors of the aboriginal race lingered on and did work for food in the dark of night. But to accept clothes might make slaves of them. The clothes themselves might by magic take possession of their bodies and souls.

One custom of the Scottish housewife which suggests the fairy connection of Hogmanay is that of cleaning the house for the New Year. No self-respecting Scots wife will let the year go out without cleaning out all her grates and putting out the ashes. In Shetland this practice is observed even more frequently, and the belief associated with it is that the fairies will be offended if a house is left uncleared at a week-end.

Whatever the origin of Hogmanay, it is probably the most popular of all the Scottish festivities.

ALBERT MACKIE

Birds, Beasts, Flowers, Insects

from *WILLIAM SOUTAR'S DIARY*

Wednesday 3 May 1934

At the moment when the earth is crying out in joy: when the prodigality of life comes up to my window—the multiplicity of leaves and wings and petals, the variety of sounds and colours and scents: all seeming to say to man, 'Be fruitful and multiply', when this earthly fullness is so evident then more than ever do the ways of modern society seem madness; the fear of life amid the largesse of nature—the lust for power rather than brotherhood and for gold rather than humanity; so that indirectly we are become lovers of barrenness instead of fellow workers in creation.

One and Only

5 July 1941

Montgomerie had been on a botany expedition and produced from his vasculum the one and only 'sma white rose of Scotland', the first time I could say with certainty I had looked on the national emblem.

WILLIAM SOUTAR

21   White Rose of Scotland. Drawing by Colin Gibson.

WHITE ROSE OF SCOTLAND

One of these islands I hold to be the most beautiful of all the islands in the West. Its shape varies according to the angle of approach but can never be mistaken because of the rock, so well known to the geologists, that crowns it. This long high ridge sometimes looks like the keel of an upended boat and sometimes like the dorsal fin of a gigantic sea monster. Buzzards nest there and ravens croak against its dark walls, while the uplands leading to it carry more wheatears and stonechats than I have ever seen elsewhere in any one place. But what distinguishes the island for me and holds it fragrant in memory is the wild Scotch rose (*Rosa spinosissima*), for it blooms here in greater abundance than anywhere else I know. It is the genius of this place. It grows near the seashore, on banks, in clefts, but above all on the little green braes bordered with hazel woods. It rarely reaches more than two feet in height; in colour, neither white nor cream so much as mellow old ivory; unassuming, modest, and known as the white rose of Scotland.

For me it has a fragrance more exquisite than that of any other rose.

NEIL GUNN

THE LITTLE WHITE ROSE

The rose of all the world is not for me.
I want for my part
Only the little white rose of Scotland
That smells sharp and sweet—and breaks the heart

HUGH MACDIARMID

MILK-WORT AND BOG-COTTON
(To Seumas O'Sullivan)

Cwa' een like milk-wort and bog-cotton hair!
I love you, earth, in this mood best o' a'
When the shy spirit like a laich wind moves
And frae the lift nae shadow can fa'
Since there's nocht left to thraw a shadow there
Owre een like milk-wort and milk-white cotton hair.

Wad that nae leaf upon anither wheeled
A shadow either and nae root need dern
In sacrifice to let sic beauty be!
But deep surroondin' darkness I discern
Is aye the price o' licht. Wad licht revealed
Naething but you, and nicht nocht else concealed.

HUGH MACDIARMID

ON HIS 'FAVOURITE THINGS'
Letter from Robert Burns to Mrs Dunlop

We know nothing or next to nothing of the substance or structure of
our Souls, so cannot account for those seeming caprices in them; that
one should be particularly pleased with this thing, or struck with that,
which on Minds of a different cast shall make no extraordinary
impression.—I have some, favorite flowers in Spring, among which
are the mountain-daisy, the hare-bell, the foxglove, the wild brier-
rose, the budding birk & the hoary hawthorn, that I view and hang
over with particular delight.—I never hear the loud, solitary whistle
of the Curlew in a Summer noon, or the wild, mixing cadence of a
troop of grey-plover in an Autumnal-morning, without feeling an
elevation of soul like the enthusiasm of Devotion or Poesy.—Tell me,
my dear Friend, to what can this be owing? Are we a piece of
machinery that, like the Eolian harp, passive, takes the impression of
the passing accident? Or do these workings argue something within
us above the trodden clod? I own myself partial to these proofs of

those aweful & important realities, a God that made all things, man's immaterial & immortal nature, & a World of weal or woe beyond death & the grave, these proofs that we deduct by dint of our own powers & observation.

ROBERT BURNS

THE COMIN' O' THE SPRING

There's no a muir in my ain land but's fu' o' sang the day,
Wi' the whaup, and the gowden plover, and the lintie upon the brae.
The birk in the glen is springin', the rowan-tree in the shaw,
And every burn is rinnin' wild wi' the meltin' o' the snaw.

The wee white cluds in the blue lift are hurryin' light and free,
Their shadows fleein' on the hills, where I, too, fain wad be;
The wind frae the west is blawing, and wi' it seems to bear
The scent o' the thyme and gowan thro' a' the caller air.

The herd doon the hillside's linkin'. O licht his heart may be
Whose step is on the heather, his glance ower muir and lea!
On the Moss are the wild ducks gatherin', whar the pules like
    diamonds lie,
And far up soar the wild geese, wi' weird unyirdly cry.

In mony a neuk the primrose lies hid frae stranger een,
An' the broom on the knowes is wavin' wi' its cludin' o' gowd and
    green;
Ower the first green springs o' heather the muir-fowl faulds his wing,
And there's nought but joy in my ain land at the comin' o' the Spring!

LADY JOHN SCOTT

THE PLANTS OF THE MOUNTAIN

All are aspects of one entity, the living mountain. The disintegrating rock, the nurturing rain, the quickening sun, the seed, the root, the bird—all are one. Eagle and alpine veronica are part of the mountain's wholeness. Saxifrage—the 'rock-breaker'—in some of its loveliest forms, *Stellaris*, that stars with its single blossoms the high rocky corrie burns, and *Azoides*, that clusters like soft sunshine in their lower reaches, cannot live apart from the mountain. As well expect the eyelid to function if cut from the eye.

Yet in the terrible blasting winds on the plateau one marvels that life can exist at all. It is not high, as height goes. Plants live far above 4,000 feet. But here there is no shelter—or only such shelter as is afforded where the threads of water run in their wide sloping channels towards the edge of the cliffs. Whatever grows, grows in exposure to the whole vast reach of the air. From Iceland, from Norway, from America, from the Pyrenees, the winds tear over it. And on its own undulating surface no rocks, or deep ravines, provide a quiet place for growth. Yet the botanist with whom I sometimes walk tells me that well over twenty species of plant grow there—many more, if each variety of moss, lichen and algae is counted. He has made me a list of them, and I can count them. Life, it seems, won't be warned off.

The tenacity of life can be seen not only on the tops but on lower shoulders where the heather has been burnt. Long before the heather itself (whose power to survive fire as well as frost, wind, and all natural inclemencies is well known) shows the least sign of life from the roots beneath its charred sticks, or has sprouted anew from seed hidden in the ground, birdsfoot trefoil, tormentil, blaeberry, the tiny genista, alpine lady's mantle, are thrusting up vigorous shoots. These mountain flowers look inexpressibly delicate; their stems are slender, their blossoms fragile; but burrow a little in the soil, and roots of a timeless endurance are found. Squat or stringy, like lumps of dead wood or bits of sinew, they conserve beneath the soil the vital energy of the plant. Even when all the upper growth is stripped—burned or frosted or withered away—these knots of life are everywhere. There is no time nor season when the mountain is not alive with them. Or if the root has perished, living seeds are in the soil, ready to begin the cycle of life afresh. Nowhere more than here is life proved invincible. Everything is against it, but it pays no heed.

The plants of the plateau are low in stature, sitting tight to the ground with no loose ends for the wind to catch. They creep, either along the surface, or under it; or they anchor themselves by a heavy root massive out of all proportion to their external growth. I have said that they have no shelter, but for the individual flower there is the shelter of its group. Thus the moss campion, *Silene*, the most startling of all the plateau flowers, that in June and early July amazes the eye by its cushions of brilliant pink scattered in the barest and most stony places, has a habit of growth as close-set as a Victorian posy. Its root too is strong and deep, anchoring it against the hurricane, and keeping its vital essence safe against frost and fiery drought, the extremes and unpredictable shifts of weather on the exposed plateau. In these ways this most characteristic of the plateau flowers is seen to be quite simply a part of the mountain. Its way of life lies in the mountain's way of life as water lies in a channel.

Even its flamboyant flowers are integral to the mountain's way of life. I do not know how old the individual clumps may be, but judging from the size to which these close-knit cushions grow, some must have endured the commotion of many winters. Most of the mountain flowers are long livers. The plant that races through its cycle in a single season could never be sure, up here, of fruition—there might be no successors. Death would dog, not only the individual, but the species. Yet even the long livers must renew themselves at times, and it is on only some of the summer days that insects can fly to the mountain top. So the *Silene* throws this ardent colour into its petals to entice the flies.

Lower on the mountain, on all the slopes and shoulders and ridges and on the moors below, the characteristic growth is heather. And this too is integral to the mountain. For heather grows in its most profuse luxuriance on granite, so that the very substance of the mountain is in its life. Of the three varieties that grow on these hills—two Ericas and the ling—the July-blooming bell heather is the least beautiful, though its clumps of hot red are like sun-bursts when the rest of the hills are still brown. The pale cross-leaved heath, that grows in small patches, often only single heads, in moist places, is an exquisite, almost waxen-still, with a honey perfume. But it is the August-blooming ling that covers the hills with amethyst. Now they look gracious and benign. For many many miles there is nothing but this soft radiance. Walk over it in a hot sun, preferably not on a path ('I like the unpath best', one of my small friends said when her father had called her to heel), and the scent rises in a heady cloud. Just as one walks on a hot day surrounded by one's own aura of flies, so one walks surrounded by one's own aura of heather scent. For as the feet brush the bloom, the pollen rises in a perfumed cloud. It settles on one's boots, or if one

22   Plants of the Mountain. Drawings by Nan Shepherd.

is walking barefoot, on feet and legs, yellowy-fawn in colour, silky to the touch, yet leaving a perceptible grit between the fingers. Miles of this, however, stupefies the body. Like too much incense in church, it blunts the sharp edge of adoration, which, at its finest, demands clarity of the intellect as well as the surge of emotion.

    To one who loves the hills at every season, the blossoming is not the best of the heather. The best of it is simply its being there—is the feel of it under the feet. To feel heather under the feet after long abstinence is one of the dearest joys I know.

NAN SHEPHERD

CROMARTY MOORLAND

Among my other favourites were the splendid dragon-flies, the crimson-speckled Burnet moths, and the small azure butterflies, that, when fluttering among delicate harebells and crimson-tipped daisies, used to suggest to me, long ere I became acquainted with the pretty figure of Moore, or even ere the figure had been produced, the idea of flowers that had taken to flying. The wild honey bees, too, in their several species, had peculiar charms for me. There were the buff-coloured carders, that erected over their honey-jars domes of moss; the lapidary red-tipped bees, that built amid the recesses of ancient cairns, and in old dry stone walls, and were so invincibly brave in defending their homesteads, that they never gave up the quarrel till they died; and, above all, the yellow zoned humble-bees, that lodged deep in the ground along the dry sides of grassy banks, and were usually wealthier in honey than any of their cogeners, and existed in larger communities.

HUGH MILLER

SPRING AT CAMUSFEÀRNA

Spring comes late to Camusfeàrna. More than one year I have motored up from the south early in April to become immobilised in snowdrifts on the passes twenty miles from it, and by then the stags are still at the roadside down the long glen that leads to the sea. By mid April there is still no tinge of green bud on the bare birches and rowans nor green underfoot, though there is often, as when I first came to Camusfeàrna, a spell of soft still weather and clear skies. The colours then are predominantly pale blues, russet browns, and purples, each with the clarity of fine enamel; pale blue of sea and sky, the russet of dead bracken and fern, deep purple-brown of unbudded birch, and the paler violets of the Skye hills and the peaks of Rhum. The landscape is lit by three whites—the pearl white of the birch trunks, the dazzle of the shell-sand beaches, and the soft filtered white of the high snows. The primroses are beginning to flower about the burn and among the island banks, though all the high hills are snow-covered and the lambs are as yet unborn. It is a time that has brought me, in all too few years, the deep contentment of knowing that the true spring and summer are still before me at Camusfeàrna, that I shall see the leaf break and the ground become green, and all the snow melt from the hills but for a few drifts that will lie summer through.

It has its own orchestration, this little prelude to the northern spring; every year there is the sound of the wild geese calling far overhead as they travel north to their thawing breeding grounds, and sometimes the wild unearthly beauty of whooper swans' voices, silver trumpets high in the clear blue air. The eider ducks have arrived to breed about the shore and the islands; they bring with them that most evocative and haunting of all sounds of the Hebridean spring and summer, the deep, echoing, wood-wind crooning of the courting drakes.

One by one the breeding bird species return to the beaches and the islands where they were hatched; the sand martins to the sand cliff at the burn foot, the wheatears to the rabbit burrows in the close-bitten turf, the black guillemots and the gulls to the Camusfeàrna islands. The herring gulls come first, to the biggest island, where the lighthouse stands, some two hundred and fifty pairs of them, and the air above the white-splashed rocks and sea pinks scattered with broken shellfish is vibrant with the clang of their calling and their wheeling white wings. Among them are two or three pairs of great black-backed gulls, massive, hoarse-voiced and vulturine. Then come the common gulls, delicate, graceful, segregated shrilly on to a neighbouring promontory, beadily mistrustful of the coarse language and predatory predilections of their neighbours; and, lastly, not until well into May, come the terns, the sea-swallows, to their own outlying skerry. They arrive in the same week as the swallows come up from Africa to nest in the old ruined croft across the field, and with the thin steel oar-beat of their wings spring has almost given place to summer.

By then the colour everywhere is green. The purple birch twigs are hidden in a soft cloud of new leaf; the curled, almond-bitter rods of young bracken have in those short weeks pushed up three feet from the earth and unfurled a canopy of green frond over the rust of last year's growth; the leaves of the yellow flag iris that margin the burn and the shore form a forest of broad bayonets, and the islands, that but for rank rooty patches of heather growing knee-deep seemed so bare in August, are smothered with a jungle-growth of goose grass and briar. To me there is always something a little stifling in this enveloping green stain, this redundant, almost Victorian, drapery over bones that need no blanketing, and were it not for the astringent presence of the sea I should find all that verdure as enervating as an Oxford water-meadow in the depths of summer. Perhaps 'depraved' is the right word after all.

GAVIN MAXWELL

FEBRUARY AND THE BIRDS

There is one annual event that never seems to stale with the years: the hearing of the first full bird's song. I don't mean the lively chattering of sparrows or yattering of starlings, heartening as these may be on a mild damp day with blinks of a living sun and promise of more to come, but the first individual song that heralds the turn of the year and has in it not a little of incantation. For it sings of spring to come, yet the memory of past springs are gathered into it. Now it may be understood the meaning of Wordsworth's line: 'That there hath passed away a glory from the earth'; because suddenly the glory is singing here and now to the mortal ear.

A memorable experience of this kind occurred many years ago in a wooded lane that bordered a nursery garden in the town of Inverness. It was the second day of January and the bare branches of great beeches were dark against the dawn in the sky; a soft mild morning in which one could imagine worms coming up to see what the iron frost had done to the earth. On a topmost twig, the thrush sang full-throated, its notes ringing out, clear and vibrant, over the awakening world. It was so unexpected on only the second day of the new year, and so triumphant, that the dullest mind would have been held spellbound, not merely by the rush of notes but by the unnameable promise that quivered at their core, quivered and travelled far over trees and blue smoke.

NEIL GUNN

JIBYDO

Jibydo is a cock chaffinch who considers it his special duty apparently to treat our house to a regular round of song. 'Round' is the only word, for he starts upon the ancient ash-tree by the north-east window, does a carefree swoop to the aged elm beyond the south-west window, and, when he has exhausted his second urgency of song there, takes a double swoop to the old plum-tree in the vegetable garden at the back, where he performs with equal vigour. Then back to the ash again. And so on and on. A merry-go-round, a ring of song, a roundelay. If

you are trying to concentrate your thoughts on a problem with too
many knots, he sings in your very ear, vibrantly. He either convinces
you of the fathomless absurdity of human worldly care or drives you
to distraction. Just as a shepherd knows the individual faces of all his
sheep, so do I know now the individual songs of all the cock
chaffinches. It is the only thing in the whole realm of bird life at which
I am really expert. We have christened him Jibydo because of a
remarkably trenchancy in his last three notes, thus: ji-*by*-do.

On his first morning this year, I heard the song with curious and
mixed feelings. It was not Jibydo, I decided, but his son. The old man's
technique was there all right, but not the finish, the splendid
assurance. Thus was the son of a MacCrimmon known from the son of
a Mackay. But I was wrong. The old pipes had needed tuning. The
reeds had been a bit dry. The bag had gone a bit crinkled on him. Now
it's the old man himself in full power and full feather. We'll have a few
words at each other this year should the heavens not fall.

NEIL GUNN

ROBIN AT MY WINDOW

The air was cleart with white and sable clouds,
Hard frost, with frequent schours of hail and snaw;
Into the nicht the stormy wind with thouds
And baleful billows on the sea did blaw;
Men, beasts and fowls unto their beilds did draw,
Fain then to find the fruct of summer thrift,
When clad with snaw was sand, wood, crag and clift.

I sat at fire weil girdit in my gown;
The starving sparrows at my window cheeped;
To read ane while I to my book was bown,
In at ane pane the pretty progne peeped
And moved me for fear I should have sleeped,
To rise and set ane casement open wide
To see gif Robin would come in and bide.

Puir progne, sweetly I have heard ye sing
There at my window on the simmer day;
And now sen winter hither does ye bring
I pray ye enter in my hous and stay
Till it be fair, and then thous go thy way,
For trowlie thous be treated courteouslie
And nothing thralled in thy libertie.

Come in, sweet Robin, welcome verilie,
Said I, and down I sat me by the fire:
Then in comes robin reidbreist mirrilie,
And sups and lodges at my heart's desire:
But on ye morn, I him perceived to tire,
For Phoebus shining sweetly him allured,
I gave him leif, and furth guid robin furd.

JAMES MELVILLE

23   Robin. Drawing by Colin Gibson.

WULLIE WAGGLETAIL

Wee Wullie Waggletail, what is a' your stishie?
Tak a sowp o' water and coorie on a stane:
Ilka tree stands dozent, and the wind without a hishie
Fitters in atween the fleurs and shogs them, ane be ane.

What whigmaleerie gars ye jowp and jink amang the duckies,
Wi' a rowsan simmer sün beekin on your croun:
Wheeple, wheeple, wheeplin like a wee burn owre the chuckies,
And wagglin here, and wagglin there, and wagglin up and doun.

WILLIAM SOUTAR

24   Grey Wagtail. Drawing by Colin Gibson.

HERON

It stands in water, wrapped in heron. It makes
An absolute exclusion of everything else
By disappearing in itself, yet is the presence
Of hidden pools and secret, reedy lakes.
It twirls small fish from the bright water flakes.

(Glog goes the small fish down). With lifted head
And no shoulders at all, it periscopes round—
Steps, like an aunty, forward—gives itself shoulders
And vanishes, a shilling in a pound,
Making no sight as other things make no sound.

Until, releasing its own spring, it fills
The air with heron, finds its height and goes,
A spear between two clouds. A cliff receives it
And it is gargoyle. All around it hills
Stand in the sea; wind from a brown sail spills.

NORMAN MACCAIG

TWO BIRDS

A single note, the cuckoo's, in the spring.
Hidden in the woods, it sends its greeting.
We are shaken wildly by the usual thing,
the possibility of a fertile meeting.

And we remember how the redbreast came
as far as the lobby with its slanted head
and how we read in some laborious tome
that after a year the little bird is dead.

IAIN CRICHTON SMITH

THE WILD GEESE

'Oh, tell me what was on yer road, ye roarin' norlan' wind
As ye cam' blawin' frae the land thats niver frae my mind?
My feet they trayvel England, but I'm deein' for the north—'
'My man, I heard the siller tides that rin up the Firth o' Forth.'

'Aye, Wind, I ken them well eneuch, and fine they fa' and rise,
And fain I'd feel the creepin' mist on yonder shore that lies,
But tell me, ere ye passed them by, what saw ye on the way?'
'My man, I rocked the rovin' gulls that sail abune the Tay.'

'But saw ye naethin', leein' Wind, afore ye cam' to Fife?
There's muckle lyin' yont the Tay that's mair to me nor life.'
'My man, I swept the Angus braes ye haena trod for years.'
'O, Wind, forgie a hameless loon that canna see for tears!'

'And far abune the Angus straths I saw the wild geese flee,
A lang, lang skein o' beatin' wings wi' their heids towards the sea,
And aye their cryin' voices trailed ahint them on the air—'
'O Wind, hae maircy, haud yer whisht, for I darna listen mair!'

VIOLET JACOB

CAW! CAW! CAW!

'Caw! Caw! Caw!'
Said an aul' dane craw,
As he dichtit his nib on a docken,
'I'm wearin awa',
But I carena a straw,
For I've tastet the tatties o' Buchan!'

JOHN C MILNE

AN DOIRBEARDAN

Tha'n doirbeardan anns an lochan fheurach
ri mion-shnàmh eadar lusan chraobhach,
is meanbh-ghlusasadan a bhith shaoghalta
air an òrdachadh;
agus ma tha a Chlach-Steinn-san air a bloigheadh
Dè 'n diofar?
Dè 'n diofar dhutsa, a dhoirbeardain na h-Albann,
a dhoirbeardain Shasainn, a dhoirbeardain an t-saoghail mhòir,
ged a bhiodh do reul-iùil a dhìth ort
's do chridhe 'na phristealan 'na do chuimhne?

RUARAIDH MACTHÒMAIS

THE MINNOW

The minnow in the grassy loch
minutely-swims between branching plants:
the tiny movements of his earthly life
are ordained;
and though his Norse Stone be shattered
what of it?
What's it to you, minnow of Scotland,
minnow of England, minnow of the wide world,
though your guiding star be lost
and your heart in shards in your memory?

DERICK THOMSON

GOLOCH

A goloch is an awesome beast,
Souple and scaly,
With a horny heid and a hantle of feet
And a forkie taily.

ANON

FROGS

Frogs sit more solid
than anything sits. In mid-leap they are
parachutists falling
in a free fall. They die on roads
with arms across their chests and
heads high.

I love frogs that sit
like Buddha, that fall without
parachutes, that die
like Italian tenors.

Above all, I love them because,
pursued in water, they never
panic so much that they fail
to make stylish triangles
with their ballet dancer's
legs.

NORMAN MACCAIG

TOAD

Stop looking like a purse. How could a purse
squeeze under the rickety door and sit,
full of satisfaction, in a man's house?

You clamber towards me on your four corners—
right hand, left foot, left hand, right foot.

I love you for being a toad,
for crawling like a Japanese wrestler,
and for not being frightened.

I put you in my purse hand, not shutting it,
and set you down outside directly under
every star.

A jewel in your head? Toad,
you've put one in mine,
a tiny radiance in a dark place.

NORMAN MACCAIG

MOLECATCHER

Strampin' the bent, like the Angel o' Daith,
  The mowdie-man staves by;
Alang his pad the mowdie-worps
  Like sma' Assyrians lie.

And where the Angel o' Daith has been,
  Yirked oot o' their yirdy hames,
Lie Sennacherib's blasted hosts
  Wi' guts dung oot o' wames.

Sma' black tramorts wi' gruntles grey,
　　Sma' weak weemin's han's,
Sma' bead-een that wid touch ilk hert
　　Binnae the mowdie-man's.

ALBERT D MACKIE

BYRE

The thatched roof rings like heaven where mice
Squeak small hosannahs all night long,
Scratching its golden pavements, skirting
The gutter's crystal river-song.

Wild kittens in the world below
Glare with one flaming eye through cracks,
Spurt in the straw, are tawny brooches
Splayed on the chests of drunken sacks.

The dimness becomes darkness as
Vast presence comes mincing in,
Swagbellied Aphrodites, swinging
A silver slaver from each chin.

And all is milky, secret, female.
Angels are hushed and plain straws shine.
And kittens miaow in circles, stalking
With tail and hindleg one straight line.

NORMAN MACCAIG

THE HARE

In the split woods a broken sapling,
Cold catkins that I stoop below.
Explosion of a blackbird's wings
Kicks up exclamatory snow.

Silence, the burden of the song,
Resumes where winds have blasted through.
The white fields swell to the dark sky,
The matrix they are frozen to.
Stopped in my fiftieth winter's track
I see the maze a March hare ran.
This wilderness supports a hare;
It also may support a man.

SYDNEY TREMAYNE

THE FOX

A vision of silence startled me:
A sinuous fox lightfooting past my door.
Out of the corner of his yellow eye
Glanced round his shoulder. Seeing nothing there,
Skirted the tall dry biscuit coloured grass
Unhurriedly, choosing the open way;
Like an hallucination passed across
To spring the trap forgotten many a day.

One who was brave and frightened, fugitive,
Fox coloured hair, eyes full of level flames,
Leaps out of buried memory to live,
The brightest thing in daylight. Swiftly comes
The verbal thought how many years she's dead.
The fox has slipped away in the dense wood.

SYDNEY TREMAYNE

TO A MOUSE

On turning her up in her nest with the plough,
November 1785

Wee, sleekit, cow'rin', tim'rous beastie,
Oh, what a panic's in thy breastie!
Thou need na start awa sae hasty,
           Wi' bickering brattle!
I wad be laith to rin an' chase thee,
           Wi' murd'ring pattle!

I'm truly sorry man's dominion
Has broken nature's social union,
An' justifies that ill opinion
           Which makes thee startle
At me, thy poor earth-born companion,
           An' fellow-mortal!

I doubt na, whyles, but thou may theive;
What then? poor beastie, thou maun live!
A daimen icker in a thrave
           'S a sma' request:
I'll get a blessin' wi' the lave,
           And never miss't!

Thy wee bit housie, too, in ruin!
Its silly wa's the win's are strewin'!
An' naething, now, to big a new ane,
           O' foggage green!
An' bleak December's winds ensuin',
           Baith snell and keen!

Thou saw the fields laid bare an' waste,
An' weary winter comin' fast,
An' cozie here, beneath the blast,
           Thou thought to dwell,
'Till crash! the cruel coulter past
           Out thro' thy cell.

That wee bit heap o' leaves an' stibble
Has cost thee mony a weary nibble!
Now thou's turn'd out, for a' thy trouble,
      But house or hald,
To thole the winter's sleety dribble,
      An' cranreuch cauld!

But, Mousie, thou art no thy lane,
In proving foresight may be vain:
The best-laid schemes o' mice an' men,
      Gang aft agley,
An' lea'e us nought but grief and pain
      For promis'd joy!

Still thou art blest, compar'd wi' me!
The present only toucheth thee:
But, och, I backward cast my ee,
      On prospects drear!
An' forward, tho' I canna see,
      I guess an' fear!

ROBERT BURNS

GULL

A seagull sits oan a cauld tin ruif
In Sutherlaun, in Sutherlaun.
He shaks his heid owre lack o pruif
It's Sutherlaun, it's Sutherlaun.
Wi heezit hulls an hazit muirs
And nae saut sea fur bliddy ours—
'It's Murderlaun,' he sichs. 'Ye hures, It's Murderlaun!'

DAVID ANGUS

SWIFTS AND AN EAGLE

The first time I found summer on the plateau—for although my earliest expeditions were all made in June or July, I experienced cloud, mist, howling wind, hailstones, rain and even a blizzard—the first time the sun blazed and the air was balmy, we were standing on the edge of an outward facing precipice, when I was startled by a whizzing sound behind me. Something dark swished past the side of my head at a speed that made me giddy. Hardly had I got back my balance when it came again, whistling through the windless air, which eddied round me with the motion. This time my eyes were ready, and I realised that a swift was sweeping in mighty curves over the edge of the plateau, plunging down the face of the rock and rising again like a jet of water. No one had told me I should find swifts on the mountain. Eagle and ptarmigan, yes: but that first sight of the mad, joyous abandon of the swift over and over the very edge of the precipice shocked me with a thrill of elation. All that volley of speed, those convolutions of delight, to catch a few flies! The discrepancy between purpose and performance made me laugh aloud—a laugh that gave the same feeling of release as though I had been dancing for a long time.

It seems odd that merely to watch the motion of flight should give the body not only vicious exhilaration but release. So urgent is the rhythm that it invades the blood. This power of flight to take us in to itself through the eyes as though we had actually shared in the motion, I have never felt so strongly as when watching swifts on the mountain top. Their headlong rush, each curve of which is at the same time a miracle of grace, the swishing sound of their cleavage of the air and the occasional high pitched cry that is hardly like the note of an earthly bird, seem to make visible and audible some essence of the free, wild spirit of the mountain.

The flight of the eagle, if less immediately exciting than that of the swifts, is more profoundly satisfying. The great spiral of his ascent, rising coil over coil in slow symmetry, has in its movement all the amplitude of space. And when he has soared to the top of his bent, there comes the level flight as far as the eye can follow, straight, clean and effortless as breathing. The wings hardly move, now and then perhaps a lazy flap as though a cyclist, free-wheeling on a gentle slope, turned the crank a time or two. The bird seems to float, but to float with a direct and undeviating force. It is only when one remarks that he is floating up-wind that the magnitude of that force becomes apparent. I stood once about the 2,500 feet level, in January when the world was quite white, and watched an eagle well below me following up the river valley in search of food. He flew right into the wind. The wings were slightly tilted, but so far as I could judge from above he held them steady. And he came on with a purposeful urgency behind which must have been the very terror of strength.

NAN SHEPHERD

THE SNOW BUNTING

In Britain a few snow birds sometimes live their summer-lives on some of the wildest hills in the Highlands of Scotland—a country of ridges and corries and steep screes—acre after acre of grey wilderness cruel in its misty desolation. Somewhere under one of tens of thousands of rocks and slabs the hen snow bird makes her nest. Whenever I think of a snow bunting's nest I begin to shiver and feel the wet and cold of a small tent on the hills and I again hear the roar of the wind, hour after hour, and day after day. For there are few days of peace and sunshine in this wild country where, if you are lucky, you may see the cock snow bird's remarkable display flight and listen to a song which is full of wildness and desire.

Before I went north I could never quite picture what these hills were like. I believed that they must be formidable, although by alpine or continental standards they were quite low. I did not then know that summer temperatures on the high tops were sometimes lower than those in west Greenland and Baffin Island. I certainly thought of mist and cloud blowing across the tops, but I also pictured days of warm sunshine. I did not know that mist sometimes came down and never lifted for weeks on end and that even in summer great winds often blew almost continuously in furious gusts that could lift a strong man from his feet and cast him down on the rocks. Somehow I never thought of June snowstorms blanketing the tops for a week or more. Yet wind, mist, sleet and snow are always part of the exacting challenge of watching snow birds in Scotland.

D NETHERSOLE-THOMPSON

THA 'N EILID ANNS AN FHRÌTH

Tha 'n eilid anns an fhrìth
    Mar bu chòir dhi bhith,
Far am faigh i mìlteach
    Glan-feòirneanach;
    Bruchorachd is cìb,
    Lusan am bi brìgh,
    Chuireadh sult is ìth
      Air a lòineanaibh;
Fuaran anns am bì
Biolaire gun dìth
'S mìlse leath' na 'm fion,
    'S e gun òladh i.
Cuiseagan is riasg,
Chinneas air an t-sliabh,
B' annsa leath' mar bhiadh
    Na na fòlaichean.
'S ann de 'n teachd-an-tìr
    A bha sòghar leath'
Sóbhrach 's eala-bhì
    'S barra neònagan;
Dóbhrach bhallach mhìn
Ghóbhlach bharrach shlìom,
Lòintean far an cinn
    I 'na mòthraichean.
Siud am pòrsan bìdh
Mheudaicheadh an clì,
Bheireadh iad a nìos
    Ri am dòilichean;
Chuireadh air an druim
Brata saille cruinn,
Air an carcais luim
    Nach bu lòdail.
B' e sin an caidreabh grinn
    Mu thràth nòine,
'N uair a thionaladh iad cruinn
    Anns a' ghlòmainn:
    Air fhad 's gum biodh an
      oidhch',

THE HIND IS IN THE FOREST

The hind is in the forest
as she ought to be,
where she may have sweet grass,
clean, fine-bladed;
    heath-rush and deer's hair grass
herbs in which strength resides,
and which would make her flanks
plump and fat-covered;
a spring in which there is
abundant water-cress,
she deems more sweet than wine,
and would drink of it;
sorrel and rye grass
which flourish on the moor,
she prefers as food
to rank field grass.
Of her fare she deemed
these the delicacies:
primrose, St John's wort
and tormentil flowers;
    tender spotted orchis,
forked, spiked and glossy,
on meadows where, in clusters,
it flourishes.
Such was the dietary
that would increase their strength,
that would pull them through
in the stormy days;
that would upon their back
amass the roll of fat,
which, over their spare frame,
was not cumbersome.
That was a comely fellowship
at eventide,
when they would assemble
in the gloaming:
    though long the night might
      be,

Dad cha tigeadh ribh,
Fasgadh bhun an tuim
  B' àite còmhnaidh dhuibh.
Leapaichean nam fiadh,
Far an robh iad riamh,
An aonach farsaing fial
  'S ann am mórmhonadh.
'S iad bu taitneach fiamh
'N uair bu daitht' am bian;
'S cha b' i 'n airc am
    miann
  Ach Beinn Dóbhrain.

no harm would come to you;
the lee base of the knoll
was your dwelling place.
Here are the beds of deer,
where they have ever been,
on a spacious, bounteous moor,
and on mountain range.
Delightful was their hue,
when vivid was their hide;
'twas no mean portion they
    desired,
it was Ben Dobhrain.

ORAIN DHONNCHAIDH BHAIN   DUNCAN BAN MACINTYRE

THE ANIMALS

They do not live in the world,
Are not in time and space.
From birth to death hurled
No word do they have, not one
To plant a foot upon,
Were never in any place.
For with names the world was called
Out of the empty air,
With names was built and walled,
Line and circle and square,
Dust and emerald;
Snatched from deceiving death
By the articulate breath.
But these have never trod
Twice the familiar track,
Never never turned back
Into the memoried day.
All is new and near
In the unchanging Here
Of the fifth great day of God,
That shall remain the same,
Never shall pass away.

On the sixth day we came.

EDWIN MUIR

THE MARRIAGE OF ROBIN REDBREAST AND THE WREN

There was an auld gray Poussie Baudrons, and she gaed awa' down by a water-side, and there she saw wee Robin Redbreast happin' on a brier; and Poussie Baudrons says: 'Where's tu gaun, wee Robin?' And wee Robin says: 'I'm gaun awa' to the king to sing him a sang this guid Yule morning.' And Poussie Baudrons says: 'Come here, wee Robin, and I'll let you see a bonny white ring round my neck.' But wee Robins says: 'Na, na! gray Poussie Baudrons; na, na! Ye worry't the wee mousie; but ye'se no worry me.'

So wee Robin flew awa' till he came to a fail fauld-dike, and there he saw a gray greedy gled sitting. And gray greedy gled says: 'Where's tu gaun, wee Robin?' And wee Robin says: 'I'm gaun awa' to the king to sing him a sang this guid Yule morning.' And gray greedy gled says: 'Come here, wee Robin, and I'll let ye see a bonny feather in my wing.'

But wee Robin says: 'Na, na! gray greedy gled; na, na! Ye pookit a' the wee lintie; but ye'se no pook me.'

So wee Robin flew awa' till he came to the cleugh o' a craig, and there he saw slee Tod Lowrie sitting. And slee Tod Lowrie says: 'Where's tu gaun, wee Robin?' And wee Robin says: 'I'm gaun awa' to the king to sing him a sang this guid Yule morning.' And slee Tod Lowrie says: 'Come here, wee Robin, and I'll let ye see a bonny spot on the tap o' my tail.' But wee Robin says: 'Na, na! slee Tod Lowrie; na, na! Ye worry't the wee lammie; but ye'se no worry me.'

So wee Robin flew awa' till he came to a bonny burn-side, and there he saw a wee callant sitting. And the wee callant says: 'Where's tu gaun, wee Robin?' And wee Robin says: 'I'm gaun awa' to the king to sing him a sang this guid Yule morning.' And the wee callant says: 'Come here, wee Robin, and I'll gie ye a wheen grand moolins out o' my pooch.' But wee Robin says: 'Na, na! wee callant; na, na! Ye speldert the gowdspink; but ye's no spelder me.'

So wee Robin flew awa' till he came to the king, and there he sat on a winnock sole, and sang the king a bonny sang. And the king says to

the queen: 'What'll we gie to wee Robin for singing us this bonny sang?' And the queen says to the king: 'I think we'll gie him the wee wran to be his wife.'

So wee Robin and the wee wran were married, and the king, and the queen, and a' the court danced at the waddin'; syne he flew awa' hame to his ain water-side, and happit on a brier.

25   The Marriage of Robin Redbreast. Drawings by Joan Hassal.
Courtesy of the Saltire Society.

The above little story is taken down from the recitation of Mrs Begg, the sister of Robert Burns. The poet was in the habit of telling it to the younger members of his father's household, and Mrs Begg's impression is, that he *made* it for their amusement.—*From* Robert Chambers's *Popular Rhymes of Scotland.*

9   Grouse Shooting over Pointers, Glen Artney, Perthshire. Photograph by Peter Davenport.

10   Red Deer Alert, Glen Artney. Photograph by Peter Davenport.

11   Loch Katrine, by Horatio McCulloch. Courtesy of Perth Museum & Art Gallery.

12   Feeding Highland Ponies in Glen Artney. Photograph by Peter Davenport.

Recreation

ON THE RANNOCH WALL IN WINTER

With nipped ears and much stamping of feet, we stood at the crossroads in brief debate. It occurred to us then that a winter ascent of the Rannoch Wall would provide high interest, and we surveyed the Buachaille to see what opportunity offered. The colours of the rock showed unnaturally clear—dove-grey, brown, and palest red, projecting through a snow-sprinkle that sparkled like salt. Here and there a smaller crag, softly black as though smoke-stained, was girdled by the white ribbon of ledge and gully. Rannoch Wall stared down at us, more free of frost than any other part of the mountain. Its angle and a day or two of sun had kept it clean, but within the groove we feared that deadly combination, ice-glaze and loose powder-snow.

We resolved to inspect the conditions more closely from the foot of Curved ridge, so turned south to Coupal Bridge in Glen Etive and thence tramped the moor for an hour and scrambled among the lower rocks to the water-slide below the ridge. There was one little mountain ash close by, miraculously springing from a ledge of solid stone. Its twigs were exquisitely beaded with ice and it looked like a crystal chandelier. I have passed beside it well over a hundred times and regard it as an old friend of heroic fortitude—how *does* it contrive to wring life from its chosen block of porphyry, winter after bitter winter? One may only marvel in vain—and pass humbly on. The water-slide was frozen and step-cutting was required. Under the swing of my axe, an icicle on the left wall, twice the size of an elephant's tusk, cracked like a rifle shot; and left a sudden silence, which for a moment seemed to brood over us like a hovering of wings, then as suddenly to vanish.

Ten minutes later our boot-nails were grating on Curved ridge and we drew up parallel to the Rannoch Wall. From all over the wall came a hard metallic glitter, emanating from invisible frost cressets. As a whole, the wall displayed a gratifying freedom from the snow that dusted the remainder of the mountain. Agag's groove looked most inviting.

'The sun has certainly been getting at it,' said Dunn with a delighted grin. 'But what about the groove? We'll probably find it lined with green ice.'

'There may be black ice at the crux,' said Mackenzie, in a tone that implied that such would be a point in its favour.

'But there's no snow,' I pointed out. 'Only the leader need carry an axe. We can always come down if it won't go.'

'At thirty-two feet per second per second!' added MacAlpine.

We honoured him with the half-laughing snort due to one's jesting friends; for in fact one may rope down the groove from any of its stances, which have first-class belays. Without more ado we crossed C gully to the cairn at the foot of the climb. We put on balaclava helmets and all available scarves and sweaters until we bulged like polar bears, then roped up with Mackenzie as leader, myself second, followed by Dunn. MacAlpine, who was suffering from a strained muscle, spent the day on Curved ridge. We all retained our rucksacks, but left two axes beside the cairn. Mackenzie carried the third slung at his waist.

The lowest end of the groove was eighty feet overhead, separated from us by a wall, which Mackenzie took in two pitches by bringing me up to a small half-way stance. That first eighty feet was not specially difficult; better than that, it was delightful. The rock lies indeed at a high angle, coarse, clean-cut, and well provided with little square holds—ideal both for boots and gloved fingers.

On joining Mackenzie in the start of the groove I at once looked around for ice, but save for straggling filaments, spreading vein-like on the main wall, there was none. No more than moderately difficult, the groove rose long, wide, and arching to the crux. At close quarters it is not so much a groove as a curving ledge, one hundred and eighty feet in length and about three feet broad, sometimes less and rarely more. As we climbed slowly upward we had a knowledge of complete safety that seemed at odd variance with our progress up the most vertical cliff in central Scotland. The feeling induced was pure elation—height and distance were a sparkling wine poured to the mind from a rock decanter. And to this blend of height and distance my attention was inevitably and repeatedly drawn as I waited on comfortable stances while the man above or below was climbing.

Near the top of the groove I came upon one especially well-upholstered couch—a hollow cushioned with crowberries, which in summer ripeness affords the climber both bed and board, but whose hoary counterpane gave me a chill welcome in frost. I sat there and first paid out Mackenzie's rope and then drew in Dunn's. I felt, perhaps, something of the pleasure of that raven, which as long as man can remember has nested on the neighbouring crags of Raven's gully—I looked straight out from the rock-wall, snugly conscious of the unseen drop below, as a man may nestle more happily in his bed when he hears the rainstorm beat upon his window. My gaze met nothing till it met the moor, lightly whitened as though veiled by frail lace, through which the brown heath glowed like an inner warmth.

Along the farthest fringe, behind Schiehallion and beyond Loch Rannoch, ran between sky and earth a broad belt of brume, the colour of the Cuillin after rain on a still evening.

Meanwhile, Mackenzie had climbed twenty-five feet to find that our protecting groove had petered out in a nest of bulging rocks. He was still a hundred feet beneath the crest of Crowberry ridge, and by a traverse to the left must now embark upon the open face. Immediately above him was the crux of the climb, twenty feet of almost vertical rock, the last fifteen of which, jutting like a squat nose, were split by a crack whence a climber may look between his legs to the screes. In this crack we anticipated ice.

'Look out for squalls,' Mackenzie said casually. 'If there's no ice then the frost has probably loosened some of the holds.' And with these parting words he stepped from the groove on to a ledge on the open wall. He climbed to the nose, where for a moment I saw him outlined against blue sky. He had stopped to strip off his gloves. Then he vanished like the boy in the Indian rope-trick.

I waited for the ominous sound of his axe, but five minutes passed without even the faintest noise from above. If there were loose holds I could trust Mackenzie not to use them; or to use them correctly. He was apt to leave loose holds rather than throw them down, arguing that loose holds are not of necessity bad holds. I was startled by a whirr, and a black shape dashed towards Curved ridge. It was my other old friend—the raven. He had watched many a climb of mine on Buachaille. He wheeled round the base of Crowberry ridge and led my eyes down to the moor. The Glencoe road ran like a grey thread to the Blackmount. It was absurd to say that this new road spoiled the scenery. As well might one say that a scratch could spoil the façade of Chartres Cathedral. The road was dominated by the scenery—lost in it. Perhaps, by comparison, it helped to lend some meaning to an immense scale of things otherwise beyond comprehension. A shout came from above. Mackenzie was up.

W H MURRAY

TO THE MOUNTAIN

Boots and ice-axe balance the suitcase
as I leave the sleeping house
by the back stair
and Long Lane
a mile long they say
to the crossroads
where traffic lights wink all night
red amber green
to little traffic

Our coach waits
I hear her heart throb

Case and rucksack on the coat rack
ice-axe and nailed boots on the floor
I sit alone
too early for talking

Through a city asleep
till Sunday newspapers
and Sabbath congregations to kirk service
after a night of prowling street cats

By a numbered bus route
we leave the city
by market gardens
raspberry canes in rows
farms named at roads' ends
and country towns

The foothills close in
with tall firs
Gaelic birchtrees against a low sky
and the first white Bens
on the dawn horizon

I spread the one-inch map on my knees
find the five glens
and to-day's mountain
a mere Munro
timed between dawn dark

The five Bens
four thousand feet and more
are for long Autumn days
or Spring
or week-ends
the Cuillins for Summer holidays

Off with my street shoes and town coat
I am water- and wind-proofed
over warm wool
up there
against ice-daggers at the heart

I don my clawed boots
to cling like an eagle
to iced crags
or wild cat to a tree

Maybe we'll climb where no stag goes

And last
my camera strap over one shoulder
the light-meter in one of my four pockets
my brown balaclava pulled over my ears
I climb down
leaving the warm coach
ice-axe at the ready as once a rifle

WILLIAM MONTGOMERIE

SPORT AN' WARK

Bit Aw'm thinkin' the time'll come fin we'll hae toon's fowk o' a kin kin' comin' oot an' takin' up fairm wark. Ye ken, richtly lookit at, plooin', an' sawin', an' mawin's sport. Ay, sport. The difference atween sport an' wark is jist a maitter o' name—a maitter o' fat wye ye look at the thing. If yer cyciclist wiz pey't for cyciclin' an' hid ti dee't as a maitter o' wark, a verra short spell o't as a riglar compuls'ry thing wid seem some like an afflickshin. Traivlin' never seems sport tull a postie: bit walkin' matches is a' the go, an' fowk'll positeevly *pey* ti gyang an' see twa lawds paddin' roon' an' roon' a ring, fair heel-an'-tae, aivn on, withoot a cheenge, for oors on en'. It's nae only sport ti the walkers, bit it's sport aivn ti the fowk 'at's only stannin' lookin' on. Sheetin's plain ivvryday *wark* tull a gamekeeper or a Red Indian; bit it's the verra best o' sport tull a loard or a poalateeshin, an they'll pey thoosans o' powins for a sax weeks' sheetin' i' the en' o' the year. Again, gairnerin's thocht a gey hard job; bit there's naething pleases a bit laddie or lassickie better than ti get a plotty o' grun' an' be tell't they can dee wi't jist fat they like. For gentle an' simple, dellin' an' weedin' an rakin' an' hyowin' micht be recreations—sport; an' in fack gairnerin' is lookit upon in that licht be some fowk as it is; bit we're maistly geylies oot o't in the vyow we tak' o' wark an' sport baith. Only that's nae my subjick, although it's a pairt o't.

The great difference atween sport an' wark is that the sport maistly goes on wi' a lot o' ye thegither an' plenty o' news an' clatter an' fun an' lauchin' gyaun on; bit wark, an country wark espeeshly, his ti gyang forrit wi' you maistly bi yersel', plooin', or pooin' frosty neeps, or castin' peats, wa' nae a sowl nearhan' ye bit the horses an' the teuchits—gien' them the benefeet o' the doot in the maitter o' sowls.

I've hid lawds 'at wid hae bann't an' curs't at Jess and Mull, at the plooin', a' day, an' aivn daudit the flunks o' the craiturs wi' clods an' steens; bit pit the same chiels intul a plooin' match, wi' ploos an' horses on ilka han' o' them, an' fowk lookin' on at the en' o' the furrs, an' they wid get through the wark in gran' style an' be the cheeriest an' best o' company. An' far'll ye get a cheerier cyarn o' fowk or mair eydent workers than the hairst han's? In spite o' jobs an' stobs in the han's, an' aivn-doon hard-pang, takin' the puff oot o' ye an' the sweyt aff o' ye, deems and chiels, aul' an' young, sing strowds an' tell stoaries nac aye fit for a Mother's Meetin'—an' faith I think the mair fun there is amo' them the mair wark ye get oot o' them. They dinna tire at it as lang as there's something ti occapee their min's.

Aw've lang thocht 'at fat wiz wintit abeen a'thing in the country wiz company at wark. Men play at cricket an' fitba' and the curlin', nae for the play itsel', bit for the company. Yarkin' a ba' or bungin' a steen upo' the ice is nae fun ava for men gin it wizna for the company. Naebody wid think o' playin' ony game bi' 'imsel. That widna be play, an' it wid be *waur* than wark, because it wid be naither pleesint nor eesefi. There wid be naither fun nor siller in't.

Weel, than, if we could hae great muckle fairms wrocht be squads o' men an' weemin—on ae bit the day, on anither the morn—that wid be ae wye o' makin' the country attractive an' garrin fowk bide in't. Wiznin't aul' Aristotle 'at said 'at man wiz mair soshl than the ants an' bees?

There's nae bonnier sicht tull a richtly constitutit man than the face o' a frien'. The face may be pock-markit; the moo may wint the teeth; the een may hae a wanderin' wye wi' them that leaves ye sometimes in doot futher yer friend's lookin' at you or the awmry far ye keep the bottle; bit a kin'ly look, a coothie word, an' a herty lauch fae a frien'—weel, nae ti pit owre fine a pint upon't, they're worth a lot. It's nae winder 'at the loons wint ti gyaung ti the toon faur a'body's aye rubbin' shoothers an' passin' the crack wi' some ane. Man, it's a lot jist ti see faces—a' kin's o' faces, a' kin' o' dresses, a' kin' o' shops, an' ships, an' cairts, an' kerriages; ti see sodgers an' sailors an' judges (sae lang as it's nae in a profeshinal capacity); ti see my leddy sailin' across the pavement tull 'er kerriage, or my leddy washin' doon the front steps, ti watch the bootcher loons an' the tellygraph loons knockin' in the time wi' their taps, an' their bools, an' their poother-deevils; ti see a' kin' o' wark gyaun on; an' ti get admittit ti a' kin' o' shows wi' the best an' the brawest—gin ye hae time an' siller. . . .

An' this is human natur', an' though it's a kin' o' richt that a body sid be self-interi, an' nae depen' upo' fowk for a' their pleeshirs in life, it's richt, at the same time, that fowk sid hae their fine-tune't social side tee. Ony wye, there it is, an' ye maun rauckn wi't gin ye want ti keep fowk in the country an' upo' the lan'. Halls an' concerts an' leeberaries an' lectirs are a' verra gweed in their place; bit the evenin's o' a man's life are a sma'er pairt o't than the moarnins, the foraneens, an' the aifterneens. Fowk wint some pleeshure in their wark as well as in their leisure. A lot o' country wark, like a lot o' toon wark, is jist plain drudgery, an' the mair sense yer fowk hae the less they'll like it. In the toons the drudgery is lichten't bi the fack 'at it's deen in company.

I've mair ti say upo' this heid; bit Aw'll hae ti keep it for anither wik. Aw doot ye've some muckle o' 'er already.

AIRCHIE TAIT

FIVE INCHES OF ICE

Unlike golf and football which in the sixteenth century were roundly and officially condemned by the law of Scotland, curling escaped stricture, and thereby identification in the dimness of past ages and it was to take religious controversy to make the first reference to curling. On the 11 December 1638, during debate in the General Assembly of the Church of Scotland, the Bishop of Orkney was attacked for being a curler on the Sabbath day. Fortunately the game itself was not decried and before the century was out powerful professional help was firmly on the way in the shape of Dr Penicuik's famous prescription. While the estimable doctor tells us what curling would do to us there yet appeared no accurate account of how the game was played. There are reports from many parts of Scotland of great stones, so famous for their predigious shape and size that they are named: of the strength required to get them to the tee and there to guard or dislodge them there can be little doubt. The rivalry of such trials kindled a strong and friendly fellowship. Leadership in the personality and commanding

26 The Curlers. by Sir George Harvey 1806–1876. Courtesy of Trustees of the National Galleries of Scotland.

nature of the skip was a most important feature. These were the days of one man one stone and eight to the side. Length of the rink was decided by the skips according to the ice available. Sometimes during a game, if players were noot up, the head by agreement was shortened.

As a fuller measure of prosperity came to Scotland in the eighteenth century and as communications improved, reports of curling stimulated the sporting inclinations of the country. Challenges were sent further afield and if an area by fortune had a larger frost than its neighbour there was nearly always to be found a greater skill and a wider and more ingenious variety of curlers' implements.

The eighteenth century saw the quite rapid growth of curling societies and clubs whose main purpose was to improve the harmony of play by adopting simple rules of conduct on the ice. One of the universal agreements at this time was that the stone should be delivered over the tee. There was a wide spread practice of tying special grips to footwear so that players could merely step to one side or another to get past some mountainous guard, but this was frowned upon and vigorously suppressed. The ultimate sanction of expulsion was not infrequently carried out, although after a year or two to calm down, many a man was wholeheartedly and generously reinstated. This summary discipline on the ice has long been a feature of the game. It simply would have been impossible to allow wordy recrimation or accusation during play. None knew when thaw would come and all must stop. These earliest rules framed on simple trust and personal integrity have stood the test of time and of artificial ice remarkably.

Curling on open deep water has many charms but, of course, one profound danger. Even today there is no way of deciding the bearing quality. From ancient times five inches of thickness was considered enough for perhaps a dozen rinks, but seven inches or more for the 650 rinks of the Grand Match. All old clubs have written records with notes and recommendations for the number of ropes and ladders which had to be brought forward before play could begin.

By the nineteenth century stones were becoming more uniform in size and shape. Local masons who were keen curlers took a pride in preparing stones most suited to there area. The old ancient splendid stones had joined together curlers in true fellowship of sport upon their own ground but now with the coming of more perfect stones curling grew nationally. Clubs could compete quite fairly and as freely and as far as they could travel. The first decades of the nineteenth century saw several clubs define their codes of rules with clarity. Among the first of these was the Duddingston Society near Edinburgh. Indeed so many were these codes and produced by such active clubs that by 1830 the formation of an overall and governing body became obvious. In 1834 the Amateur Curling Club of Scotland was proposed for promoting and cherishing the noble national game of curling. An anonymous letter in the North British Advertiser finally brought 36 clubs together on 25 July 1838, and these clubs determined upon the formation of the Grand Curling Club. A surge of enthusiasm followed and this event soon brought royal approbation to the Grand Club.

The antiquity of the game perhaps we cannot prove, but we do know that the spirit of many old curling clubs in Scotland built the strength of the game on nothing more than the chance of natural ice. We who inherit this spirit may now in the artificial circumstances of today share the game with many other nations.

EARL OF ELGIN

INLAND GOLF COURSES

These spreads, mounds, terraces and ridges, produced by the meltwaters of the last ice sheet to cover Scotland, have been extensively used as sites for golf courses. They represent the nearest inland equivalent to the classic links ground of the coastal golf courses. The similarities between windblown-sand landforms (links) and fluvioglacial sand and gravel landforms (sandar, kames, terraces, eskers) are numerous. Both sets of landforms are well-drained and support firm turf. Both sets of landforms are characterised by ridges and hollows and by short steep slopes which frequently change direction. Both sets of landforms consist of materials (sand and gravel) easily worked by man either with or without mechanical assistance. Many of the early inland golf courses in Scotland were established on these relatively easily managed fluvioglacial deposits. It would appear that golfers and golf course architects have a considerable affinity for fine grained unconsolidated sediments whether they are deposited by wind or water.

ROBERT PRICE

GOLF

In Winter, too, when hoary frosts o'er spread
The verdant turf, and naked lay the mead,
The vig'rous youth commence the sportive war,
And, arm'd with lead, their jointed clubs prepare;
The timber curve to leathern orbs apply,
Compact, elastic, to pervade the sky:
These to the distant hole direct they drive;
They claim the stakes who hither first arrive.
Intent his ball the eager gamester eyes,
His muscles strains, and various postures tries
Th' impelling blow to strike with greater force,
And shape the motive orb's projective course.
If with due strength the weighty engine fall,
Discharged obliquely, and impinge the ball,
It winding mounts aloft, and sings in air;
And wondering crowds the gamester's skill declare.
But when some luckless wayward stroke descends,
Whose force the ball in running quickly spends,
The foes triumph, the club is cursed in vain;
Spectators scoff, and e'en allies complain.

Thus still success is followed with applause;
But ah! how few espouse a vanquished cause.

JAMES ARBUCKLE

GOLFING AT DELVINE

To John Mackenzie   *University of St Andrews 1691*

. . . Receive from the bearer, our post, ane sett of Golfe-clubs
consisting of three, viz. an play club, ane scraper, and ane tin fac'd
club. I might have made the set to consist of more, but I know not your
play, and if you stand in need of more, I think you should call for them
from me. Tho I know you may be served there, yet I presumed that

such a present from this place, the metropolis of Golfing, may not be unsuitable for these fields, especially when it's come from a friend. Upon the same consideration I have also sent you ane dozen of Golfe balls which receive with the clubs. I am told they are good, but that will prove according to your play and the fields. If the size do not suite, were you so free with me I would mend it with the next . . .

PROFESSOR ALEXANDER MUNRO

THE FIRST SALMON

How carefully one fishes the first pool! And reflects at the end of it that it would be wrong to get anything in the first pool. Nothing worth doing should be easy. One salmon a day should satisfy any man. And it should be caught at some moment when he would almost have been justified in being careless—but wasn't. Yet truth compels me to say that I once caught an eighteen-pounder in my second full cast, that I have never forgotten it, and that I am dogged by an unworthy desire to find out again precisely how it felt.

There was to be no eighteen-pounder this day. And by the time I had finished the pool, the vertebral bones were creaking, certain muscles were tremulous, and the wind performed its only useful service by drying a bared forehead. Hitherto I had thought the wind rather cold, but now as I sat down to change my fly, I realised that it was a spring wind full of promise of long days to come. The year was opening its slow door to summer pastures. There is an emotion of gratitude to this old scarred earth that runs very deep. Or is it very high, like blown thistledown in a sunny wind? About as light as that, anyhow, and with an echo of laughter blown with it.

And so to the next pool. And to the next. With never a tug or a swirl or a rise anywhere. No, the salmon cannot have started running yet. In the last few years, I was told, the salmon in this river have decidedly been running later—to the extent even of affecting the letting. No reason could be given for this. And the whim might pass.

'Have you no special theory?' I asked my host, making my last cast at the tail of the pool and half turning my head. But I never got the answer, for in the same instant I was 'in him'.

A kelt? No, said my host. No, said the gillie. Decidedly no, thought I, as he took the current with a strong head. There had been no turn-over, with the silver gleaming ruddy through the brown water— a thing one should not see until the fight is ending. After five minutes I would have offered fantastic odds that I was in a clean fish, had there been anyone to take me. Indeed I had landed many clean fish that had behaved with even slower stubbornness. I could not get him to show himself. And when at last he was tiring, I began to grow anxious. My host was ready with the gaff. The gillie was all eyes. I brought him in. He showed himself. It was a kelt—foul-hooked!

The gillie tailed him, undid the hook, and he sailed away into deep water, none the worse.

The first part of my prophecy had come true.

And the second part followed in due course, for my friend got into a salmon. Again speculation was favourable—but this time with the mighty difference that it was correct. A clean-run hen fish of seven pounds, exquisite in line as anything that was ever created. The first fish of the season, of the year. The river was at last open.

It was an occasion to be toasted properly, with bonnets off. Even to be toasted twice. Nature was fulfilling her ancient contract to man. The local reporter could put his paragraph in the press.

We got no more fish that day. Which was right and proper. We had started in the half-light of the morning, full of hope. We left in the half-light of the evening, full of blessed tiredness and hospitality, convinced that fine men lived in a fine world—whose life-streams are its rivers.

NEIL GUNN

HEAD FISHING GILLIE

The knowledge a good gillie carries in his head about his river is enormous. Quite frankly there is so much I doubt if I could explain even the half of it. It takes years and years of patient study. It just goes on and on. And it will never end. I'm certain of this. I am still learning something fresh and new about methods of fishing and about the river and the fish themselves. A gillie must be prepared to adapt and as far as possible keep an open mind. This is especially so when it comes to dealing with the differing abilities of the many guests I have fishing here with me every year. I think the main thing is that a gillie must be a bit of a diplomat in order to do his job properly. All the same he must never be afraid to speak his mind if a guest steps out of line and is not obeying the rules of fishing as they apply to the river here on this estate. He carries a trump card all the time: this knowledge of the river he possesses. It can mean everything to the guest if he is going to start catching fish without wasting too much time. I always think that the sooner a guest realises and appreciates this fact then the better for all concerned.

A gillie has to know and understand many things. He has to know when the fish are running, where and when they will rest at different times of the year and how they are likely to be affected by changing conditions in the level of the river and the temperature of the water. The temperature must be taken every day. There's a great deal of information to be gained from it and depending on what it is the gillie will have some idea of what size of fly to recommend or, if in the early part of the year, whether or not it is only worthwhile because of the cold to use a spinning rod. A gillie who is really absorbed in his job will take every opportunity to watch the river, the fish and the direction of the wind. He should also be fully familiar with every pool and stream on his beat on the river—their depth, the lie of the fish and the state of the river which suits the fish best of all. In addition to this he must know the effect of the sun upon the pools (there's nothing worse for frightening salmon away), the direction of the wind that catches certain of them and the best side from which the pool can be fished at any particular time of the day.

Every day before going to the river—his first job in the morning—he has to check tackle, rods, reels, lines, flies, casts and baits which have been provided for the fishing. He will then be able to advise the guests about the best rod to use, the most suitable line—either one that floats on the surface or one that sinks well beneath it—the particular size of fly for the height of the water that day. He has one hundred and one things to remember to do and years ago there was a rhyme which young gillies used to be advised to learn by heart to help them become familiar with this part of their day's work. It goes like this:

> Rods, reels and hooks,
> Nets, bait and baskets,
> Gaff, baton, books,
> Coats, lunch and flaskets.

The gaff—a long pole with a sharp metal hook—is what is used to lift the fish out of the water and on to the bank after the fisherman has tired the salmon sufficiently in order to bring it close-in to the water's edge. It's often used in preference to a net. The baton referred to is a short, truncheon-like club for striking the head of the salmon in order to kill it. Books aren't what most folks will think—for reading when the fishing is poor— but fly books containing dozens of different salmon flies in all sizes and colours. Flaskets is just another word for whisky flasks—spirit flasks really, but as whisky is the most popular drink among anglers in these parts then this is what they would contain. Mind you, today he doesn't have to worry about the flaskets. That's a throw-back to the old days when the gillie was looking after the laird and his personal guests staying in the Big House. Today's guests are different. They are paying for their sport. They bring their own whisky and dispense it according to their own nature—generous or otherwise.

ANDREW FRASER

AT THE MOUTH OF THE ARDYNE

The water rubs against itself,
glancing many faces at me.
One winces as the dropped fly
tears its tension. Then it heals.

Being torn doesn't matter.
The water just goes on saying
all that water has to say,
what the dead come back to.

Then a scar opens.
Something of water is ripped out,
a struggle with swung air.
I batter it on a loaf of stone.

The water turns passing faces,
innumerable pieces of silver.
I wash my hands, pack up, and
go home wishing I hadn't come.

Later, I eat my guilt.

MAURICE LINDSAY

THE BEATER

For the first year or so after I left school at the age of fourteen—in the mid 1920s—I had to work on a farm until a place could be found for me in the game department. . . .

My chance came during the grouse shooting season which begins every year on 12 August. I was hired to go as a beater and right from the start found myself enjoying every moment of my new temporary job. Now, for anyone who doesn't know what a beater does, it involves being part of a long line of men (well in my young days it was mostly all men though now quite a few women take part) advancing spread out across the face of a particular part of the moor, waving sticks with coloured flags attached to them. The aim is to make the grouse, lying low among the tussocks of heather, rise up and fly off towards and over the guns, waiting hidden in the butts, constructions of stone or netting wire faced with turf and heather so that they are camouflaged with the background. It may sound like a jolly easy day's work, all this walking about and waving of flags. But believe me, nothing could be further from the truth. You have to keep position with the beater on either side of you, but take your pace not from him but from the man on the flank, usually the head gamekeeper himself or one of his more experienced under-keepers, sometimes a trusted and reliable beater from former years.

RODERICK GRANT

THE SHOOT

The first heather to bloom was the crimson bell-heather, but when autumn came, the moors were richly purple with ling, and the sound of shots echoed over the landscape, sending grouse toppling out of a blue sky, to be retrieved by the gun-dogs from the keeper's kennels and brought to the feet of the marksmen.

The latter were known as the guns and those at Gairnshiel, as I remember them, had a decided look of a gathering of variously-built editions of Sherlock Holmes, enveloped in immense ulsters of a style and material familiar to all readers of early illustrated productions of Conan Doyle's masterpiece, and since copied, more or less accurately, on television. Breeches and Norfolk jackets, and thick-knit stockings were weightier than anything worn nowadays, and must have felt like chain-mail when rain-soaked; peaty soil clung to the hand-made, well-oiled boots built like battleships, with soles encrusted with enormous tackets. At a grouse-drive the guns stayed in the butts with loaders, and beaters drove the birds in the approved direction. Because of the way the butts were sited, the hill was no place for the foolhardy; only by continual alertness and strict adherence to discipline were shooting accidents avoided. Any gun who followed a bird beyond the line of safety was a source of constant worry to the keeper. It was every gun's ambition and expectation to bring grouse down right and left when they swerved in hundred-miles-an-hour pace over a wind-swept ridge. The joys were not confined to those who carried a gun; ladies who were not 'out with the guns' joined them for lunch, and stayed to watch the well-trained labradors at work on the sun-dappled moors. At Gairnshiel the game-larder was outside the kitchen door. It was made of metal gauze. In it the game-birds were left hanging by their necks for perhaps a week, and were then considered fit to prepare for the table. In that primitive larder, long before deep-freeze methods were practised, the game actually kept for months.

In the grouse-driving season, men who could be spared from farm work were glad to earn money as loaders, gillies and beaters. All the boys were engaged as beaters at five shillings a day (and bring your own flag), their mothers depending on their earning enough to get new suits and winter boots. They took a 'piece' to the hill and were 'gey hungert and trauchled' when they got home at the end of the day. When it was a royal shoot, lunch was provided, men getting in addition a bottle of beer apiece.

The small farmer, also, took his sheltie to the hill to bring down the game in panniers, which were covered baskets shaped to lie on the pony's sides, but I remember, long before Land Rovers were designed, a car with caterpillar wheels, built for Alexander Keillor of Morven, crawled over the hills on that estate, bringing down the day's bag, thus outmoding the panniered-pony.

In his youth King Edward VII had been tireless on the hills, but when he came to the throne he was close on sixty and had become stout. In spite of this, he liked to be out on the hills and moors, seated on a pony with his Inverness cape wrapped about him. When he used to shoot over Geallaig a sturdy pony was provided to carry him up the quarry road to the Royal Butt above Delnabo. On the Gairnside moors he had the reputation of being the cheeriest of the party, and his geniality made the day enjoyable for all who served him. It amused him to use the speech of the locality, which he did with a faultless accent. On one occasion he noticed among the gillies, Peter Robertson, who for years had been his personal servant at Abergeldie Castle and had long retired. Delighted, he at once approached him and shaking his hand vigorously he exclaimed, 'Man, Peter, foo are ye?'

AMY STEWART FRASER

27   Capercaillie. Drawing by Colin Gibson.

PROTECTIT BIRD

Pass the word
I'm a protectit bird.
They're setting girns for vermin
Like stoats and their kin;
The fox is huntit and shot doun
And aa to keep me safe and soun.
Pass the word
I'm a protectit bird.
You micht say I'm august
And that is surely just.
Aa is for my health
And a pairty on the twelfth!

DUNCAN GLEN

HIGHLAND STALKER

Even without firing a shot at a beast nothing could be more enjoyable than climbing the hills in the early morning, watching the quiet herds taking up their position for the day just between the winds. You can lie there in the heather and watch the little ones playing, scampering about, kicking their hind legs in the air, while the older deer are perhaps wallowing in a mud bath where there is boggy ground near to a burn. One or two of the old hinds will be to one side on sentry duty. Then, as you sit and watch, spying on them through your telescope, trying to count the heads, spot the best heads among them, the sun will be starting to warm you and you are aware of nothing in the world except the sight of those creatures and the sounds of the upland birds, a raven croaking, a grouse chattering in a hollow; perhaps, if you're lucky, the echoing call of an eagle perched on the very top of a nearby crag. No matter how down-hearted I might be about some mundane problem at home, once I get up on to the mountain, once I get into the heart of the place where the deer are, all my worries fade away. They cease to exist in such surroundings. It's the most wonderful place in the world to me.

During the course of the year, apart from looking after a beat on the moor, keeping down vermin and predators in search of the grouse, I became stalking gillie to one of the estate deerstalkers. Now, as a gillie I had an important part to play in the stalking team. The stalker of the beat did all the actual stalking of the deer. He carried the rifle, took the guest right in to the beast, sometimes over miles of difficult terrain, then handed over the rifle for him to take a shot at it. The guest then took his shot at the stag and either hit it or missed, according to how good an eye he had. As the gillie I went with the stalking party and carried the lunch bag; and when the stag was killed I had to bleed it by cutting its throat (gralloching is what we call this) then go and make contact with the ponyman and help him to load the beast on to the pony's back.

When we returned to the Big House in the evening we all had to muck-in and skin the deer. The skull head was always placed to one side. At the end of the week it was my job to gather up all the heads that had been skulled and boil the flesh off them, ready for the guests who had been out stalking to take their trophies away with them when they departed at the week end. Some left them behind for the laird to mount and hang if he wished, but they usually took them away. Each guest was allowed at least one good trophy head and the main thing was to keep up the standard of the stags in the deer forest by killing out all the deer with narrow heads and leave the big stags with the wide heads. Royals and Imperials, they weren't touched, except for special guests whom the laird respected as being first-rate shots and who would appreciate the magnificence of owning such a splendid trophy.

A Royal is a stag with twelve points on his antlers—that's six points on each horn—and an Imperial has seven points on each horn. With fourteen points on a splendid head he really is an awe-inspiring beast when you see him through a telescope, perhaps standing there on the fringe of a herd scattered along a ridge against the skyline.

The stalking and shooting of stags can usually start about the end of August. They've got clear of their 'velvet' by then (the soft growth which protects their newly-emerging horns which are freshly grown each year). By then the horns have turned brown and become hard. It is then possible to stalk right through to around 20 October, but on most estates it stops around the 10th because the rutting season is starting to get underway. The stags start to roar, challenging other males to fight, and seeking mates. What a fantastic sound it is—this roaring. To anyone hearing it for the first time it can be quite frightening and unless you know what you're doing it's best to keep out of the way of the stags when they are in this state.

RODERICK GRANT

HUNTERS
from 'To Circumjack Cencrastus'

Hunters were oot on a Scottish hill
Ae day when the sun stude suddenly still
At noon and turned the colour o' port
A perfect nuisance, spoilin their sport.
Syne it gaed pitch black a' thegither.
Isn't that jist like oor Scottish weather.

'Ae day'—the day of Christ's crucifixion.

HUGH MACDIARMID

THE STAG HUNT AS WITNESSED BY QUEEN VICTORIA

We scrambled up an almost perpendicular place to where there was a box, made of hurdles and interwoven with branches of fir and heather, about five feet in height. There we seated ourselves, . . . Macdonald (one of the gillies) lying in the heather near us, watching and quite concealed; some had gone round to beat, and others again were at a little distance. We sat quite still, and sketched a little: I drawing the landscape, and some trees, Albert drawing Macdonald as he lay there. This lasted for nearly an hour, when Albert fancied he heard a distant sound, and in a few minutes Macdonald whispered that he saw stags, and that Albert should wait and take a steady aim. We then heard them coming past. Albert did not look over the box, but through it, and fired through the branches, and then again over the box. The deer retreated; but Albert felt certain he had hit a stag. He ran up to the keepers, and at that moment they called from below that 'they had got him', and Albert ran on to see. I waited for a bit; but soon scrambled on with Bertie (the Prince of Wales and future King Edward VII) and Macdonald's help; and Albert joined me directly, and we all went down and saw a magnificent stag, a 'royal' (a stag with twelve points to its antlers) which had dropped, soon after Albert had hit him, at one of the men's feet. The sport was successful, and everyone was delighted—Macdonald and the keepers in particular—the former saying: 'that it was her Majesty's coming out that had brought the good luck'. I was supposed to have 'a lucky foot', of which the Highlanders 'think a great deal'.

Leaves from the Journal of our Life in the Highlands

VICTORIA

28   A Stag from The Royal Forest, Glen Etive.

BLOODSPORTS ON DEESIDE

I do not understand blood sports very well; and in so far as I do understand I deplore them. Not that I can take up a high moral attitude in the matter. As a farmer I breed cattle that eventually go to the butcher. As one who likes a good diet of meat I will wring the neck of a duck. Indeed, all who like a steak or a cut off the breast should have to kill and disembowel occasionally in case they become over-refined. I have killed birds and beasts, but always with a sense of regret, or even guilt. When you take a trout from the water and that most exquisite agility dies between your hands, you have destroyed something you can never replace. There is no essential difference between taking the life of a bird or a fish and the life of a man or a woman; the difference is only in degree. In our defence we can quote only the necessity that knows no law greater than itself. It is part of the human predicament that there is so often a conflict among our instincts and impulses. I destroy the lovely caterpillars that strip the leaves from my young poplar trees because I am in great need of trees for shelter, but as I destroy them I feel a slight chill, an intimate desolation, at the ruin of those innocent and lovely creatures. I doubt if there is any escape from the predicament. We live only by the death of others. Of course the vegetarians have an answer; but how valid is it? Who knows what agonies the cabbage suffers as the reticulations of its heart are shredded down to recreate a classical economist? We must accept the fact that we are beasts of prey and live by murder . . .

The slaughterer kills because it is his living. What can we make of the people who kill wholesale in the name of sport? When a gentleman goes to the moor with several friends and they shoot two hundred grouse and various other birds and creatures they can hardly plead necessity. On the contrary, the fact that the killers are neither hungry, nor forced to kill for a living, is a mark of very high social position. To enjoy a successful day with the guns must require a great atrophy of feeling, an advanced state of decadence. As for the idea that there is something manly about shooting game, it is a little comic. What fortitude is required to hit a bird with shot scientifically prepared to be propelled out of an expensive gun? Fortitude—there was a lot more shown by the fine old sportswoman the farmer's wife when she cut off the tails of the three blind mice.

The great grouse shoots were one of those forms of vulgarity that sometimes become marks of social distinction. They were marks of conspicuous waste and very expensive at that. The grouse shooters were often rather pathetic people, going through a ritual imposed on them because they could afford it. They came north to live in draughty castles and damp, dark shooting lodges. They dressed themselves in tweeds and trudged through the heather, drenched by mists or tortured by horseflies. They were stung, by everything and everybody. From the laird who let his moor for £3,000 and the grocer who charged quite as fantastically, down to the youngest beater with an eye for a shilling, the countryside knew the sporting tenants were their game. That is not an honest way for a countryside to live. And how pathetic that for fifty years only the rents from the moors kept many estates from total bankruptcy. In days when it did not pay to feed a bullock for the professional slaughterer there was good money in raising a grouse for the amateur one.

The days of the big house parties and the organised shoots would seem to be over. When cattle and sheep are more important than grouse on the hills again, Deeside will be a sweeter and a saner place to live in.

JOHN R ALLAN

HIGHLAND GAMES

The scene is always the same, though it may vary in small details. A green field—perhaps a pleasure ground, or just a field from which the cows, but not their traces, were removed last night. A marquee for teas. Another for bottled refreshments. A tent for the judges. A tent for the competitors. A few sideshows put up by travelling showmen. The vans of sixteen ice-cream hawkers, and a fried potato man. Hundreds of motor-cars, from the large and glossy to the kind that rattle in the wind. Some thousands of people sitting or standing round the wide ring in the middle of the field. Over all the windy summer sky, with the threat of a shower blowing up from the west.

Affairs proceed briskly inside the ring, for there are usually two or three things happening at one time. Sprinters sprint; slow-bicyclists totter on the active side of inertia; girl dancers, hideously dressed in kilts and velvet and hung with little silver medals, posture and pirouette to a monotonous highland noise from the bagpipes. And all the time the heavyweights go about their ponderous business, like mountains at labour. They are of course very big men, with great knees and calves displayed by the kilt, and great biceps and abdominal muscles that bulge out of their woollen sweaters. Not the sort of fellows to move in an athletic way; nor do they. Throwing the hammer as they do it must be about the slowest sport on earth. Each competitor is allowed three attempts. The first man comes forward, making the ground tremble as he walks. He takes off his sweater, eases his muscles, takes up the hammer, examines it, polishes the shaft, tests the balance in his hands, looks over the ring, the crowd and the distant hills, as if doubting the occasion worthy of him; then just as you fear he will decide to go home in disgust, he suddenly whirls round and round, winding himself up faster and faster, while the hammer rises to shoulder height, until the man, having spun himself into a blur of kilts and thighs and muscles, lets go and the hammer flies a great distance through the air. Small boys cry 'ooooooh' and sound critics say 'Ayyyyeeee'. Stewards run forward and stick a peg in the dent made by the hammer head as it landed. It was a great moment but it is past and time slows down to a crawl again. The champion resumes his sweater and withdraws, either to inspect the place where the hammer landed or to join the other champions, while the second comes ponderously forward.

JOHN R ALLAN

A BAGPIPE COMPETITION IN 1784

A few moments later, a folding door opened at the bottom of the room, and to my great surprise, I saw a Scottish Highlander enter . . . playing upon the bagpipe, and walking up and down an empty space with rapid steps and a military air, blowing the noisiest and most discordant sounds from an instrument which lacerates the ear. The air he played was a kind of sonata, divided into three parts. Smith begged me to give it my whole attention, and to tell him afterwards the impression it made on me.

But I confess at first I could distinguish neither air nor design. I only saw the piper marching away with rapidity, and with the same warlike countenance. He made incredible efforts both with his body and his fingers to bring into play at once the different pipes of his instrument, which made an insupportable uproar.

He received nevertheless great applause from all sides. A second musician followed into the arena, wearing the same martial look and walking to and fro with the same martial air . . .

After having listened to eight pipers in succession, I began to suspect that the first part was connected with a warlike march and military evolutions: the second with a sanguinary battle, which the musician sought to depict by the noise and rapidity of his playing and by his loud cries. He seemed then to be convulsed; his pantomimical gestures resembled those of a man engaged in combat; his arms, his hands, his head, his legs, were all in motion; the sounds of his instrument were all called forth and confounded together at the same moment. This fine disorder seemed keenly to interest every one. The piper then passed, without transition, to a kind of andante; his convulsions suddenly ceased; the sounds of his instrument were plaintive, languishing, as if lamenting the slain who were being carried off from the field of battle. This was the part which drew tears from the eyes of the beautiful Scottish ladies. But the whole was so uncouth and extraordinary; the impression which this wild music made upon me contrasted so strongly with that which it made upon the inhabitants of the country, that I am convinced we should look upon this strange composition not as essentially belonging to music, but to history . . .

The same air was played by each competitor, of whom there was a considerable number. The most perfect equality was maintained among them; the son of the laird stood on the same footing with the simple shepherd, often belonging to the same clan, bearing the same name, and having the same garb. No preference was shown here save to talent, as I could judge from the hearty plaudits given to some who seemed to excel in that art. I confess it was impossible for me to admire any of them. I thought them all of equal proficiency: that is to say, the one was as bad as the other; and the air that was played as well as the instrument itself involuntarily put me in mind of a bear's dance.

B FAUJAIS ST FOND

PIBROCH

pibroch &c ['pibrox] *n* the music of the Scottish bagpipe, *now* limited to traditional *gatherings* (GAITHER), marches, salutes, laments etc (in Gaelic called *ceol mor* literally = great music); a piece of this, consisting of a theme (the URLAR) and a series of variations 18–. [Gael *piobaireachd* piping]

CONCISE SCOTS DICTIONARY

SALUTES, LAMENTS, INCITEMENTS

By the eighteenth century many of the clan chiefs had their hereditary family pipers. The best known of these were the MacCrimmons, hereditary pipers to the MacLeods of Dunvegan. There is a story that they were of Italian origin from Cremona. It is said also that they first of all were harpers and later turned to the pipes. What is certain is that they established a school of piping at Boreraig from which many of the traditional methods of piping have been handed down. They developed a classical music of the pipes quite distinct from the marches, reels and strathspeys which are the more popular products of piping. Their more elaborate type of composition is the *piobaireachd* which we know in English as the pibroch (a fair shot at the pronunciation of the Gaelic, properly pronounced 'peeper-achk', and meaning 'pipership'). The pibroch includes salutes, laments and incitements to battle. It is made up of three movements, two of them usually recurrent, and the third the most elaborate.

The *urlar* (this Gaelic word means the floor) sets the theme. Next comes the *siubhal* (pronounced 'shoo-al'), which means a wandering. This is the first variation, and there may be several alternations of *urlar* and *siubhal* resembling that of the verse and chorus of a song melody. Last of all comes the *crunluadh*, a crowning or rounding-off, but often with variations of its own. Good pibroch calls for skilful fingering and the playing of these compositions is prominently featured in piping contests. To the mass of Scots it is the lively marches, strathspeys and reels which have the most immediate appeal. Pibroch is a cultivated taste, but true Highlanders are wildly enthusiastic about good playing in this Gaelic grand style.

The MacCrimmons used a bagpipe notation which the older generations of pipers, many of them unlettered men, would commit to memory as was the custom of the Gael. This was the *canntaireachd*. It was made up of combinations of syllables such as

> *Hi o dro hi ri, hi an an in ha ra,*
> *Hi o dto ha chin, ha chin hi a chin.*

Pipers became famous people in their day and generation, and stories were told about their deeds and their sayings, and especially about their tunes and how they came to compose them. When Donald

Ban MacCrimmon left Dunvegan with the MacLeod chief who was opposed to the Jacobites in the 1745 Rising, the piper composed a lament on the theme, 'I shall not come back'. He was killed at the Rout of Moy. Afterwards a lyric was fitted to his melody and it became the favourite concert song, 'MacCrimmon's Lament'.

ALBERT MACKIE

CHALLENGING COMPOSITIONS

Each clan has its salute, gathering tune, march and lament. The MacFarlanes, whose lantern was the moon, marched to *'Togail nam bo'*, which means 'lifting the cattle'. The Clan Cameron gathering song has the ferocious title, *'A chlanna nan con, thigibh a so, is gheibh sibh feoil'* (Children of the dogs, come hither and ye shall have flesh). It arose when the Earl of Atholl, chief of Clan Murray, disputed grazing rights with Sir Ewen Cameron. He was having an argument on the question with Cameron out on the hills, and suddenly, to prove his point, he called up his men, who were lying in ambush, and told the rival chiefs, 'These are a few of my hoggs [young sheep] come across the hills to grow fat on their proper grazings.' Cameron whistled up his own men, who suddenly appeared from their hiding places. 'These,' he said, 'are a few Lochaber hounds eager to taste the flesh of your Atholl hoggs.' Since the Camerons outnumbered the Murrays, or at least looked the stronger force, there was no further dispute that day. The Camerons' piper, on the spot, it is said, struck up the challenging composition.

The tune used to incite a clan to battle is called a *brosnachadh*. A lament or dirge is a *cumha* or a *coronach*. There are about a hundred clan tunes.

ALBERT MACKIE

A DIFFERENT QUALITY

On the whole it would seem that the pipers of lowland Scotland occupied a fairly well-defined position in society. As town pipers, as performers at weddings and feasts, at fairs and holidays, they formed an integral if not all that highly respected part of the social life of the time. All this is not to denigrate the Scots lowland piper—he was no worse and perhaps a good deal better at times than the pipers of England or France or any other country. But of one thing we can be sure: in all these centuries there did not exist one single 'master piper' for the lowland pipe. There were no schools of piping, no recognised periods of apprenticeship, and no incentive in the form of high position for those who excelled in the art. No great music was composed for or played by these lowland pipers. Their repertoire consisted of songs and dance music, and with that they and their audiences were well pleased.

At this same period of time, in the same country of Scotland, separated in places by a bare ten or twenty miles, there lived other pipers of an entirely different calibre. They spoke a different language, wore a different dress and in their remote mountain glens and isolated islands followed a vastly different way of life from that of their southern neighbours. It might be imagined that with less of the obvious trappings of civilisation these Highlanders would play a cruder bagpipe and produce less sophisticated music, but this was not so. Their bagpipe was different in some respects, and superior in all. Indeed this is the one which was eventually to displace all other forms of bagpipe from the face of the earth.

The reasons for the greatness of the Highland pipe are varied, and at times elusive. Possibly the most basic and important one is to be found in the strange musical genius of these Highland people—not that they had better musical appreciation than other people, but simply the kind of music they preferred was different. There are hundreds of beautiful lowland Scots songs, with melodies to warm the heart or set the feet tapping, but the Highland songs have an entirely different and mystical quality. They send a shiver down the spine, even when the words are not understood. Matthew Arnold wrote that the Celtic culture has all the beauty of classical Greece, plus one extra ingredient—magic. It is this which makes us feel that the land of the ever-young really is just over the western horizon, that the haunting Gaelic melodies are not entirely of this earth, that the singer—and the piper—stands in an in-between world, half-remembering visions from another dimension.

S MACNEILL AND F RICHARDSON

TO PLAY A PIBROCH

We stood under the branches of a tree on the Balmoral Estate waiting for the rain to moderate. A blackie sang from another tree, and there were cushie doos making their presence known from the other side of the clearing. The rain went off. Mist hung about the trees in still air and blanketed the hills. Pipe Major Robert U Brown walked into the clearing, tuned his pipes, and began to play *Lament for the Children*. It seemed all other sounds had stopped. Could the blackies and the doos be listening too, as the music left the piper, and lifted itself into the hills. No other music could pay such respect to the nativity of the land as it made the past present nor record with such sadness the originating event.

For a time nothing was said until I asked the piper:
   'How long does it take to learn to play a pibroch?'
He answered:
   'It takes seven years to learn to play the pipes, and seven years to learn to play a pibroch, and then you need the poetry.'

And the skill and the poetry, and the virtue of the man, were in that playing.

Interview with Pip Major Robert U Brown
recorded and edited by GEORGE BRUCE

AN T-EARRACH 1937   SPRING 1937

Air an raon fhada leathann	*On the long wide field*
An eur-thuath air Port-righ,	*North-east of Portree,*
Shuas air cùl a' bhaile,	*Up behind the village*
Raon mór iomain na Bòrlainn,	*The big Home Farm shinty field,*
Sgioba Sgoilearan Phort-righ:	*The Portree School Team:*
Gillean mu shia-diag's mu	*Boys about sixteen and*
sheachd-diag,	*seventeen,*
Iad uile dèante is sgairteil,	*All well-made and full of vigour,*

Cruadalach agus tapaidh,
Sgitheanaich, Ratharsairich, agus
      fear dhiù
Leodhasach mór socair làidir.

Latha o chionn lethchiad
      bliadhna,
Latha grianach ciùin,
Gun snàithnean ceòtha air a'
      Chuilhionn
No air claigeann a' Stòir.

Ach an diugh ceò eile
Air raon mór na Bòrlainn
Ceò na lathaichean a dh fhalbh
Ciar thar nah- òigridh a chaill an
      òige
Is ochdnar dhen dà-dhiag marbh.

Chaill iad uile an òige
'S i 'n toiseach mar linn
      eile,
Ach an ceann dà bhliadhna
Borb le cunnartan a'
      Chogaidh,
Le tinneas, leòintean agus bàs,
A shearg flùraichean na
      h-àbhaist
Ged a thàrr a' mhor-chuid as.

Am bliadhna tha buidheann eile
A cheart cho gleusda 'n Sgoil
      Phort-righ,
A cheart cho calma ris an sgioba
A bha 'san t-stri air Raòn na
      Bòrlainn
Mun do bhàrc an leth-chiad
      bliadhna
Air an linn làidir ud de
      dhòigridh.

Hardy and courageous,
From Skye and Raasay, and
      one,
Big, strong and gentle from Lewis

A day fifty years
      ago,
A calm sunny day,
Without a thread of mist on the
      Cuillins
Or on the Skull of the Storr.

But today another mist
On the big Home Farm field,
Mist of the days that have gone,
Dim over the youth who lost their
      youth,
And eight of the twelve dead.

They all lost their youth,
Which was at first like another
      generation,
But before two years ended
Barbarous with the dangers of the
      war,
Sickness, wounds and death,
Which withered the flowers of
      the customary
Though the majority survived.

This year there is another band
Quite as skilled in the School of
      Portree,
Quite as hardy as the team
That stood on the Home Farm
      field,
Before the fifty years
      surged
On that strong generation of the
      young.

SOMHAIRLE MACGILL-EAIN   **SORLEY MACLEAN**

13   Wild Flowers by a Barley Field, East Neuk of Fife. Photograph by
Peter Davenport.

14   Lambs folded on turnips, Glen Lednock, Perthshire. Photograph
by Peter Davenport.

15   Aberfoyle, Loch Ard, The Trossachs. Photograph by Mike Guy.

16   Winning the Cup. Skye Camanachd wins the Cup, June 1990. Courtesy of William Urquhart, *West Highland Free Press*.

IN FROM THE COLD

Today, win or lose, Skye Camanachd comes in from the cold. For the first time in its 98-year history the club appears in shinty's most prestigious event, the Glenmorangie Camanachd Cup Final.

Between them the teams that line up on Fort William's Aird Park at 3pm will embody much of the character and history of the game.

Newtonmore's claims are the more obvious. Their record of 46 appearances in the final, winning 28 of them, speaks of an unrivalled supremacy in shinty annals. Even in a lean patch they demand, and will be given, respect.

Skye's honours, despite occasional forays among the trophies, are less tangible, though no less real. Down the years the team has mirrored the island community's hopes and fortunes, and engaged its loyalty; more than any other organisation it has been a focus for island identity.

At a time of uncertainties and tensions born of rapid demographic change—two-fifths of the population are incomers—that role becomes accentuated. The 12 who will wear the traditional white strip on the Aird today are reassuring emblems of continuity.

They bear familiar names like MacDougall, MacKenzie, Maclean, MacDonald, Murchison . . . names that have graced Skye teams since the turn of the century. Many of them can look back to parents and grandparents who played in these same white colours.

Team Manager Ross Cowie's great-grandfather, Billy Ross, was captain of the Skye team which brought the club's first trophy, the MacTavish Cup, back to the island in April 1898, having handsomely defeated Inverness by a 7–2 margin.

As they stepped onto flag-bedecked Portree pier they were greeted with a 10-volley salute from the Cameron Highlanders' Volunteers and marched through the town with a pipe band at their head. 'The recent successes of the team will doubtless go far to thoroughly re-establish the popularity of shinty in the island,' the local paper forecast.

For Skye, as for other shinty districts, the First World War brought that era to a close. A generation of young players died at Festubert, where the local territorial battalion of the 4th Camerons was decimated overnight in May, 1915.

The postwar revival was still fraught with travel difficulties, but at least the Camanachd Association had relented on its ban on home games, and the team found a beneficent sponsor in Duncan MacLeod of Skeabost, a local whisky magnate.

In the 1920s there were some memorable encounters with northern teams like Beauly and Caberfeidh, and if the scores were not always to the islanders' liking, post-match socialising with 'copious exchanges of felicities' more than made up for them.

Occasionally the hospitality was misplaced. Down Foyers way they still talk of the time the Boleskine team travelled to Portree in 1929 to find a pre-match lunch set for them with four bottles of whisky on the table! To the chagrin of the Skyemen the Boleskine manager confiscated them for post-match consumption.

But economic reality put paid to the parties. As the 1920s drew to a close men moved south in search of jobs; the names that graced Skye's postwar teams could now be found in the ranks of the Glasgow Skye club.

And so to today and a Newtonmore team hitting unwonted doldrums, and already twice defeated by Skye in league competition.

'They have a formidable cup record which we ignore at our peril,' says Ross Cowie. 'But we're happy to be out there challenging.' As also no doubt is the Gaelic exodus that will have crossed the ferry from Skye this morning in support, leaving the incomers to look after the tourists for a day.

Who says the faint echo of a 10-volley victory salute won't roll down the generations in Portree tonight?

MARTIN MACDONALD

A NEW NAME ON THE CUP

History was made at An Aird, Fort William, on Saturday 2 June 1990. It was a great day for shinty, and a great day for Skye Camanachd who lifted the coveted Camanachd Cup for the first time in the club's 98-year history.

Before a ball was struck, the match had already created more interest than any final in the recent history of the game. And the estimated 5,000–6,000 spectators who made their way to An Aird, most of them urging on Skye against Camanachd Cup veterans Newtonmore, were treated to a game which in skill and excitement at least lived up to expectations.

WEST HIGHLAND FREE PRESS

Whose Land?

MY OWN, MY NATIVE LAND!

Breathes there the man with soul so dead,
Who never to himself hath said,
This is my own, my native land!
Whose heart hath ne'er within him burn'd
As home his footsteps he hath turn'd,
    From wandering on a foreign strand!
If such there breathe, go, mark him well;
For him no minstrel raptures swell;
High though his titles, proud his name,
Boundless his wealth as wish can claim;
Despite these titles, power, and pelf,
The wretch, concentrated all in self,
Living, shall forfeit fair renown,
And, doubly dying, shall go down
To the vile dust, from whence he sprung,
Unwept, unhonour'd, and unsung.

O Caledonia! stern and wild,
Meet nurse for a poetic child!
Land of brown heath and shaggy wood,
Land of the mountain and the flood,
Land of my sires! what mortal hand
Can e'er untie the filial band
That knits me to thy rugged strand?
Still, as I view each well-known scene,
Think of what is now, and what hath been,
Seems as, to me, of all bereft,
Sole friends thy woods and streams were left;
And thus I love them better still,
Even in extremity of ill.

SIR WALTER SCOTT

from *AN CUILITHIONN*
EARRANN II

A Chuilithinn chreagaich an uamhais
Tha thusa mar rium dh' aindeoin fuathais.
A'cheud la dhìrich mi do mhùr dubh
Shaoil leam am Breitheanas bhith tùirling;
A'cheud la phòg mi do ghruaidh
B'e choimeas fiamh an Tuile Ruaidh;
A'cheud la phòg mi do bhial
Dh'fhosgail Iutharn a dhà ghiall;
A'cheud la laigh mi air d'uchd-sa
Ar leam gum faca mi an luchdadh
Aig na speuran troma, falbhaidh
Gu crith sgriosail na talmhainn.
'S mi ruigheachd roinn-dhruim Bruach na Frìthe
Nochd mi allaidheachd na tìre:
Brat throm, dhubh-dhearg air na neòil,
Doineannachd nan gaoth 'nam beòil.
Mu bhàrr cearcall nan sgùrr iargalt
Fosgladh lachdunn anns an iarmailt
Fo bhrat ìosal, dearg-dhubh, dùmhail
Nan sgóth riabhach, dorcha mùgach,
Coimthional uamhas nan dùilean,
Cruinneachadh nan sian gu lùth-chleas.
Strannaich ghaillionach gach sgalla
Mu na biodan gruamach, allaidh,
Crathadh is crith na h-osaig-éighich
Mu bhaidealan gach creachainn léithe,
Sliosan is sléisdean a' Chuilithinn
Lom, nochdte ri gleachd an fhuirbidh,
Gun de fheòil orra ach an sgàirneach
A thilgeadh comhair a cinn 'na càrnaich
Bho do chruachann 's bho do ghlùinean
Sìos gu grunnd nan glomhar ùdlaidh.
Ris an fhaobairne, Mac Cuilithinn
Cha robh Goll no Fionn no uilebheist
A dheachdadh le macmeanmna daonnda
Ach mar mhìol air druim na daolaig
Ri Cu-chulainn 'na àrm-aodach.

Dé an coimeas glùn no calpa,
Uchd, sliasaid no ghuala thalmhaidh
Ri ballachan nan stalla gruamach
Dubh le deigh no snighe fuaraidh,
Ri uchdaich nam fireach àrda
'Nan creagan uamharra bàrcadh
Mar chìochan-màthar an t-saoghail
Stòite 's an cruinne-cé ri gaoladh.
Chunnaic mi Adharc an Sgùrr Dheirg
Ag éirigh ann an dùbhlan feirg
Anns an deifir bh' air na speuran,
'S 'nan cathadh a thilgeil nan reultan
Trianaid an Sgumain air éirigh.

Air Sgurr Dubh an Dà Bheinn
Thàinig guth gu m' chluais a' seinn,
Pàdraig Mór 's a cheòl ag caoineadh
Uile chlann a' chinne daonna.
Agus feasgar air a' Ghàrsbheinn
Bha ceòl eile ann a thàinig,
Maol Donn agus ùrlar sàth-ghaoil
A' bristeadh cridhe nam fonn àlainn.
Ann an laighe geal na gréine
Bha an áird an iar à toirt do m'léirsinn
Lainnir a' chuain air cùl Bharraidh
'S e 'g iathadh eileanan ar fala;
Agus an t-Eilean mór 'na shiantan
Mar chunnacas le sùil na h-iargain
A nochd Aimereaga 's i 'g iarraidh
Grùla, Brunnal, Dà Chnoc Scarrail,
A bhàrc am plosgartaich na fala,
Diùirinis nan rubhachan àrda,
Minginis a' bhroillich lànmhoir,
Bràcadal bhog nan cìoch-lag àlainn
'Gan nighe le falach-phòig an t-sàile;
Agus Aird mhór Shrath Shuardail,
Sliasaid fhada réidh nam fuar bheann,
Fraoch is feur 'nan leugan shuas oirr'
Mar chiabhan òr-laist ceann mo luaidhe.
'S ag éirigh bho roid Rudha 'n Dùnain
Anns na tlàman geura cùbhraidh
Gaol is bròn tuath na dùthcha
A sgapadh le beairteas an spùillidh.

Air na leathadan uaine
Ceò na h-eachdraidh 'ga shuaineadh,
Cridh, fuil is feòil mo dhaoine
'Nan trom-laighe air na raointean;
Minginis ag crodhadh le chéile
Bhatairnis agus Sléite,
Tròndairnis, Ratharsair is Rònaidh,
Diùirinis, an Srath is Sòghaidh
Anns a' mhiath chiùran còmhla.
Agus trom air suain na frìthe
Cruaidh-chàs is bochdainn nam mìltean
De thuath 's de mhith-shluagh na tìre,
Mo cháirdean is mo chuideachd fhìn iad.
Agus ged nach d' rinn an càs-san
Gaoir ghoirt saoghail na Spàinne
Agus, ged nach d' rinn an dìol-san
Brat fala air aodann na h-iarmailt,
Mar chunnaic Marlowe fuil Chrìosda
Agus Leonhardt fuil Liebknecht,
Agus ged nach d' fhuaradh fios
Air oidhche challa an sgrios,
A ràinig gal saoghail a' bhròin,
Tuiteam nan Asturaidheach 'nan glòir,
B'e 'n càs-san càs nan uile bhochd,
An cruaidh-chàs, a' ghainne is an lochd
On mhealladh ìochdarain gach tìre
Le uachdarain, le stàt 's lagh sìobhalt
Agus leis gach ioma strìopach
a reic an anam air a' phrìs ud
A fhuair gallachan ant-saoghail
On bhuadhaich urrachan na maoine.

SOMHAIRLE MACGILL-EAIN

from THE CUILLIN
PART II

Rocky terrible Cuillin
you are with me in spite of life's horror.
The first day I ascended your black wall
I thought the judgement was descending;
the first day I kissed your cheek
its likeness was the face of the Great Flood;
the first day I kissed your mouth
Hell opened its two jaws;
the first day I lay on your breast
I thought I saw the loading
of the heavy swift skies
for the destructive shaking of the earth.
Reaching the blade-back of Bruach na Frithe
I came in sight of the savageness of the country:
a heavy black-red mantle of the clouds,
the storm winds in their mouths;
about the girdling summits of the awesome scurrs
a dun opening in the firmament
under the low red-black dense pall
of brindled dark surly clouds,
congregation of the horrors of the elements
gathering of the storms for exercise;
hurricane clangour of every blast
about the grim savage pinnacles;
shaking and quivering of the yelling blast
about the battlements of every grey bare-swept summit.
The sides and thighs of the Cuillin
stripped naked for the giant wrestling
with no flesh on them but the scree
thrown headlong in cairns
from hips and knees
down to the depth of the gloomy abysses.
Compared with the giant Son of Cuillin
neither Goll nor Fionn nor monster
devised by man's imagination
was more than a louse on a beetle's back
compared with Cuchulain in his war gear.

What likeness knee or calf,
chest thigh or mortal shoulder
to the ramparts of grim precipices
black with ice or with cold wet ooze,
to the heaving chest of the high mountain bluffs
surging in proud crags
like the mother-breasts of the world
erect with the universe's concupiscence.
I saw the horn of Sgurr Dearg
rising in furious challenge
in the haste of the skies;
and throwing the stars in spindrift
the trinity of the Sguman risen.

On Sgurr Dubh of the Two Hills
a voice came to my ear singing
Patrick Mor and his music mourning
all the children of mankind;
and an evening on the Garsven
there was another music that came,
'Maol Donn' and its theme of love-fullness
breaking the hearts of lovely tunes.
In the white lying down of the sun
the west gave to my sight
the gleam of seas behind Barra
going round the islands of our blood
and the great Island in its storm-showers
as seen by the homesick eye
that looked upon America while it desired
Grula, Brunnal, and the two Hills of Scarral
that surged in the pulsations of the blood;
Duirinish of the high headlands,
Minginish of the abundant breast,
soft Bracadale of the lovely pap hollows
washed by the hidden kiss of the sea;
and the great Aird of Strath Swordale
the long smooth thigh of the cold mountains
on which heather and grass lie high in jewels
like the clustered gold-lit hair of my beloved.
Rising from the bog-myrtle of Rudha an Dunain
in sharp fragrant wafts
the love and grief of the peasants of the land
scattered for exploiters' wealth;

on the green hill-slopes
the mists of history wound,
the heart, blood and flesh of my people
in a nightmare on the fields:
Minginish gathering into a fold
Waternish and Sleat,
Trotternish, Raasay and Rona,
Duirinish, the Strath and Soay
In the soft smirr of rain.
And heavy on the slumber of the moorland
the hardship and poverty of the thousands
of crofters and the lowly of the lands,
my kin and my own people.
And though their fate did not make
the sore world cry of Spain;
and through their dispensation did not make
a mantle of blood on the face of the firmament,
as Marlowe saw the blood of Christ
and Leonhardt the blood of Liebknecht,
and though no news came
of their destruction's night
to reach the world agony of grief,
the fall of the Asturians in their glory,
their lot was the lot of all poor people,
hardship, want and injury,
ever since the humble of every land
were deceived by ruling-class, State and Civil Law,
and by every prostitute
who sold their souls for that price
that the bitches of the world have earned
since the great people of wealth have triumphed.

SORLEY MACLEAN

JOHNSON AND MACLEOD OF DUNVEGAN

We had a fine sail this day. There cannot be a finer harbour than the basin which we saw sheltered from every wind. MacLeod showed us an arm of the sea which runs up with very deep water for a mile, upon which he intends to build a town. We sailed up another arm. The shore was varied with hills and rocks and cornfields, and natural wood or bushes. We landed near to the house of Fernilea. He himself was waiting on the shore, with a horse for Mr Johnson. The rest of us walked up. We found at Fernilea a very comfortable house. His wife is daughter to Bernera. When I took off my *scalck*, with hearty readiness he said, 'Fare fa' you!'* His parlour was paved with flagstones, not in squares, but just in the shapes which they naturally had in the quarry. I liked this better. It had more variety. I preferred it by the same rule that Mr Johnson prefers the variety of the English conclusions of letters to the common style, 'I am, etc.' We had here an excellent dinner, in particular a remarkable leg of boiled mutton with turnips and carrots. MacLeod has really shown us a chief and his clan. We saw some of them with him at Dunvegan. We now saw him with some of them. On both sides there was the most agreeable kindness. I expressed to MacLeod the joy which I had in seeing this. Said he, 'Government has deprived us of our ancient power, but it cannot deprive us of our domestic satisfactions. I would rather drink a bottle of punch in one of their houses' (meaning his people) 'than a bottle of claret in my own.' Here he said at once what every chieftain should think. All that he can get by raising his rents is more luxury in his own house. Is it not far better to share the profits of his estate to a certain degree with his kinsmen, and so have both social intercourse and patriarchal influence? Fernilea seemed to be a worthy, sensible, kind man.

JAMES BOSWELL

* 'Fair fall you.' Burns, *To a Haggis*: 'Fair fa' your honest, sonsie face.' In *fare*, Boswell may be attempting to reproduce a Hebridean pronunciation, or he may have confused the word with the first syllable of *farewell*.

MR REA AND HIS COLLEAGUE CRAIG LEARN ABOUT FISHING RIGHTS

We had the whole day before us; consequently there was no need for us to hasten on our way, so we talked and smoked, as we strolled along; now and then the ground, rising a little, gave us a glimpse of the blue, summer sea; we stopped at times to gather some of the rarer flowers or to listen to the carolling of the skylarks, or to watch the flight of heron, plover, hawk, or of the skua.

Some two miles had been covered when Craig, who was a short way ahead, stopped and stood looking downwards, at the same time giving to us a low call 'Come here'. Quietly hastening to his side we found that he was looking intently into a stream that was running towards the sea, and directly across our path. The stream was about six or seven feet in width and running in a clean-cut channel across the 'machair'. At first I did not see what he was gazing at; then I became aware that hundreds and hundreds of trout were rushing inland up the stream; they were so closely packed that the water seemed scarcely sufficient to contain them. We all three stood silently watching them as they sped past us at our feet: all sizes of fish from a foot to three or four feet in length were hurrying madly upstream: so thick were they in the water that even the big fish seemed to find difficulty in getting past their smaller brethren and, by sheer strength and their weight, they forced their way through the packs of speeding fish.

We stood watching them for nearly an hour, and still then the stream was packed as full of them—there must have been thousands of them—I remember remarking to my companions: 'We could almost walk across the stream on their backs!' Craig, at last, gave a deep breath and said in a voice full of feeling: 'Well, boy and man I have fished the eastern rivers of Scotland, from the Ythan to the Tweed, but I have never seen such a sight as this before.' Alasdair told us that this stream was an effluent of the Howmore River and these waters were strictly watched and preserved for the sport of the proprietor and his friends. He had often seen the trout ascending the stream, but he had never seen them in such numbers before. Here we had to part with our friend; so, giving one last look at the fine fish we so much coveted, we each stepped back a few paces, took a run forward and leapt the stream. Not trusting ourselves to look into it again we waved to Alasdair and resumed our way homeward.

A few days later, meeting the factor, he was interested in my account of the stream packed with rushing fish. He said that we should have got into serious trouble had we attempted to interfere with the fish. I asked him whether anyone had been able to obtain permission to fish the Howmore River. 'Only once,' was the reply. He then told me that one of the anglers at the hotel, a very rich man from London who came every year for the fishing, had often importuned him to try and get him permission from the proprietor to fish the river, but though the landowner was so seldom on the island, permission was always refused by him when approached. The London man told the factor that he would not mind what he paid, and he told the factor to ask the proprietor how much he would take for a permit for a week's fishing on the river. So, on the next occasion that the landlord was leaving the island the factor spoke to him on the matter again. 'Oh! Choke him off and tell him that I should want £200,' was the reply. When the man from London heard of this, he was delighted and paid the money cheerfully. 'And it was well worth it,' was the verdict of this angler after his week's fishing.

FG REA

Note. There was no big farmer called MacLeod in South Uist in Rea's time. He must either have forgotten the right name, or be trying to conceal the person's identity.

ISLAND FARM

I cannot well describe my own feelings that night and shortly afterwards when the deeds were finally transferred. Now, a little while before I was thirty-five, an island property had become a fact, a bare fact in truth, but the place was there and our own. We owned part of one of the British Isles and at least a quarter of a mile of British coastline. Ownership of land in Scotland consists of two parts, the superiority and the *dominium utile*. A superior may sell the *dominium utile* for the full worth of the land and still retain the valuable superiority which gives him the title 'of' So-and-so, which means much in Scotland, and the right to charge the owner of the *dominium utile* a feu duty. The superiority of Tigh an Quay is worth £2. 10s. a year. This means nothing at all monetarily as long as we continue to live in the place, but had we not had the superiority granted to us we should have had to pay Dundonnell the £2.10s. each year.

But to come back to my feelings: there was this exultation of ownership of land of our very own, won after a period of years of intense longing; and there was a more defensible emotion of gratitude. I have taken the path in life of not accumulating worldly goods, of actually choosing poverty in return for the right to live as I wish. I believe that to take joy in gathering riches is bad and exultation in ownership is bad. Yet here was I exulting, and I asked myself how it squared with my philosophy of life. Land, land; what it has meant to me and my family! A fierce love of land above all other riches, and a pride in the ownership of good animals. I should be just as high-chested about a herd of cattle (if I had bred them myself) as about the land on which they fed. Land and stock are in a category by themselves. All this I feel deeply, but if I consider the subject objectively I cannot defend my feeling. It is primitive and not abreast of man's spiritual development, and yet there is undoubtedly a voice inside me which says, 'Never you mind, me lad, it may be primitive, but it's good common sense.' The very fact that I love land so dearly is sufficient reason for my renouncing it. I overcame that first exultation very quickly, or perhaps it passed of itself, being mere froth, and Bobbie and I have both been left with the enduring feeling that ownership is really custodianship. I have always said that this should be the attitude to ownership of land, but now I do more than state it academically, I feel it through and through. That custodianship is not merely for Alasdair, whose name is in the deeds as heir to Tigh an Quay, not merely for the British nation, but for posterity. We have become more and more humble in our tiny ownership and are grateful for the chance of work it offers.

F FRASER DARLING

THE LAIRD

You stride on, wearing the trappings of their toil,
Wearing your assumptions lightly,
Telling others what is right, what due,
And what is worse, imagining you know,
And by a mental sleight, to see
In the age-old submission,
A proper deference, a seemly order.
Supremely happy in your blithe assumptions
Of blithe untruths.

Your dress, your speech, your style,
Your mannered ill-manners to the lower orders,
Making your money talk for you,
Not talking yourself, or if you do,
To fool yourself the more.
Surprised, hurt even at reaction,
Angry at reply, and arrogant
Above all knowledge.
Disallowing others the pride
You so unassumingly allow yourself.

Discounting truth
With unwarrantable presuppositions
Of order, right, propriety,
The just deserts of effort.
Imagining yourself seeing, all-seeing,
But your sight is barred
By the myopic vision of your subconscious
Whose inverted optics deliberately deny
The unpleasant premises of your rule.

DENIS RIXSON

THE HIGHLAND CROFTER

Frae Kenmore tae Ben More
The land is a' the Marquis's;
The mossy howes, the heathery knowes
An' ilka bonnie park is his;
The bearded goats, the towsie stots,
An' a' the braxie carcases;
Ilk crofter's rent, ilk tinkler's tent,
An ilka collie's bark is his;
The muir-cock's craw, the piper's blaw,
The ghillie's hard day's wark is his;
Frae Kenmore tae Ben More
The warld is a' the Marquis's.

The fish that swim, the birds that skim,
The fir, the ash, the birk is his;
The Castle ha' sae big and braw,
Yon diamond-crusted dirk is his;
The roofless hame, a burning shame,
The factor's dirty wark is his;
The poor folk vexed, the lawyer's text,
Yon smirking legal shark is his;
Frae Kenmore tae Ben More
The warld is a' the Marquis's.

But near, mair near, God's voice we hear—
The dawn as weel's the dark is His;
The poet's dream, the patriot's theme,
The fire that lights the mirk is His.
They clearly show God's mills are slow
But sure the handiwork is His;
And in His grace our hope we place;
Fair Freedom's sheltering ark is His.
The men that toil should own the soil—
A note as clear's the lark is this—
Breadalbane's land–the fair, the grand—
Will no' be aye the Marquis's.

                                        ANON

JOHN MACDONALD, CROFTER, SOUTH DELL (57)—EXAMINED

15738. *The Chairman.*—Where is South Dell?—About three miles west of this.

15739. Were you freely elected by the people?—Yes.

15740. Have you got a statement to make?—Regarding their poverty, I have more than time will allow me to tell. You have heard already of the small holdings and the very high rents, and I need not enter into details on that matter. They are very poor. Some are in want of food. That is their sorest cry. The land is so heavily burdened that it cannot yield crop, and just as that is the case the land that is pastured on by the sheep is, as it were, crying out to be cultivated. We complain of the heavy assessments. The schools are a very great burden upon us. We were not used to that burden, and our poverty scarcely can bear it well. We prefer the schools we had before. Our objection to the present mode of education is that the rule which the Almighty has given us for our salvation is treated as a boy plays at 'skippack,'—just a slap and be done with it. . . .

15743. Do they learn the Shorter Catechism?—A small portion at the beginning—the easy bit.

15744. Do they learn it in English or learn it in Gaelic?—Oh! what but English, that they don't understand.

15745. Do they learn to read the Bible in Gaelic?—No, not at all.

15760. You complain about the school rate being so heavy. Now the minister told us yesterday that if all the children in the parish went to school the Government grant would be so large that there would scarcely be any rate at all. Have you ever been told that?—Yes, I heard that, but every person in this district is not a minister, and as such, able to shoe his children so that they can go to school.

15761. But the children all over Scotland, at least in many parts, go to school without shoes?—That is the case. There is no man here who is more anxious that children should be educated than I am, but I see clearly that cannot be done.

15766. How many people are now living in your township?—Forty-five.

15767. Were you born there?—No.

15768. How long have you been there?—Fourteen years.

15769. How many were there fourteen years ago?—Forty-one.

15770. Do you know how many were there fifty years ago?—
Thirty.   15771. Do you complain of being over-crowded as well as of
high rent?—Yes, we are.

15772. Do you know about the people who were removed from
Galston?—I ought to. I was born there, and my ancestors lived there.

15773. What was the name of the town you lived in?—North
Galston.

15774. How many families were removed from that town?—There
were over sixty of them. Fifty-four paid rent.

15775. Were there any more townships cleared besides North
Galston?—Other three.

15776. Name them?—Balmeanach, Melbost, and South Galston. In
Balmeanach there were ten families, in Melbost twenty-five, and in
South Galston thirteen.

15777. Were these removed at one time, or did it run over several
years—Over several years.

15778. How long altogether?—Would it take ten years?—They
were removed at intervals during a period of twelve years.

15779. How long is it since the last clearance?—Twenty years ago.

15780. Was the whole of this done in Sir James Matheson's time?—
The whole of it, and without his knowledge.

15781. Was it all done under the one chamberlain?—No.

15782. Who were the two?—Mr Murdo Mackenzie to begin with,
and then Mr Munro.

15783. What was done with the land from which these families
were cleared?—It was given to the tacksman.

15784. Was it the case that as each successive clearance took place
the tack was enlarged?—Yes, that was the case.

15785. Were you well off when you were living at North Galston?—
I could not ask to be better off.

15786. Was that the case with your co-crofters generally at the
time?—Almost the whole of them were so at first, but at a later period
the tenants of South Galston were added on to them, and then they
were not so well off.

15787. There seem to have been 108 families altogether,—we shall
say upwards of 100. What became of those families?—About forty of
them went to America. The rest was scattered all over the country.

15788. Was it against their will that they were put out of Galston?—
Yes, it was against our will, but we went away without being summoned.

15789. Was it for the benefit of the Galston people that they were
turned out in this way and went some to America, and some to other
places?—I don't know one who benefited by it except one family.

HIGHLANDS AND ISLANDS COMMISSION

CRUAIDH?

Cuil-lodair, is Briseadh na h-Eaglaise,
is briseadh nan tacannan-
làmhachas-làidir dà thrian de ar coms;
's e seòltachd tha dhìth oirnn.
Nuair a theirgeas a' chruaidh air faobhar na speala
caith bhuat a' chlach-lìomhaidh;
chan eil agad ach iarann bog
mur eil de chruas nad innleachd na nì sgathadh.

Is caith bhuat briathran mìne
oir chan fhada bhios briathran agad;
tha Tuatha Dè Danann fon talamh,
tha Tìr nan Og anns an Fhraing,
's nuair a ruigeas tu Tìr a' Gheallaidh,
mura bi thu air t'aire,
coinnichidh Sasannach riut is plìon air,
a dh'innse dhut gun tug Dia, brathair athar, còir dha anns an fhearann.

RUARAIDH MACTHÒMAIS

STEEL

Culloden, the Disruption,
and the breaking up of the tack-farms—
two thirds of our power is violence;
it is cunning we need.
When the tempered steel near the edge of the scythe-blade is worn
throw away the whetstone;
you have nothing left but soft iron
unless your intellect has a steel edge that will cut clean.

And throw away soft words,
for soon you will have no words left;
the *Tuatha De Danann** are underground,
the Land of the Ever-Young is in France,
and when you reach the Promised Land,
unless you are on your toes,
a bland Englishman will meet you,
and say to you that God, his uncle, has given him a title to the land.

DERICK THOMSON

*Tuatha De Danann, a supernatural race in Ireland, sometimes said tc be the progenitors of the fairies.

COUNTRY LIFE

GOD DAMN this earth, when not alive
with stones, it's bog, and always greedy
for dung. there aren't cows here
to shit a breakfast for spiky acres
that clamour for feast.

not since the great war
have i had peace. each year
this place commits me
to trench warfare
and what i win, i lose.

it broke my beth, long time ago, it drove
our sons away. she's dead
who with me made that dyke
with stones we broke
from tillage.
            and still the wind
lays flat the half-ripe corn,
                    and still
it's stony ground,
and still, each year i scrape
a few potatoes from among the stones

and now that man
in the big black shining limousine, he says
            the land
is his, whom i've never seen
before. he wants to rob
me of over fifty years
of sweat and pain.

this is the only war i know, how can i
make him understand
i am too old for armistice.

AONGHAS MACNEACAIL

KEEP AFF THE GIRSS

Ye ken hou thae Gaelic place-names discryve the places?
Aweill, Ah speir'd of a man that nas the Gaelic,
whit wad be the names, wad dae fir thon estate:
to win thair, ken, ye oar owre Loch Private,
or soom owre the River Keep Out,
syne ye're at liberty to sclimm Ben Nae Trespassing,
and if ye see a rabbit, or a bit stag,
juist mind it's no yours, nor Gode's;
it langs til Lord Muck of that ilk,
or til a London company, mair like,
Wad ye believe it?
He cuidnae gie me the word fir *Private*,
and Gaelic had niver heard tell of *Trespassing*.
The anerlie word of that naitur,
sae he tellt me,
was niver yaised, binna fir yae thing:
to fence the Heathen out of Free-Kirk prayer-meetings.

ROBERT GARIOCH

A QUESTION

A question which must be asked is the effect of the land raids on Highland land settlement. It was claimed in the islands that the illegal seizure of land was the one sure way of getting it, and this was absolutely true, no matter how often the Scottish Office denied it. But this must be seen in the light of the post-First World War situation. Although on a small scale land raids had proved an effective weapon before the war, it was the enormous public sympathy for the men who had survived the appalling carnage of the war which gave the land raids their enormous impact. The constant stress on the promise of land to men when they returned from the war made public pressure impossible for the government to withstand.

What about this promise then? The powerful land hunger in the Highlands and Islands was certainly capitalised on by recruiting agents at the outbreak of the First World War, and there is no doubt that the pledge of land for men who served their country in the war was an intrinsic part of government policy. It is clear that as early as 1915 legislation was being prepared to fulfil that pledge. The Coalition Government's election manifesto after the armistice reiterated this promise, and even those like the K & LTR who loathed the policy never doubted that the government was honour-bound to fulfil its pledge. The impossibility of providing a holding for every ex-serviceman who wanted one was never faced up to.

Did ex-servicemen believe the promise made when they enlisted? Certainly the memory has remained. In the 1970s a man in Tiree said: 'The land was promised to the boys when they joined the First World War. When they would come back they would get land. Anybody who had so much, the land would be taken from him and given to the ex-servicemen.' However, HM Conacher shrewdly observed that the war had simply given Highlanders 'a new "formula" to be used in support of their claims'.

LEAH LENEMAN

WHAT WE WANT IS THE LAND

And it was at this point that Leverhulme's ambitions and those of Lewis' large landless population came into—as it proved—irreconcilable conflict: a conflict beautifully preserved in this account, by one of the Board of Agriculture's representatives, of a meeting between Lord Leverhulme and a group of his dissident tenantry. Leverhulme is addressing the crowd:

And then there appeared in the next few minutes the most graphic word picture it is possible to imagine—a great fleet of fishing boats—a large fish-canning factory (already started)—railways—an electric power station; then one could see the garden city grow—steady work, steady pay, beautiful houses for all—every modern convenience and comfort. The insecurity of their present income was referred to; the squalor of their present houses deftly compared with the conditions in the new earthly paradise. Altogether it was a masterpiece; and it produced its effect; little cheers came involuntarily from a few here and there—more cheers!—general cheers!! . . .

And just then, while the artist was still adding skilful detail, there was a dramatic interruption.

One of the ringleaders managed to rouse himself from the spell, and in an impassioned voice addressed the crowd in Gaelic, and this is what he said:

'*So so, fhiribh! Cha dean so gnotach! Bheireadh am bodach mil-bheulach sin chreidsinn oirnn gu 'm bheil dubh geal 's geal dubh! Ciod e dhuinn na bruadairean briagha aige, a thig no nach tig? 'Se am fearann tha sinn ag iarraidh. Agus 'se tha mise a faighneachd* (turning to face Lord Leverhulme and pointing dramatically towards him): *an toir thu dhuinn am fearann?'* The effect was electrical. The crowd roared their approbation.

Lord Leverhulme looked bewildered at this, to him, torrent of unintelligible sounds, but when the frenzied cheering with which it was greeted died down he spoke.

'I am sorry! It is my great misfortune that I do not understand the Gaelic language. But perhaps my interpreter will translate for me what has been said?'

Said the interpreter: 'I am afraid, Lord Leverhulme, that it will be impossible for me to convey to you in English what has been so forcefully said in the older tongue; but I will do my best'—and his best was a masterpiece, not only in words but in tone and gesture and general effect:

'Come, come, men! This will not do! This honeymouthed man would have us believe that black is white and white is black. We are not concerned with his fancy dreams that may or may not come true. What we want is the *land*—and the question I put to him now is: *will you give us the land?*'

The translation evoked a further round of cheering. A voice was heard to say:

'Not so bad for a poor language like the English!'

Lord Leverhulme's picture, so skilfully painted was shattered in the artist's hand!

JAMES HUNTER

A FUTURE FOR CROFTING

A nation's survival as a free, independent, and self-respecting entity hangs on the ability of its people to nourish and protect themselves; to provide the means of building and maintaining healthy minds in healthy bodies, and to develop the enterprise, resilience, and determination to surmount natural disasters and adapt to ever-changing conditions.

These introductory sentences to a practical manual for the would-be smallholder were not written in 1905 but in 1985. Although this sounds more like a bugle call to bygone values than the genuine reveille of a new generation of smallholders, that author is not alone in his belief that in years to come more and more people will again wish to return to the land. Disenchantment with cities, urban overcrowding and unemployment, and a simple wish to breathe fresh country air are leading many to try their luck at small scale agriculture, and indeed there is now a helpful journal called *The Smallholder*. If this trend continues then there are many lessons to be learned from the land settlement experience of the first half of the century.

LEAH LENEMAN

A FEELING FOR THE LAND

Unfortunately, many people persist in thinking of crofting as simply some sort of primitive farming activity. True, agriculture is a major part of crofting, but it is by no means the sole component. Most of Scotland's 18,000 or so crofts are worked on a part-time, or even spare-time basis. The crofters who work them are involved in an enormous variety of other professions, from the traditional weaving and fishing industries to Local Authority jobs, bankers, mechanics, shop-keepers, electricians, and so on.

You would indeed find it hard to expose an occupation which, given the motivation, is incompatible with running a croft. In this situation it is the full-time crofter who is the most disadvantaged, neither big enough to compete on an equal footing with the larger mainland producers, nor small enough to permit taking on a regular job to supplement the croft income.

The link-pin in this social system is the access to the land and its security of tenure. Traditionally, many crofts were subdivided longitudinally among the surviving members of a family, to give each descendant a piece of the moor, a piece of the good blackland, a piece of the machair, and so on.

This practice is no longer legal, but it has left a patchwork of essentially independent, small family units. These crofts were never meant to support the family without additional employment (usually provided by the landlord) but they were, and still are, able to contribute to the family diet, and, by selling the surplus, to the family income.

But where does conservation stand in all this? There is no doubt that much of the variety and types of wildlife species which make the crofting lands so attractive to conservationists stems directly from the nature of crofting land-use itself. The low intensity, low input, low output style of agricultural activity is less harsh on the natural environment than large-scale factory farming. The small-scale, compartmentalised structure of croftland also means that a wide variety of wildlife habitats exist in a very small geographical area.

Permanent grassland, turnips, potatoes, hay/silage and heather moorland all support subtly different communities of species, which in turn provide food and shelter for higher organisms. The fact that crops are not saturated with weedkillers sprayed from tractors with boom mounts (in many cases because the fields are too rough and/or small for heavy machinery to operate), is healthier both for humans and wildlife. Even where weedkillers and fertilisers are used, they are usually applied using knapsack sprayers and on such a small scale that to compare crofting with modern mechanised farming is spurious and farcical.

One common concern is the question of getting more cattle back onto the land. In Lewis and Harris, one of the bastions of the crofting culture, there were nearly 15,000 cattle and 78,000 sheep in 1911, a cattle/sheep ratio of 1:5. By 1986 there were 720 cattle and 113,000 sheep, a ratio of 1:158. The IDP can claim to have halted the decline temporarily, but it would be rash to expect too much from this.

There is a strange law on the Statute Books that prohibits a crofter from qualifying for suckler cow premium payments if more than 50 per cent of his income does not come directly from the croft. Crofters with a full-time job (as most of us are), or even a good part-time one, are immediately debarred. It would create unimaginable havoc if this precedent was extended to the non-agricultural activities of farmers as well, and it clearly flies in the face of the government's rhetoric on agricultural diversification.

As well as the potential income to the stockholder, the environmental benefits from cattle can be substantial. A good grazing mix of one cow for every four or five sheep gives a far greater diversity of herbs and flowering plants. On the lime-rich machair grasslands of the west coast and Western Islands, cattle have ensured a rich botanical interest and have helped to keep down pest species such as butterburr (*Petasites hybridus*) by crushing the large leaves underfoot.

It is obvious that the spread of this plant is most virulent in areas devoid of cattle. On the damper areas of the machair, the footprints made by the browsing cattle are frequently used for shelter by delicate wader chicks before fledging: a complex mixture of nature benefiting through man's exploitation.

Not so the interface between crofting and forestry. Archie Gillespie, a former member of the Scottish Land Court, has described the wholesale loss of crofting land to blanket forestry as the biggest threat to these communities since the clearances.

The loss of croftland is the biggest worry, though, for once it has been removed from crofting tenure there is no way under the present legal structure that this land can ever be returned to crofting. Compare the diversity—ecological, social, and economic—between a thriving crofting community in Lewis and a mono-use mainland estate. Whether it is under forestry or simply grouse-moor you must surely deplore the continued erosion in the stock of croftland and, like me, seek legislation to permit the creation of more croftlands.

With the continuing fall in farm profits it would seem only natural to divide at least some of these estates and large farms into croft-sized units and to encourage families to settle on them. This view has been echoed by John MacDonald, Chairman of the East Sutherland Area of the SCU, who said: 'I want to make clear my own view that no trees should ever be planted on much of the Flow Country. That landscape is a precious, living thing. But all around it there are empty places where our people used to live. I see no reason why they shouldn't be able to live there again'.

There is a good case to be made that development schemes which revitalise and strengthen crofting land-use patterns are also good for the natural environment. We have meddled with the landscape too much for it to be left simply to look after itself, and healthy rural communities in sympathy with the land are our only real hope for a healthy natural environment.

FRANK RENNIE

BEN COUTTS, FARMER

Alan Wright   Ben, where did your love of the land come from?

Ben Coutts   Probably from my grandfather who was a crofter's son . . .
My father always loved the hills dearly and to his dying day did
a lot of walking in them. I never thought of anything else but
farming, I just adored the land . . . it's a way of life. There's
something about struggling with nature. You remember 1985
when we'd that ghastly summer. I remember 1947, that terrible
winter. You know these things, you come up against it and you
find it's not just yourself. In business nowadays when you're
working with computers and figures you can do a lot with these
but when you're working with the land you're up against a
challenge the whole time and I love it. Living in the country, to
me, is life. It's not all beer and skittles. I was coming back in the
car the other night from Crieff and popping along the country
road as I always do and heard on my wireless that there was a
queue of five miles on the M4 and a queue of six miles on the
M6. I thanked God literally that I was sitting and living where I
was. The reason townies think it's as much theirs as those of us
who work there is that they have this feeling of democracy—
what's mine is yours and we have as much right as the other
person. Which is a pity in a way because it's so essential that we
in the farming industry, in the nicest possible way, instruct
people from the urban population on how they should behave.
We love seeing them if they behave. When I had the farm I'd a
mile on a B-road. Along that mile every Autumn my old man
and I used to collect a bogey load of rubbish—tins and bottles,
plastic, paper, fish and chip things. How sad! Why can't they
take their rubbish home? All that sort of thing, people wandering in through sheep with their dog. 'Little Fifi never looks at a
sheep, she wouldn't dream of it.' What they don't realise is that
sheep, because of the way they're bred, think of dogs as
relations of wolves. If they see a dog they push off in a corner
and if they're very heavily in lamb it can do these sheep an
awful lot of harm. Stop things like that, but if they behave we
love seeing them.

AW   In Scotland we have enjoyed more or less freedom of access so long as we're not destroying a graining crop. We can pretty much walk where we like. We don't have the antagonisms they have in England about bridal paths and foothpaths and things like that.

BC   The main reason, as you know, is that we don't have as many people up here as they do in the South. We don't have the antagonisms. It's only a small percentage that make it bad for the rest. I managed the Blackmount Estate up in the Bridge of Orchy for the Fleming family, the bankers, for 25 years. It's a great stalking estate, a beautiful part of the country. Old Major Fleming, before he died, said he'd had only one stalk spoilt and it wasn't even then completely spoilt. He'd been there from 1923 until he died, a good 50 years. Nowadays the West Highland Way has gone through—a marvellous idea. People get out of Glasgow, Liverpool and all these big cities and come and walk up that lovely country from Loch Lomond right up to Fort William—and it goes bang through Blackmount Estate. Ninety-nine per cent of the people behave superbly: 1 per cent have to push off the West Highland Way and go into the hills to see what it's all about. We've a big notice up saying, Please, if you're walking between the dates of the stalking, about 10 August–20 October, please tell the stalker. It tells you where his house is and all the rest. But that 1 per cent don't bother, it's sad, they spoil it for the rest. Major Fleming was a lovely man, he always used to say, 'I love seeing people enjoy themselves'. He never turned anybody off that Estate in all the years that I looked after it for him. And his son is doing the same thing. There are hundreds of nice landlords. Again it's just a small percentage of landlords who spoil it for the rest.

INTERVIEW WITH ALAN WRIGHT FOR BBC RADIO SCOTLAND

OBSERVATIONS FROM BEN COUTTS' DIARY

In every walk of life there have always been different sorts in the landed gentry class. Highland Estates especially have depended on money from other sources to prime the pump so to speak. In my time I have seen Glasgow ship-building money, Bristol tobacco money, London banking money etc. In fact in the Highlands they said 'where there's a will they're away'. All kinds of money have been pumped into the rural economy, and a dashed good thing too. Now we have

German, Dutch and French money flooding in as Europeans realise what a lovely countryside we have and how good our sport can be. A constant change of ownership from all sources. but it was ever thus.

But through all this change there has run a seam of Scottish Lairds who have lived on their Estates and run them from home. Among the bigger ones the Buccleuchs and Douglas Homes in the Borders and the Lochiels and Lovats in the Highlands and many more besides. But the interesting change to me is how the young modern lairds are training themselves to run their family Estates. One of the curses of the pre-war and just post-war days was that the laird's son went to an English Public school then possibly Oxbridge and in later days Cirencester; came home with a pair of cricket pads, green wellie boots and a yearning to go back South to the flesh pots, but had lost the touch to manage his men, with perhaps the exception of the head keeper or stalker. But this is changing rapidly and I think one of the reasons is the ease of transport to Australia and New Zealand. Why? because in my young day it took weeks not hours to get there, and if a young man went out there he usually stayed out there, whereas now he goes out, learns to work with stock, and be one of Jock Tamson's bairns—for there is no doffing of bonnets out there—and he'll probably wonder if he has a father or mother as their term of endearment questions one's parentage.

I had reason to meet one of these modern lairds last week when I went to see his mother's Highland ponies, one of the few studs left that are genuinely reared on hill ground, consequently slower to mature, but as a result famed for their longevity. This young laird knew his sheep, was building a new shed along with his two men, was telling a fencer where he wanted the fence to go and during the hour I was in the house was booking in someone for the salmon fishing and arranging for their Australian help to go to a local ceilidh by talking on christian name terms to the organiser. In fact a laird who knew his job and was acceptable in the district. What a change, and for the better. And most important of all are the modern lairds' wives, no longer house proud but lambers, calvers, ghillies, cooks, mothers and general supporters. Although only a laird of few acres, I've got one too. God bless her!

BEN COUTTS

29 Private—No Hill Walking. Photograph Sam Maynard/Eolas
Photography.

from A MAN IN ASSYNT

Glaciers, grinding West, gouged out
these valleys, rasping the brown sandstone,
and left, on the hard rock below—the
ruffled foreland—
this frieze of mountains, filed
on the blue air—Stac Polly,
Cul Beag, Cul Mor, Suilven,
Canisp—a frieze and
a litany.

Who owns this landscape?
Has owning anything to do with love?
For it and I have a love-affair, so nearly human
we even have quarrels.—
When I intrude too confidently
it rebuffs me with a wind like a hand
or puts in my way
a quaking bog or a loch
where no loch should be. Or I turn stonily
away, refusing to notice
the rouged rocks, the mascara
under a dripping ledge, even
the tossed, the stony limbs waiting.

I can't pretend
it gets sick for me in my absence,
though I get
sick for it. Yet I love it
with special gratitude, since
it sends me no letters, is never
jealous and, expecting nothing
from me, gets nothing but
cigarette packets and footprints.

Who owns this landscape—
The millionaire who bought it or
the poacher staggering downhill in the early morning
with a deer on his back?

Who possesses this landscape?—
The man who bought it or
I who am possessed by it?
False questions, for
this landscape is
masterless
and intractable in any terms
that are human.
It is docile only to the weather
and its indefatigable lieutenants—
wind, water and frost.
The wind whets the high ridges
and stunts silver birches and alders.
Rain falling down meets
springs gushing up—
they gather and carry down to the Minch
tons of sour soil, making bald
the bony scalp of Cul Mor. And frost
thrusts his hand in cracks and, clenching his fist,
bursts open the sandstone plates,
the armour of Suilven:
he bleeds stones down chutes and screes,
smelling of gunpowder.

Or has it come to this,
that this dying landscape belongs
to the dead, the crofters and fighters
and fishermen whose larochs
sink into the bracken
by Loch Assynt and Loch Crocach?—
to men trampled under the hoofs of sheep
and driven by deer to
the ends of the earth—to men whose loyalty
was so great it accepted their own betrayal
by their own chiefs and whose descendants now
are kept in their place
by English businessmen and the indifference
of a remote and ignorant government.

Where have they gone, the people
who lived between here and
Quinag, that tall
huddle of anvils that puffs out

two ravens into the blue and
looks down on the lochs of Stoer
where trout idle among reeds and
waterlilies—take one of them home
and smell, in a flower
the sepulchral smell of water.

Beyond Fewin lies the Veyatie Burn—fine
crossing place for deer, they trot over
with frills of water flouncing
at their knees. That water rests in Fewin
beneath the sandstone hulk
of Suilven, not knowing what's to come—
the clattering horserush down
the Kirkaig gorge, the sixty-foot
Falls . . . There are twenty-one pools
on the Kirkaig . . . Since
before empires were possible
till now, when so many have died
in their own dust,
the Kirkaig Falls have been walking backwards—
twenty-one paces up their own stream.
Salmon lie
in each of the huge footprints.
You can try to catch them—
at a price.
The man whose generations of ancestors
fished this, their own river,
can catch them still—
at a price . . .

Greenshank, adder, wildcat, guillemot, seatrout,
fox and falcon—the list winds through
all the crooks and crannies of this landscape, all
the subtleties and shifts of its waters and
the prevarications of its air—
while roofs fall in, walls crumble, gables
die last of all, and man becomes,
in this most beautiful corner of the land,
one of the rare animals.
Up there, the scraping light
whittles the cloud edges till, like thin bone,
they're bright with their own opaque selves. Down here,

a skinny rosebush is an eccentric jug
of air. They make me,
somewhere between them,
a visiting eye,
an unrequited passion,
watching the tide glittering backward and making
its huge withdrawal from beaches
and kilted rocks. And the mind
behind the eye, within the passion,
remembers with certainty that the tide will return
and thinks, with hope, that that other ebb,
that sad withdrawal of people, may, too,
reverse itself and flood
the bays and the sheltered glens
with new generations replenishing the land
with its richest of riches and coming, at last,
into their own again.

NORMAN MACCAIG

30 'Master of all he Surveys', Cartoon by Christ Tyler.
*A company based in Northampton is offering Americans the chance to become
a 'laird' in Wester Ross for $29. . . . . This will give them title to a one square
foot plot of land and details of the 'exact location' will be forwarded along with
a photograph.*

Land and 'The Seeing Eye'

SCOTLAND SMALL?

Scotland Small? Our multiform, our infinite Scotland *small?*
Only as a patch of hillside may be a cliché corner
To a fool who cries 'Nothing but heather!' where in September another
Sitting there and resting and gazing round
Sees not only the heather but blaeberries
With bright green leaves and leaves already turned scarlet
Hiding ripe blue berries; and amongst the sage-green leaves
Of the bog-myrtle the golden flowers of the tormentil shining;
And on the small bare places, where the little Blackface sheep
Found grazing, milkworts blue as summer skies;
And down in neglected peat-hags, not worked
Within living memory, sphagnum moss in pastel shades
Of yellow, green, and pink; sundew and butterwort
Waiting with wide-open sticky leaves for their tiny winged prey;
And nodding harebells vying in their colour
With the blue butterflies that poise themselves delicately upon them;
And stunted rowans with harsh dry leaves of glorious colour.
'Nothing but heather!'—How marvellously descriptive! And
   incomplete!

HUGH MACDIARMID

LANDSCAPE AND THE SEEING EYE

Now it is the peculiar character of Scottish as distinct from all other
scenery on a small scale in north Europe, to have these distinctively
'mindable' features. One range of coteau by a French river is exaclty
like another; one turn of glen in the Black Forest is only the last turn
re-turned; one sweep of Jura pasture and crag, the mere echo of the
fields and crags of ten miles away. But in the whole course of Tweed,
Teviot, Gala, Tay, Forth, and Clyde, there is perhaps scarcely a bend
of ravine, or nook of valey, which would not be recognisable by its
inhabitants from every other. And there is no other country in which

the roots of memory are so entwined with the beauty of nature, instead of the pride of men; no other in which the song of 'Auld lang syne' could have been written—or Lady Nairn's ballad of 'The Auld House.'

JOHN RUSKIN

A RAMBLE WITH SIR WALTER SCOTT

August 1817. Abottsford

His domestic animals were his friends. Everything about him seemed to rejoice in the light of his countenance. Our ramble took us on the hills commanding an extensive prospect. 'Now,' said Scott, 'I have brought you, like the pilgrim in the Pilgrim's Progress, to the top of the Delectable Mountains, that I may show you all the goodly regions hereabouts.' . . . I gazed about me for a time with mute surprise. I may almost say with disappointment. I beheld a mere succession of grey waving hills, line beyond line, as far as my eye could reach, monotonous in their aspect, and so destitute of trees, that one could almost see a stout fly walking along their profile; and the far-famed Tweed appeared a naked stream, flowing between bare hills, without a tree or thicket on its banks; and yet such had been the magic web of poetry and romance thrown over the whole, that it had a greater charm for me than the richest scenery I had beheld in England. I could not help giving utterance to my thoughts. Scott hummed for a moment to himself, and looked grave; he had no idea of having his muse complimented at the expense of his native hills. 'It may be pertinacity,' said he at length; 'but to my eye, these grey hills, and all this wild border country, have beauties peculiar to themselves. I like the very nakedness of the land; it has something bold, and stern, and solitary about it. When I have been for some time in the rich scenery about Edinburgh, which is like ornamented garden land, I begin to wish myself back again among my own honest grey hills; and if I did not see the heather, at least once a-year, *I think I should die!*'

WASHINGTON IRVING

ON WASHINGTON IRVING'S COMMENTS ON 'SCOTT'S VIEW'

The casual traveller to this region usually finds at least three fundamental faults with it—featurelessness, treelessness, and monotony. To him it is a smooth bare sweep of bushless hills, rising ridge beyond ridge, interminable in their continuity of tame outline and oppressive in their sameness of colour.

For my own part, I have never been able to understand the charge of want of feature. True, the hills do not mount into crests or peaks, nor are their sides abundantly gashed with ravines, or roughened with many crags and precipices. Yet, of feature, and most expressive feature, every one of them is full. Nowhere else in Scotland can the exquisite modelling of flowing curves in hills forms, due partly to the contours of underlying solid rock, and partly to the lines assumed by accumulating detritus, be so conspicuously seen. These characters are not obtrusive, indeed, but perhaps on that very ground they afford a keener pleasure to the eye that has been trained to detect them.

With regard to the charge of treelessness, it should be borne in mind, I think, by those who make it that trees have their appointed places in landscape, where they are altogether admirable, but that there are other places where their presence in any number is felt to be inappropriate. Much, of course, depends upon personal taste and habit in such matters. To my own eye, for example, the hills in Rhineland, so densely wooded to the top that not a single feature of them can be seen, are examples of the abuse of trees in landscape. It would be intolerable so to bury up the beauty of the Border hills. All that a true lover of that region will allow in a straggling copse of pensive birks, creeping upward from the valley, or nestling green in some shady stream-watered dell on the bare hill-side. To imagine that we should improve the look of the landscape there by large plantations of timber, would be about as natural as to believe that we should add to the grace of the Apollo Belvedere by putting him into a greatcoat.

The so-called monotony of these softly undulating hills constitutes, I do not doubt, one main element in the peculiar fascination which they have always exercised upon minds of a poetic cast. From the sky-line on either side, gentle but boldly drawn curves of bent-covered moorland sweep down into the grassy meadow on the floor of the valley. These are architectural forms of the hill-slopes, and remain distinct at all seasons of the year. But their beauty and impressiveness vary from month to month, almost from hour to hour. For the most part they are aglow with colour, now purple with heather-blooms, now bright-green with bracken, now yellow with golden bent, now deepening into orange and russet as the early frosts of autumn lay their fingers on the ferns. And these colours are suffused, as it were, over the slopes, like a thin enamel, that never conceals the modulations of their form. In winter, when the ground is covered with snow, the endless diversity and grace of the curves stand out in naked beauty and offer to the student of hill-forms an admirable lesson. I cherish, as a lifelong possession, the recollection of the winter aspect of these uplands when I was snowed-up for a week under the hospitable roof of old Tibbie Shiels at St Mary's.

The long sweeping lines of form and colour, which would be utterly lost under a covering of trees, plunge down into the flat meadows of the valley through which a clear stream is ever murmuring. We wander down the valley, and find other similar streams emerging from narrower valleys, on either hand, where still the same forms of slope and ridge rise against the sky. The very barrenness of the landscape becomes itself a charm, allowing the soft gentle outlines of the hills to have full play upon the fancy. There is a tender grace in the landscape that is offended by the protrusion of no harsh feature, no abrupt crag or yawning ravine. Moreover a pleasing loneliness broods over it all, which, in the case of sterner scenery, becomes oppressive and almost insupportable. The silence is broken fitfully by the breeze as it bears back the murmur of the distant brook, or by the curlew screaming from the nearer hill. The very sounds of the valley—the plaintive cadence of the river, and the low sad sough of the wind along the slopes—combine to produce that tone of melancholy which seems so characteristic and so inseparable from these pastoral valleys.

But who can wander by Yarrow or Ettrick without feeling that the strange witchery with which the scenery fascinates us, springs mainly from what can neither be seen nor heard—from the human associations that have consecrated every spot within its borders. No one can feel this more deeply and gratefully than I. And yet am I none the less convinced that these human associations, in so far as they are the offspring of poetic imagination, owe far more than is generally recognised to the peculiar physical features of the region in which they took their birth, and which, indeed, often suggested as well as coloured them. To the influence of the scenery, amid which the deeds of daring were done, and the tales of love were told, the ballads and songs owe much of the distinguishing qualities of the border minstrelsy. The recognition of this influence, however, will in no way lessen the pleasure with which, indulging in dreamy thoughts of the past, we linger by Gala and Tweed, Ettrick and Yarrow, with their castles, and peels, and chapels, lonely and grey, and the traditions that seem to cling with a living power to every ruin and hillside. And though, sharing in Wordsworth's experience, we may 'see but not by sight alone,' and allow 'a ray of fancy' to mingle with all our seeing, we come back to these bare hills and quiet green valleys ever with fresh delight, and find that as we grow older they seem to grow greener, and to enter with a renewed sympathy into the musings of the hour.

ARCHIBALD GEIKIE

BENNACHIE

There's Tap o' Noth, the Buck, Ben Newe,
  Lonach, Benrinnes, Lochnagar,
Mount Keen, an' mony a Carn I trow
  That's smored in mist ayont Braemar.
Bauld Ben Muich Dhui towers, until
  Ben Nevis looms the laird o' a';
But Bennachie! Faith, yon's the hill
  Rugs at the hairt when ye're awa'!

Schiehallion,—ay, I've heard the name—
  Ben More, the Ochils, Arthur's Seat,
Tak' them an' a' your hills o' fame
  Wi' lochans leamin' at their feet;
But set me doon by Gadie side,
  Or whaur the Glenton lies by Don—
The muir-cock an' the whaup for guide
  Up Bennachie I'm rivin' on.

Syne on the Mither Tap sae far
  Win'-cairdit clouds drift by abeen,
An' wast ower Keig stands Callievar
  Wi' a' the warl' to me, atween.
There's braver mountains ower the sea,
  An' fairer haughs I've kent, but still
The Vale o' Alford! Bennachie!
  Yon is the Howe, an' this the Hill!

CHARLES MURRAY

31 Scots Firs, Loch Lomond. Reproduced with permission from the George Washington Wilson Collection in Aberdeen University Library.

LOCH LOMOND

The superb Loch Lomond, the fine sunlight that gilded its waters, the silvery rocks that skirted its shores, the flowery and verdant mosses, the black oxen, the white sheep, the shepherds beneath the pines, the perfume of the tea poured into cups that had been given by kindness, and received with gratitude, will never be effaced from my memory, and make me cherish the desire not to die before seeing Tarbet. I shall often dream of Tarbet, even in the midst of lovely Italy with its oranges, its myrtles, its laurels, and its jessamines.

B FAUJAIS ST FOND

THE APPROACH TO THE LOCH

The coachman walked alongside the horse; one moment we reeled and jolted down hill at a wild speed, the next, we were slowly being tugged up hill; it was a journey the likes of which I have never seen elsewhere. There was not a house to be seen, and we did not meet a soul; all around us there were the silent, gloomy mountains shrouded in mist; monotonous and always the same. The one and only living creature we saw for miles was a lonely shepherd, who was bitterly cold, and wrapped himself in his grey plaid. Silence reigned over all the landscape. Ben Lomond, the highest mountains peak, finally broke through the mist, and soon we could see Loch Lomond below us. Although there was a sort of road leading down, the descent was so steep that it was extremely dangerous to go with a carriage; it had to be left behind, and on foot we approached the well-equipped inn where a crowd of people were waiting for the steamer to arrive.

HANS CHRISTIAN ANDERSEN

WE LAND ON THE ISLAND OF INCH-TA-VANACH ON LOCH LOMOND.

We had not climbed far before we were stopped by a sudden burst of prospect, so singular and beautiful that it was like a flash of images from another world. We stood with our backs to the hill of the island, which we were ascending, and which shut out Ben Lomond entirely, and all the upper part of the lake, and we looked towards the foot of the lake, scattered over with islands without beginning and without end. The sun shone, and the distant hills were visible, some through sunny mists, others in gloom with patches of sunshine; the lake was lost under the low and distant hills, and the islands lost in the lake, which was all in motion with travelling fields of light, or dark shadows under rainy clouds. There are many hills, but no commanding eminence at a distance to confine the prospect, so that the land seemed endless as the water.

DOROTHY WORDSWORTH

FAREWELL TO BEN LOMOND

It is one of those moments which I shall not easily forget, when at that point from which a step or two would have carried us out of sight of the green fields of Glenfalloch, being at a great height on the mountain, we sate down, and heard, as if from the heart of the earth, the sound of torrents ascending out of the long hollow glen. To the eye all was motionless, a perfect stillness. The noise of waters did not appear to come this way or that, from any particular quarter: it was everywhere, almost, one might say, as if 'exhaled' through the whole surface of the green earth. Glenfalloch, Coleridge has since told me, signifies the Hidden Vale; but William says, if we were to name it from our recollections of that time, we should call it the Vale of Awful Sound.

DOROTHY WORDSWORTH

INVERSNAID*

The day was dark and partly hid the lake, yet it did not altogether disfigure it, but gave a pensive, or solemn beauty which left a lasting impression on me.

This darksome burn, horseback brown,
His rollrock highroad roaring down.
In coop and in comb the fleece of his foam
Flutes and low to the lake falls home.

No wind-puff bonnet of fawn-froth
Turns and twindles over the broth
Of a pool so pitchback, fell-frowning.
It rounds and rounds Despair to drowning.

Degged with dew, dappled with dew
Are the groins of the brae that the brook treads through,
Wiry heathpacks, flitches of fern,
And the beadbonny ash that sits over the burn.

What would the world do, once bereft
Of wet and of wilderness? Let them be left,
O let them be left, wildness and wet;
Long live the weeds and the wilderness yet.

GERARD MANLEY HOPKINS

* Gerald Manley Hopkins visited Loch Lomond in the Summer of 1881.

THE TROSSACHS

My course lies round the left flank of Benledi, straight on for the Trosachs and Loch Katrine. Leaving Callander, you cross the waters of the Leny—changed now from the fury that, with raised voice and streaming tresses, leaped from rock to rock in the glen above—and walk into the country made immortal by the Lady of the Lake. The loveliest sight on the route to the Trosachs is about to present itself. At a turn of the road Loch Achray is before you. Beyond expression beautiful is that smiling lake, mirroring the hills, whether bare and green or plumaged with woods from base to crest. Fair azure gem in a setting of mountains! the traveller—even if a bagman—cannot but pause to drink in its fairy beauty; cannot but remember it when far away amid other scenes and associations. At every step the scenery grows wilder. Loch Achray disappears. High in upper air tower the summits of Ben-Aan and Ben-Venue. You pass through the gorge of the Trossachs, whose rocky walls, born in earthquake and fiery deluge, the fanciful summer has been dressing these thousand years, clothing their feet with drooping ferns and rods of foxglove bells, blackening their breasts with pines, feathering their pinnacles with airy birches, that dance in the breeze like plumage on a warrior's helm. The wind here becomes a musician. Echo sits babbling beneath the rock. The gorge, too, is but the prelude to a finer charm; for before you are aware, doubling her beauty with surprise, there breaks on the right the silver sheet of Loch Katrine, with a dozen woody islands, sleeping peacefully on their shadows.

ALEXANDER SMITH

THE LADY OF THE LAKE

Onward, amid the copse 'gan peep
A narrow inlet still and deep,
Affording scarce such breadth of brim
As served the wild-duck's brood to swim;
Lost for a space, through thickets veering,
But broader when again appearing,
Tall rocks and tufted knolls their face
Could on the dark-blue mirror trace;
And farther as the hunger strayed,
Still broader sweep its channels made.
The shaggy mounds no longer stood,
Emerging from entangled wood,
But, wave-encircled, seemed to float,
Like castle girdled with its moat;
Yet broader floods extending still,
Divide them from their parent hill,
Till each, retiring, claims to be
An islet in an inland sea.

And now, to issue from the glen,
No pathway meets the wanderer's ken,
Unless he climb, with footing nice,
A far projecting precipice.
The broom's tough roots his ladder made,
The hazel saplings lent their aid;
And thus an airy point he won,
Where, gleaming with the setting sun,
One burnish'd sheet of living gold,
Loch-Katrine lay beneath him rolled;
In all her length far winding lay,
With promontory, creek, and bay,
And islands that, empurpled bright,
Floated amid the livelier light;
And mountains, that like giants stand,
To sentinel enchanted land.

High on the south, huge Benvenue
Down to the lake in masses threw
Crags, knolls, and mounds, confusedly hurled,
The fragments of an earlier world;
A wildering forest feathered o'er
His ruined sides and summit hoar,
While on the north, through middle air,
Ben-an heaved high his forehead bare.

SIR WALTER SCOTT

IN LOVELY TRUTH

It is of little use to the reader now to tell him that still at that date the
shore of Loch Katrine, at the east extremity of the lake, was exactly as
Scott had seen it, and described,

Onward, amid the copse 'gan peep,
A narrow inlet, still and deep.

In literal and lovely truth, that was so:—by the side of the footpath (it
was no more) which wound through the Trosachs, deep and calm
under the blaeberry bushes, a dark winding clear-brown pool, not five
feet wide at first, reflected the entangled moss of its margin, and arch
of branches above, with scarcely a gleam of sky.

That inlet of Loch Katrine was in itself an extremely rare thing; I
have never myself seen the like of it in lake shores. A winding recess of
deep water, without any entering stream to account for it—possible
only, I imagine, among rocks of the quite abnormal confusion of the
Trosachs; and besides the natural sweetness and wonder of it, made
sacred by the most beautiful poem that Scotland ever sang by her
stream sides. And all that the nineteenth century conceived of wise
and right to do with this piece of mountain inheritance, was to thrust
the nose of a steamer into it, plank its blaeberries over with a platform
past it as fast as they can scuffle.

JOHN RUSKIN

NINE DAYS IN THE HIGHLANDS

MAISTER EDITUR, I've just come hame frae a grand pedestrian tour i' the Hielands. . . .

There's the sweet little Loch Achray, about a mile or so lang, an' hardly three quarters broad: an' maybe you'll see the coos wadin' across to a little island covered wi' trees—no the coos, sir, the island; an' shuttin' up the view, the Trossachs, wi' 'huge Benvenue' on the sooth, an' Ben A'an rearin' its 'forehead bare' on the north. This is as lovely a picture on a sma' scale as nature can furnish ony gate.

Afore the present road was made it wad be next to impossible to get alang this side o' the loch. The ither side is quite open an' bare.

Passin' the kirk on the left, an' opposite a hoose as big again, the manse, I suppose (for ye'll often see in the country the minister's dwallin' bigger than the kirk he preaches in), an' syne that thing like a sham castle (the grand hotel), we entered the Trossachs. This is certainly a strange place, but, in a' humility, I wad venture to say I dinna think it deserves a' the worship it gets. I've been there three times noo, an' have explored the whole place near, an' canna see what the fouk mak' sic a sang aboot. Scott's 'Lady o' the Lake,' I suspect, has to do considerably wi' the great popularity o'd. An' alloo me to observe, sir, that the hotel-keepers are under the deepest obligations to the fictionist for the lift he has gi'en them. His description o' the place is fine to read, but it's just barely true. I'm no an admirer o' Wattie's poetry tho', an' so I'm maybe prejudiced. I winna attempt to describe the place, but wad like just to gie' ye my theory o'd. Imagine, then, twa great mountains, ane on the north, an' ane on the sooth, wi' a valley aboot a quarter o' a mile broad atween them. an' a loch in'd. Suppose, noo, some great convulsion o' nature has shattered the northmost mountain, an' great masses o' rock are flung doon fae the tap an' sides; that the mountain has been torn to pieces in fact, an' been thrown doon into the loch. The loch is divided in twa in consequence aboot a mile or so abune the fit o'd. The upper, an' by far the larger pairt o' the loch, seeks an ootlat an' finds it, on the sooth side o' the soothmost rock, just at the fit o' the opposite mountain, that's never been affected wi' the shock, or very little at least. Then suppose a lang, lang time to elapse—an age or twa say—the grund dries; the sees tak' root, an' spring up into trees; the heather, brackins, an' ither plants grow up around: an' ye hae the Trossachs as they appear 'ithenoo. We gaed alang the side o' Loch Katrine aboot a mile, saw Ellen's Isle, 'coir nan Urskin', the gobblin's den, an' up the loch a great lump. There's a better view up the loch to be gotten a mile farer up, but we hadna time to gae sae far. By-the-bye, there's anither island just aside Ellen's noo, that Wattie Scott never saw. The Glasgow fouk, gettin' water fae this loch, are obleeged to keep the level o' the loch higher than what it was afore, an' what was twa year syne a promontory is noo surrounded wi' water, an' converted into an island.

TAMMY TRAMPALOT

LOCH MAREE

It was a delightful evening—still, breathless, clear—as we swept slowly across the broad breast of Loch Maree; and the red light of sinking sun fell on many a sweet wild recess, amid the labyrinth of islands purple with heath, and overhung by the birch and mountain-ash; or slanted along the broken glades of the ancient forest; or lighted up into a blush the pale stony faces of the tall pyramidal hills. A boat bearing a wedding party was crossing the lake to the white house on the opposite side, and a piper stationed in the bows, was discoursing sweet music, that, softened by distance, and caught up by the echoes of the rocks, resembled no strain I had ever heard from the bagpipe before. Even the boatmen rested on their oars, and I had just enough of Gaelic to know that they were remarking how very beautiful it was. I wish, said my comrade, you understood these men: they have a great many curious stories about the loch, that I am sure you would like. See you that large island? It is Island-Maree. There is, they tell me, an old burying-ground on it, in which the Danes used to bury long ages ago, and whose ancient tomb-stones no man can read. And yon other island beside it is famous as the place in which the good people meet, every year to make submission to their queen. There is, they say, a little loch in the island, and another little island in the loch; and it is under a tree on that inner island that the queen sits and gathers kain for the Evil One. They tell me that, for certain, the fairies have not left this part of the country yet.

HUGH MILLER

A VIEW FROM SGURR ALASDAIR

From Dreadh III

Here in this simple place of clean rock and crystal water,
With something of the cold purity of ice in its appearance,
Inhuman and yet friendly,
Undecorated by nature or by man
And yet with a subtle and unchanging beauty
Which seems the antithesis of every form of art,

Here near the summit of Sgurr Alasdair
The air is very still and warm.
The Outer Isles look as though
They were cut out of black paper
And stuck on a brilliant silver background,
(Even as I have seen the snow-capped ridges of Peninsula
Stand out stark and clear in the pellucid Arctic atmosphere
Or, after a wild and foggy night, in the dawn
Seen the jagged line of the Tierra del Fuego cliffs
Looking for all the world as if they were cut out of tin,
Extending gaunt and desolate),
The western sea and sky undivided by horizon,
So dazzling is the sun
And its glass image in the sea.
The Cuillin peaks seem miniature
And nearer than is natural
And they move like liquid ripples
In the molten breath
Of the corries which divide them.
I light my pipe and the match burns steadily
Without the shielding of my hands,
The flame hardly visible in the intensity of light
Which drenches the mountain top.

I lie here like the cool and gracious greenery
Of the water-crowfoot leafage, streaming
In the roping crystalline currents,
And set all about on its upper surface
With flecks of snow blossom that, on closer looking,
Shows a dust of gold.

The blossoms are fragile to the touch
And yet possess such strength and elasticity
That they issue from the submergence of a long spate
Without appreciable hurt—indeed, the whole plant
Displays marvellous endurance in maintaining
A rooting during the raging winter torrents.
Our rivers would lose much if the snowy blossom
And green waving leafage of the water-crowfoot
Were absent—aye, and be barer of trout too!
And so it is with the treasures of the Gaelic genius
So little regarded in Scotland to-day.
Yet emerging unscathed from their long submergence,
Impregnably rooted in the most monstrous torrents
—The cataracting centuries cannot rive them away—
And productive of endless practical good,
Even to people unaware of their existence,
In the most seemingly—unlikely connections.
I am possessed by this purity here
As in a welling of stainless water
Trembling and pure like a body of light
Are the webs of feathery weeds all waving,
Which it traverses with its deep threads of clearness
Like the chalcedony in moss agate
Starred here and there with grenouillette.

HUGH MACDIARMID

32 The Old Man of Storr from the North, Skye. Reproduced with
permission from the George Washington Wilson Collection in
Aberdeen University Library.

SHETLAND AND PONIES

Light—when you come to this place—
light is falling from the sky
and the water is returning it;
the land, wrinkled and dark, a dead skin
that might crack open with no sound
and the bright water drain into that breathless dark,
lost like a single life in emptiness,
and not a tree to bless with its gentle growth,
but the bone of the world pressing through,
the stone face to which the human face returns.
Inhospitable but splendid—this North land
that tells the cosmic tale
of earth and sky and water.

Water—in the beginning a drop of water
and the light was in the water and there
each stone was shaped to be itself and none other,
each shell to be itself and none other,
each creature to be itself and none other,
peerie fish and crab and whale
seen and known and named,
yet unknown as the round of the sea.

I look into that glass that is water
and know I am a stranger to this place.
I look into light upon light
and know it is not of me.
I look on to the waste of land.
I do not belong, but these

fourlegs make the spaces their own,
a backyard for their games,
a stamping ground for their romp,
a prancing place for their pride.
They populate it with their warmth,
make jokes about the mountains—
this universe is their home.

GEORGE BRUCE

SHETLAND

The appeal of the Shetlands is not so facile as that of the Hebrides, nor has it been eked out with so many adventitious aids. This is not altogether a misfortune. If the Shetlands are much less known they have at all events escaped the dangers of superficial and generally false enthusiasm and have nothing to correspond to 'Celtic Twilight-ism'. If the fake-glamour of the Hebrides has become a weariness to the flesh and a real obstacle to their true appreciation, an insistence on the claims of the Shetlands may now prove a useful corrective and help to establish a properly balanced conception of Scotland as a whole. A sense of actuality will serve us better than any artificial allure.

It is all the more regrettable that so few holiday-makers come to the Shetlands since the essence of a holiday is a complete change, and this the Shetland Islands offer to mainland dwellers to a far greater extent than is obtainable anywhere else within easy reach, which is to say, at moderate cost. Superficially even, the Shetlands are quite unlike Scotland, and, unless the visitor has been prepared in advance, he or she may find it difficult to account for the sense of something very different—the sense of something wanting. It may take them a little time to realise that what is affecting them is the total absence of trees and of running water. But one quickly gets accustomed to that, and appreciates that, even if trees and singing streams could be introduced, they would be no improvement; they would simply make the Shetlands like other places we know, whereas, without them, the Shetlands are complete in themselves, and the absence of these usual features of the countryside does not involve any deficiency or monotony. There is no less variety of form and colour; just as we find it difficult in other connections to imagine how we could get on without certain things we are accustomed to, so here it surprises one to discover how easily even the presence of trees and rivers can be dispensed with and how, instead of a sense of loss, we soon realise that their absence throws into relief features we seldom see or underprize because of them—the infinite beauties of the bare land and the shapes and colours of the rocks which first of all impress one with a sense of sameness and next delight one with a revelation of the endless resource of Nature albeit in subtler and less showy or sensational forms than we are accustomed to appreciate in regions of more profuse development. It is in fact the treasures and rich lessons of a certain asceticism the Shetlands provide, and these offset in an invaluable way our normal indulgences in scenic display. But the spirit of the Shetlands is not easily or speedily apprehended; one must accustom oneself patiently to a different aspect of the world, a different rhythm of life, before one can fully understand how its variations from what we have been used to are counter-balanced by its own essential qualities. The lack of ostentatious appearances, the seeming bareness and reserve, make the Shetlands insusceptible of being readily or quickly understood; one must steep oneself in them, let them grow upon one, to savour them properly. It is a splendid discipline.

HUGH MACDIARMID

ENDURING FASCINATIONS

It is, of course, merely stupid to suppose that the record-breakers do not love the hills. Those who do not love them don't go up, and those who do can never have enough of it. It is an appetite that grows in feeding. Like drink and passion, it intesifies life to the point of glory. In the Scots term, used for the man who nis *abune himsel'* with drink, one is *raised; fey;* a little mad, in the eyes of the folk who do not climb.

The *feyness* itself seems to me to have a physiological origin. Those who undergo it have the particular bodily make-up that functions at its most free and most live upon heights (although this, it is obvious, refers only to heights manageable to man and not at all to those for which a slow and painful acclimitisation is needful). As they ascend, the air grows rarer and more stimulating, the body feels lighter and they climb with less effort, till Dante's law of ascent on the Mount of Purgation seems to become a physical truth:

> This mountain is such, that ever at the beginning below 'tis
> toilsome, and the more a man ascends the less it wearies.

At first I had thought that this lightness of body was a universal reaction to rarer air. It surprised me to discover that some people suffered malaise at attitudes that released me, but were happy in low valleys where I felt extinguished. Then I began to see that our devotions have more to do with our physiological peculiarities than we admit. I am a mountain lover because my body is at its best in the rarer air of the heights and communicates its elation to the mind. The obverse of this would seem to be exemplified in the extreme of fatigue I suffered while walking some two miles underground in the Ardennes caverns. This was plainly no case of a weary mind communicating its fatigue to the body, since I was enthralled by the strangeness and beauty of these underground cavities. Add to this eyes the normal focus of which is for distance, and my delight in the expanse of space opened up from the mountain tops becomes also a perfect physiological adjustment. The short-sighted cannot love mountains as the long-sighted do. The sustained rhythm of movement in a long climb has also its part in inducing the sense of physical well-being, and this cannot be captured by any mechanical mode of ascent.

This bodily lightness, then, in the rarefied air, combines with the liberation of space to give mountain *feyness* to those who are susceptible to such a malady. For it is a malady, subverting the will and superceding the judgement: but a malady of which the afflicted will never ask to be cured. For this nonsense of physiology does not really explain it all. What! am I such a slave that unless my flesh feels buoyant I cannot be free? No, there is more in the lust for a mountain top than a perfect physiological adjustment. What more there is lies within the mountain. Something moves between me and it. Place and a mind may interpenetrate till the nature of both is altered. I cannot tell what this movement is except by recounting it.

NAN SHEPHERD

LANDSCAPE INSIDE

Or, again, in Skye. Many years ago, I was staying in a small hotel at Carbost. The only other guest was Professor Collie of London University, the distinguished mountaineer, who charmed more than one evening with descriptions of climbs in the Himalayas, the Rockies, and elsewhere. His quiet precise manner gave an extraordinarily vivid versimilitude to the solution of sudden rock-face problems of great difficulty and danger; in particular a certain feat of endurance can still haunt me. Once, when the talk must have veered to the local scene, he told me that the most memorable stretch of colour he had ever seen anywhere was on the moor in front of the Cuillin—on the Glenbrittle side, as you come up from Talisker. I had seen it the day before. Its tone was somewhere between amontillado and a medium or richer sherry, but it looked like an immense living golden hide. The wind rippled and played on it in a light-hearted frolic. The glow of life was there, as if the earth were a beast. Perhaps the earth has a life of its own. Every new physical fact discovered by the scientists is more astonishing than the last.

However, there is something further here that I hesitate to mention because it is so elusive, so difficult to convey.

Have you ever, as a small boy, wandered farther from home than you meant to or were aware of—say, up a strath or valley—until you found yourself in a place where you had never been before? All at once you realise that *you* are in this strange place. Stock still, not breathing so that you can listen, you stare at grey rocks with whorls of lichen on them like faces, tree-roots like snakes, the trees themselves heavy with leaves and silent. Your heart comes into your throat. Quietly, very quietly, you get back onto the path, then take to your toes for all you are worth. This may have been the first experience of panic fear—the first meeting with the old Greek god. But you also met someone else there, much nearer to you than Pan: you met yourself.

There is nothing mysterious in coming to a standstill. To stand and not to think, receptive to the influences of earth and sky, scent and sound and silence, is easy and natural. But something then comes seeping in, sometimes very slight, so slight that it scarcely seems to come at all; and yet, *if the pause be held*, there supervenes a delicacy of tension, a certain strangeness within oneself and going out through the far reaches of the world; and the burden of the day's care slowly falls away like the leaf.

To be concerned with the solidly calculable things all the time is surely literally, arithmetically, to become lop-sided, to know only one aspect of living. It came to me with a small shock the other day that I had, for example, missed the autumn bird-life, the wheeling of great flocks of plovers over the uplands, the gatherings of excited swallows, particular grouse and partridge coveys, the new strategic disposal of the pigeon clan. I felt as if I had been robbed of something I could never hope to recover! So much had been filched away by a too material preoccupation with affairs. Grey-brown backs went running in a field in the deep dusk. They got up. Curlew. They affected me with a feeling of remoteness, of experiencing a life that I had forgotten, far back in the past—or on some other place. The touch of dismay seemed absurd, but it was there nevertheless, like a warning!

The only bird I can properly say I have seen these many weeks is the robin. That brings me back to the twilight again—and no doubt to what some southern critics, in an apprehension of mystery beyond our feeble reach, call the Celtic Twilight.

NEIL GUNN

A GEOLOGICAL VISION

Among the many forms of scenery that vary the surface of the earth, mountains and ravines have from time immemorial impressed most vividly the human imagination. The lower grounds where man passes his existence are liable to continual change. He sees the shores worn away by the sea, the plains strewn with debris by the streams, and the meadows torn open by the inroads of floods. He himself too helps to transform the landscape. He ploughs up peat mosses, turns wet bogs into fertile farms, cuts down forests, plants new woodlands, covers the valleys with cornfields and orchards, graves the country with lines of roadway, and builds all over the land his cottages, villages, and towns. But high above the din and stir of his feverish life, the great mountains rise before him with still the same forms of peak and crag that were familiar to his ancestors long centuries ago. While the outlines of the lowlands are touched with the instability that marks everything human, these far heights seem to remain impassive and unaffected, as if the hand of time had passed them by. Hence the everlasting hills have ever been favourite emblems, not only of grandeur but of immutable permanence.

And yet the mountains bear on their fronts the memorials of change which have not altogether failed to catch the eye even of the most untutored races. Their grim, naked cliffs and splintered precipices, their yawning defiles and heaps of ruins, have always appealed to the fancy and the fears of men. These striking natural features in old days suggested legends and superstitions which are of interest, not only as the characteristic mental efforts of an early stage of human progress, but as embodying the special parts of mountainous landscape that most potently excite the imagination in the childhood of a people. The days of legend and superstition have passed away, but the lonely glens and dark precipices of a mountainous region still make their mute appeal to us, as they did to our forefathers. We have cast aside the old fables and romances, but the same ineradicable desire to find an explanation of natural appearances, which prompted these fanciful inventions, still burns within us, and compels us to ask in our own way the same questions. We cannot shake off the feeling of vague awe which falls upon us in a great mountain range, as we stand face to face with some of the sublimest scenery on the earth's surface. The magnitude of the scale of nature and the utter loneliness of the vast mountain-world powerfully affect us. But deep beneath the feelings thus evoked lies the mental unrest in presence of the mystery of the cause of such stupendous features. The gentle undulations of a lowland landscape may never start in the mind a passing thought as to how they came into existence. The stern broken features of the mountains, however, arrest our attention and press home upon us the question of their origin.

ARCHIBALD GEIKIE

IONA

We were now treading that illustrious Island, which was once the luminary of the Caledonian regions, whence savage clans and roving barbarians derived the benefits of knowledge, and the blessings of religion. To abstract the mind from all local emotion would be impossible, if it were endeavoured, and would be foolish, if it were possible. Whatever withdraws us from the power of our senses; whatever makes the past, the distant, or the future predominate over the present, advances us in the dignity of thinking beings. Far from me and from my friends, be such frigid philosophy as may conduct us indifferent and unmoved over any ground which has been dignified by wisdom, bravery, or virtue. That man is little to be envied, whose patriotism would not gain force upon the plain of Marathon, or whose piety would not grow warmer among the ruins of Iona!

SAMUEL JOHNSON

A POET'S VISIONS

An T-Eilean

Nuair a ràinig sinn an t-eilean
bha feasgar ann
's bha sinn aig fois,
a' ghrian a' dol a laighe
fo chuibhrig cuain
's am bruadar a' tòiseachadh as ùr.

Ach anns a' mhadainn
shad sinn dhinn a' chuibhrig
's anns an t-solus gheal sin
chunnaic sinn loch anns an eilean
is eilean anns an loch,
is chunnaic sinn
gun do theich am bruadar pios eile bhuainn.

Tha an staran cugallach
chon an dàrna eilein,
tha a' chlach air uideil
tha a' dìon nan dearcag,
tha chraobh chaorainn a' crìonadh,
Fàileadh na h-iadhshlait a' faileachdainn oirnn a nis.

Leodhas As T-samhradh

An iarmailt cho soilleir tana
mar gum biodh am brat-sgàile air a reubadh
's an Cruthaidhear 'na shuidhe am fianuis a shluaigh
aig a' bhuntàt 's a sgadan,
gun duine ris an dèan E altachadh.
'S iongantach gu bheil iarmailt air an t-saoghal
tha cur cho beag a bhacadh air daoine
sealltainn a-steach dha'n an t-sìorruidheachd;
chan eil feum air feallsanachd
far an dèan thu chùis le do phrosbaig.

RUARAIDH MACTHÒMAIS

The Island

When we reached the island
it was evening
and we were at peace,
the sun lying down
under the sea's quilt
and the dream beginning anew.

But in the morning
we tossed the cover aside
and in that white light
saw a loch in the island,
and an island in the loch,
and we recognised
that the dream had moved away from us again.

The stepping-stones are chancy
to the second island,
the stone totters
that guards the berries,
the rowan withers,
we have lost now the scent of the honeysuckle.

Lewis in Summer

The atmosphere clear and transparent
as though the veil had been rent
and the Creator were sitting in full view of His people
eating potatoes and herring,
with no man to whom He can say grace.
Probably there's no other sky in the world
that makes it so easy for people
to look in on eternity;
you don't need philosophy
where you can make do with binoculars.

DERICK THOMSON

EPILOGUE

9 March 1938

All the manifestations of the creative urge are but variations upon the single theme—the glory of life—that consummation of joy and generosity; that magnificence and magnanimity which is yet embodied in the simplest form, the clearest gesture. Silence is, perhaps, the greatest hallelujah; the silent hosannas of the sun, the stars, the trees and the flowers. But silence is not enough—the innumerable songs of earth mingle with the acclamations of the serene witnesses. The wind, the water, the cries of bird and beast and the thoughtful utterance of humanity: each day is life's messiah and at its feet are leaves and about its head are the canticles of joy. Joy is met and is shared—it cannot be buried or hoarded.

WILLIAM SOUTAR

33   Mist on the Glencoe Hills from the top of Ben Nevis. Reproduced with permission from the George Washington Wilson Collection in Aberdeen Unversity Library

GLOSSARY

abeen above
agley askew
ain own
aince once
aivn even
anerlie only

bailie cattleman
bannets bonnets
bean rannie pottach kindly gentleman
beets boots
beenwood ragwort
bickering brattle hurrying scamper
big build
bike rest
binnin binding
binnae except
birk birch
birns crowds
blae hard blue clay
bleezin blazing
bleggartin getting up to mischief
boontree elder
brak break
braid broad
bran'it brawny, sturdy
branks bridee
braxie diseased
breem broom
breets brutes
breenged barged
Broch Fraserburgh
brods boards
budder bother
bungin throwing
bursen bursting
buss bush
but without

ca' knock or push
callour fresh
callant boy
cannas breid canvas breadth
carl doddie rib grass
chappit knocked
chavie young person
chaumer chamber
cheenge change
chine chain
claes clothes
clash gossip
cleugh gorge
clootie dumplin steam pudding made in a cloth
clorty muddy
clossacht enclosed
cloupit curved
cog bowl
coorie squat
coupin upsetting
cove man
conkers a game played with horse chestnuts
crack gossip
cranreuch hoar-frost
craps crops
cried called
crochlie crippled
croodit crowded
Crowdieknowe—the graveyard where lie ancestors of MacDiarmid
cyarn group

daimen icker odd ear
daudit struck
deeked looked
deein dying
deid dead

dellin digging
dern hide
dichtit wiped, sprinkled
dilse dulse
dook bathe
dozent dozing
dreel drill
druchtit dried out
dul woe
dwebble feeble

earin ploughing
echteen eighteen
een eyes
eezin eves of as house
eident busy
emmerteen ant
er there

fails sods of turf
fauld-dike wall for penning sheep
feck plenty
feck an exclamation
fee'd hired
finicky fussy
fin when
flyting calling abusive names
fite white
fly-cup a cup of tea
forfochen tired
foggage coarse grass
furrs furrows
fut what
fykie triky
fyles whines

gadgie man
gadie lad
gang/gyang go
gar/garrin —make, compel
gedderin gathering
geylies somewhat
gie give
gin if

girnie complaining
girns snares
girss grass
gizzent dried up
gowan marguerite
gowdspink goldfinch
gled kite
gollach earwig
grat wept
grun ground
gruntle snout
guff smell
gullion slight bog
gweed good

had haud, hold, keep
hairst harvest
hake hook
hantel people
hantle quantity
hap over
hail hypothec the whole lot
haveless incompetent
havered shared
haughs level ground by a stream
heuk reaping-hook
heeze hoist
heids heads
hinna have not
histit hoisted
hyowin hoeing
hysters stumbles

ilka each

kebbock cheese
ken know
knablich stone, stony
knowes knolls

laarik larch wood
laich low
laith loth
lang-nebbit long-nosed

laivin sinking
lave remainder
leein lying
lichtit alighted
lick speed
lift the sky
lippen peel a pool to be trusted
loons boys
loupin' leaping
lowsened loosened
lowsin time time to finish work
lows't unharnessed

maazie jersey
mail hammer
mairch boundary
maleen alone
manging talking, yearning
maukins rats
maulins hares
maun face
mauts malts
mawin mowing
meshanter mistake
micht might
mislippen mistrust
mou mouth
moolins crumbs
mowdieworp mole
muckle large
muir-cock male grouse
mull tin box
mutchkin pint

neap turnip
news talk
nieve fist
niffer haggle
nowt cattle

ower too
oo wool
orra loon odd jobs boy
oxterfou armful

paidle hoe
pang pain
pattle tool for cleaning plough share
pawkie shrewd
peeweep lapwing
pilget struggle
pint point
plype plump
poddock frog
pookit put in a bag
puddick steels toad stools
puckle few
progne robin
pyock bag

queets ankles
quine girl

raivelin your noddle confusing your brains
rax reach, stretch
ream cream
redd clear
reets roots
richt right
roosty rusty
rottan rat
ruggit pulled

sae so
scaldie non-traveller
shannish an exclamation
shaw grove
sheen shoes
sheetin shooting
sheugh ditch
shooder shoulder
siccar secure
sklentin obliquely
skinklan shining
skraiks screeches
skweel school
skyrie glowing

slap gap
slocken slake
sleekit sly
smoore smother
sna snow
sned chop
snell bitter
sooman swimming
spangs jerks
speen spoon
speld split open
speired asked
speugies sparrows
spewin vomitting
sprots coarse grass
stane dykes stone walls
steen stone
stirk steer
stishie disturbance
stecht overheated
stookies starlings
stoor dust, smoke
stoot stout
strabs pieces of corn stalk
streekin stretching
stott young bull
stroud song
styoo dust
swyte sweat
syne ago, since

tapner tappit
tatties potatoes
teuchat lapwing
thole endure
thoom thumb

thrapple throat
thrang busy
thrave twenty-four sheeves
thrawn obstinate
tichter tighter
tirrin removing the surface
tint lost
toom empty
toon town
tousy toosled
tramort carcase
trunkle trinkle
tuggery clothes
tyauved laboured

unyirdly unearthly

vratch brat

waa wall
waar seaweed
whaup curlew
wheddled spoke
whigmaleerie fanciful notion
winnock soll window sill
winna will not
wised guided
wuppit bound together with string
wuts wits

yaavins awns
yarkin jerking out
yin one
yirdy earthy
yokie itchy
yokit worked

INDEX OF AUTHORS AND SOURCES

The editors and publisher are grateful to all authors, agents, publishers and other copyright holders who have given permission to print copyright material. Every effort has been made to trace copyright holders, and where this has proved impossible, and the work has been included in the anthology, it is with apologies and in the hope that such use will be welcomed.

All the authors in this anthology are listed below in alphabetical order, followed by the title of prose or poem in this work, the titles (in brackets) of books or journals in which they have already appeared, then by the page number in this book where they are to be found. Names of copyright holders are added where appropriate.